Creating Jesus

Books by Dennis Kennedy

*The Spectator and the Spectacle:
Audiences in Modernity and Postmodernity*

*Looking at Shakespeare:
A Visual History of Twentieth-Century Performance*

The Oxford Encyclopedia of Theatre and Performance

The Oxford Companion to Theatre and Performance

Foreign Shakespeare

Shakespeare in Asia (with Yong Li Lan)

Granville Barker and the Dream of Theatre

Plays by Harley Granville Barker

Fossil Light: A Novel in Films

Creating Jesus

The Earliest Record of Yeshua of Nazareth

DENNIS KENNEDY

RESOURCE *Publications* · Eugene, Oregon

CREATING JESUS
The Earliest Record of Yeshua of Nazareth

Copyright © 2024 Dennis Kennedy. All rights reserved. Except for brief quotations in critical publications or reviews, no part of this book may be reproduced in any manner without prior written permission from the publisher. Write: Permissions, Wipf and Stock Publishers, 199 W. 8th Ave., Suite 3, Eugene, OR 97401.

Resource Publications
An Imprint of Wipf and Stock Publishers
199 W. 8th Ave., Suite 3
Eugene, OR 97401

www.wipfandstock.com

PAPERBACK ISBN: 979-8-3852-2459-3
HARDCOVER ISBN: 979-8-3852-2460-9
EBOOK ISBN: 979-8-3852-2461-6

An exemption applies to the translation of The Good Message According to Mark in chapter 3 herein, which may be quoted without written permission in extracts that total no more than fifty verses, providing acknowledgment is given in this form: "Translated by Dennis Kennedy from his book *Creating Jesus*, copyright © 2024, used by permission."

A few quotations from the Old Testament contained herein are from the New Revised Standard Version Bible, copyright © 1989, by the Division of Christian Education of the National Council of the Churches of Christ in the U.S.A., and are used by permission. All rights reserved.

The image in Figure 7 is reproduced under free licence from the Classical Numismatic Group, Inc. www.cngcoins.com

Artificial intelligence disclaimer. The author has used Microsoft Office spell check and various internet and library search engines in preparing this book. No other part of the research or composition was generated or assisted by artificial intelligence.

For Annie

Contents

List of Figures viii

Foreword ix

Prologue 1

1 The Gospel Truth: An Introduction 5
2 Reading Mark 28
3 The Good Message According to Mark: A Literal Translation 50
4 Mark as Literary Object 87
5 The Oral Tradition 114
6 Myth and History 139
7 Tragedy and Epic 166

Epilogue 189

Bibliography 197

Index 203

List of Figures

1. The Two-Document Hypothesis | 17
2. Conjectured Dates: Paul and the Evangelists | 22
3. The Nicene Creed of 325 | 35
4. Ending of the Constantinopolitan Creed of 381 | 36
5. Not in Mark | 40
6. Structure of Mark | 89
7. Divus Iuliu(s) | 100
8. The Pauline Kerygma | 144

Foreword

THIS IS A BOOK for general readers on the gospel of Mark as the earliest surviving witness of the life of Yeshua of Nazareth. It is not a running commentary but an investigation of Mark as a literary and historical document. My main concerns are how Mark came to be written, what it meant in its time, how it differs from the other gospels, and how it was used (or misused) in history to certify a belief system. Though the book is based on considerable research, my goal is to make those main concerns as plain as I can. The four gospels grew out of a small offshoot of Judaism, a minor sect that did not have an official name or status but is fairly well documented when compared to other cults in the Roman empire of the first and second centuries. Yet hardly anything can be said about those founding documents, which together are called the New Testament, that hasn't been complicated by someone at some time. The texts available—their dates, their authors, their audiences, their meanings—are matters of persistent debate. Sometimes it has been necessary to enter the frame of those debates, but more often I have left the finer arguments to others, who are acknowledged in the notes.

    We do not know the exact year of the birth of Yeshua of Nazareth, though it is generally thought to have been about five years before what is conventionally called AD 1. Thus for dating it is more sensible to use the abbreviations BCE (Before the Common Era) and CE (Common Era) than to use BC (Before Christ) and AD (Anno Domini, in the Year of the Lord), though the labels refer to the same calendar scheme. There is also a little trouble about the terms Old Testament and New Testament. Obviously what Christians call the Old Testament has not, for Jews, been displaced by a later one. Because of wide use there is no satisfactory way around this difficulty; calling one the First Testament and the other the Second Testament, as some scholars do, is a bit disingenuous since they too are just different terms for the same things. I have compromised and used "Hebrew scriptures" when referring to the collection of Jewish writings (the Tanakh) in a Jewish historical context, and "Old Testament" when speaking in the context of the New Testament.

All translations from the New Testament are my own, including quotations used by Paul and the evangelists from the Septuagint, the Greek version of the Hebrew scriptures. Most of the other Old Testament passages quoted here are from the New Revised Standard Version (NRSV).

Thanks are due to a number of people who have helped me with this book, particularly Matthew Causey, Annie Tyrrell Kennedy, Miranda Kennedy, Patrick Mason, and the late Ronald Vince. Richard Lehnert has read a number of drafts and made many useful suggestions with a poetic editor's eye; I owe him a great debt. My colleague Daniele Pevarello has been a wonderful source of encouragement, and his knowledge and wisdom about the New Testament and early Christianity have saved me from many mistakes. Those that remain are not his.

Prologue

LAST WEEK I WENT to a funeral at a local Catholic parish in Dublin. I haven't attended any church regularly for a long time and funerals are about the only occasions when I am at Mass. I didn't know the deceased well; he was a professional colleague and I felt no particular grief at his passing. The service was boring, the sermon tedious, the eulogy conventional, the music misguided. Even a final blessing by a retired bishop sounded off the cuff. But then the incense was lit, scenting the coffin and the people, and I was sent back to childhood.

Though I am descended from an Irish family and have lived in Ireland for three decades, I was born in Cincinnati, a city on the Ohio River settled heavily by Germans and Irish in the second half of the nineteenth century. My father was a plumber and a strictly observant Catholic, my mother was very pious, and my learning was in Catholic schools, right through university. I began at the Saint Francis de Sales school, taught by the Ursuline nuns, attached to a gorgeous pseudo-gothic church. The children started each school day in that church where, probably for unrelated reasons, the service was usually a Requiem Mass said for the intention of some departed soul. A strange way for a youngster to welcome the day, participating in the rite for the dead. In those years the priest wore purple or black vestments for the Requiem and the general tone of the service was fear and woe. A little later I joined the children's choir, singing about doomsday, the forbidding rhythms of the Gregorian *Dies Irae* battered into my brain:

> Dies irae, dies illa
> Solvet saeclum in favilla
> Teste David cum Sibylla.

> Day of wrath, that day
> The age dissolved to ashes
> Testified by David with the Sibyl.

End-of-the-world prophesy delivered daily for six-year-olds.

Because it was delivered inside the padded glove of Latin, the blow was softened. I grew up in a Catholicism that was linguistically bifurcated, our children's missals offering side-by-side English with the Latin spoken at the altar, which seemed all the more authentic because incomprehensible. As an altar boy like thousands of others I learned the Latin responses by heart and can still say some of them, along with my Paters, Aves, and Glorias. Or I *could* say them, since I do not—not deliberately, though sometimes they pop into my head unrequested and I run through them in a sentimental attachment to Latin.

My father moved us to Santa Barbara in southern California in the 1950s in time to catch the housing-construction boom—not to that wealthy suburb now the province of Hollywood royalty and disgruntled British royalty, but to a working-class district populated by immigrants and their descendants from Italy, Ireland, and Mexico. I finished elementary education at Our Lady of Guadalupe school, named for an appearance of the Virgin Mary in sixteenth-century Mexico that few in Cincinnati had heard of. As a result, Spanish was added to church Latin and church English, and in my uncritical mind became part of the sacredness, or otherness, of the liturgy. High school was staffed by more nuns with dissatisfied faces, who regularly encouraged me to become a priest; religion was taught by local Jesuits. Then I was off to the Jesuit University of San Francisco, where we were required to take a course every semester in Thomistic philosophy and one in Catholic theology.

In my uninterrupted sixteen years of Catholic instruction I cannot remember a single nun or priest encouraging me to read a gospel from start to finish. The idea would have seemed outlandish. In fact there was little encouragement to read the bible at all. That fits with the stereotyped view of the Roman church, which from the middle ages worried that reading the bible was a double-edged pursuit for ordinary mortals—not because it was evil or mistaken, but because it is so easy to misunderstand, which for the church meant it could be construed in an unorthodox fashion. In tune with its dogmatic and paternalistic establishment in the fourth century, the pre-Reformation church thought its duty was to guide the (illiterate, uninformed) faithful through the complications of belief. Established doctrine was more important than the founding documents. The Old Testament was good for poetic prayer from Isaiah or the Psalms, and the New Testament was useful for theological instruction from the gospel of John and the epistles, but generally biblical matters were best contained in brief passages inserted in Mass, where their editorial selection and liturgical placement already circumscribed their meaning. Missals and lectionaries were more reliable than bibles.

The Reformation changed this for the sects that withdrew from Roman authority, and should have changed it for Catholicism more than it did. Luther's and Calvin's insistence on *sola scriptura* (by scripture alone) radically altered twelve hundred years of ecclesiastic emphasis on tradition and interpretative doctrine. After Luther the New Testament was to be the guide for understanding the nature of the Messiah and his offer of salvation. No priest, no pope, no church, no appeal to tradition should stand between the minds and souls of human beings and their intimate relation to God. Ironically, by enforcing what they thought a return to origins the reformers actually were going against how the earliest Christian communities viewed the gospels: as notes for preaching and discussion rather than absolute truths. That there were four of them, that they often contradicted each other in detail, and that none of the four was ever suppressed, those facts suggest that the basic declaration of faith, the core belief in the actuality of the Resurrection, mattered more to early Christians than the biography of its fountainhead. How and why this happened, and the part that the evangelist Mark played in it, are the main themes of the work that follows.

First, though, it is fair to ask why a lapsed Catholic agnostic should undertake to write such a book as this one. No doubt there are psychological reasons that revolve around my past; it would be as tedious for me to dig in that soil as it would be for you to sift through it. At death I think we go into nothingness, the emptiness of a universe that has no clue we ever existed. I know that the belief in an afterlife is a source of comfort for many people, whether Muslim or Christian or other, and I have no desire to deny anyone the sense of hope, belonging, and community that the practice of religion can give. This book is not for or against religion; it is designed as a work of historical and literary analysis that looks at the earliest gospel as a remarkable document in its own right. Of course we can't separate the gospels from the faith that gave rise to them, but it is possible, and desirable, to investigate them without recourse to preexisting thesis or a predetermined outcome.

A second question is also legitimate. Since I'm not a biblical scholar by training, what expertise can I bring to a subject already overloaded with commentary and remarkable research? My professional schooling was in literature and history, and in many ways this book falls inside those subjects. In practice I became a historian of performance in an academic field usually called theatre and performance studies. I have researched and written about performance of many types: not just the presentation of plays in playhouses but also other types of performance, such as television game shows, public gambling, museum displays, and religious rituals. Later in the book I will bring that experience to aspects of Mark relating to the oral tradition, the performance of the gospel, and the celebration of the eucharist; for now I'll simply note that my sense of the pervasiveness of performance in the past and present will help uncover aspects of New Testament analysis that might be new to some readers.

Thanks to the Jesuits I learned classical languages, but decades of neglect have left me, as Ben Jonson said of Shakespeare, with small Latin and less Greek. I have worked hard at Greek over the past few years and managed, with a good deal of help, to make the translation of Mark that appears as chapter 3. That effort brought me more deeply into the gospel, since the act of translating requires an understanding of a text that goes beyond ordinary reading and even thorough study. I have also dug deeply into New Testament scholarship and the history of early Christianity, subjects that intrigued me long before I thought of writing this book. A historian looks at how a moment in the past or present became itself, how the past and the understanding of the past determined the condition that later prevailed. Few things in history are inevitable; almost everything that happens has a context, a set of causes, actors, and an element of chance. Understanding it requires a measure of creative interpretation. How did one of the itinerant Jewish teachers in rural Galilee become the catalyst for a new way of understanding human purpose? How did first-century belief in his power become solidified around an idea of salvation and eternal life? No one has objective answers to those questions, but trying to answer them is what a historian of Christianity ought to do.

In the end what draws me to the gospel of Mark is a conviction that it is an extraordinary document. Whether considered as a work or literature, a text for performance, a historical treatise, or a religious manifesto, Mark was unparalled in previous culture, and has had influence as great as any single text in world history.

1

The Gospel Truth: An Introduction

Both read the Bible day and night,
But thou read'st black where I read white.

—William Blake, "The Everlasting Gospel"

From its start Christianity depended on translation. The Mediterranean world of the first century of the Common Era was a multiethnic, multireligious, and multilingual mix of societies and nations, some of them displaced by war and exile, all of them conquered by a brutal and unforgiving occupier. The eastern regions of what became the Roman Empire had been thoroughly Hellenized by the conquests of Alexander the Great in the fourth century BCE, and ever since Greek had been the lingua franca for a variety of peoples, many of whom spoke something else at home. Koine Greek, it was called—"common" Greek, a simplified form of classical Greek, useful for trade, for interrogation by the empire's officials, and for written communication. That is the simple reason why the gospels were written in Greek, along with all of the rest of the New Testament.

The central figure of Christianity was born a Jew in the northern sector of the ancient Israelite nation, which had been long divided into three or more parts ruled by invading forces and shifting alliances. Raised in Aramaic, a northwest Semitic language prevalent from eastern Anatolia and Syria to the Levant and Mesopotamia, he spoke the Galilean dialect, readily mocked in Jerusalem. By the standards of the southern region of Judea, Galilee was a backwater, important for fishing and farming but suspiciously corrupted by the many Hellenized non-Jews who lived around its large lake. Whether he could read or write Aramaic or Hebrew is an open question. The word used in the gospels to describe his occupation and economic class is *tekton*, which can mean any kind of artisan or craftsman, including carpenter, mason, or metal worker. "Builder" is probably the best translation.[1] If he was a builder or the son of a builder it is unlikely he was educated in any formal way, though he might have become literate with the help of a synagogue teacher.

The third language of the region was Hebrew. In the same Semitic group as Aramaic, it was no longer spoken regularly in Galilee but known to Jews everywhere through quotations from the scriptures, hymns, and religious terms. It was used in Jerusalem and the Temple, though it was regular practice to comment on the biblical texts in Aramaic and to translate scriptural Hebrew into Aramaic as well. In the gospel of John, Pilate writes out a famous inscription, "The King of the Jews," and has it fastened to the cross. John comments: "Many Jews read this inscription because the place where Iesous was crucified was near the city and it had been written in Hebrew, Latin, and Greek" (19.20). When the evangelist wrote "Hebrew" he actually meant Aramaic. Aramaic for locals, Latin for Romans, and Greek for everybody else.

The fourth language, then, was the Latin of Roman officials, used among themselves, for communication with Rome, and for inscriptions on monuments. Elite Romans learned Greek, which was considered more refined, backed by a large ancient literature that provided a model for Latin. In practice Greek would have been necessary for any administrator posted to the eastern Mediterranean. Contrary to Mel Gibson's film *The Passion of the Christ* (2004), the trial before Pilate would have been conducted in Greek, not Latin. The ordinary Roman soldiers in Galilee were most likely not Roman at all but mercenary legionnaires hired from a variety of eastern ethnic groups, perhaps Aramaic speakers, but with at least some Greek as a shared tongue.

Four languages around a lake where Jews and gentiles, Phoenicians and Syrians, Pereans and Persians, Macedonians and Romans crossed

---

1. *Tekton* is used in Mark 6.3 and Matthew 13.55. Two incidents in the gospels show Yeshua as literate. Luke (4.16–20) has him begin his ministry in the Nazareth synagogue by reading a passage from the scroll of Isaiah and commenting on it. In the scene of the woman caught in adultery, John (8.6–8) has him write with his finger in the earth, though what he writes is not mentioned. On the linguistic and social meaning of *tekton* see Campbell, "What Was Jesus' Occupation?"

and recrossed in trade, manufacture, politics, conflict, and religion. People were translating all the time, usually into Greek. Throughout the New Testament "a Greek" is used to identify a gentile, referring both to the language and the Hellenized situation, but educated Jews knew Greek as well, and had used it regularly for some centuries in speech and writing.

Names. Let's start with a name. Known around the world as Jesus Christ, or in some fair variant, neither word was his actual name. The world, Christian and non-Christian, is so used to hearing that name in praise, submission, invocation, and hope, or in anger, curse, denigration, pain, and oath, that it is very difficult for anyone to approach it objectively. "Jesus Christ!" I can say, and mean many things, some of them completely opposite each other. To get beyond our anesthetized use, it might help to use his real name, which was Yeshua. Yeshua, or Yehosshua, with variant transliterations from Hebrew, was the name of a number of biblical characters, most prominently the successor to Moses in the book of Exodus. The standard English equivalent is Joshua, he who "fit the battle of Jericho," in the words of the Black American Spiritual. Joshua's Hebrew name was translated into the Greek version of the Hebrew scripture, the Septuagint, as Iesous (Ἰησοῦς—the final sigma is the Greek masculine singular), and the New Testament writers followed the precedent. It went into Latin as IESVS or Iesus, and then into English and many European tongues with an initial J. Because there are very few other biblical figures whose names in modern languages are rendered as Jesus, the word has achieved a special quality as an independent signifier, sacred, unique, pervasive, and in one sense, incorrect.

The second word, Christ, is not a name at all but a title. Christos in Greek (Χριστός) means "anointed" and translates Hebrew Mashiah, or Messiah. The term refers to the ancient Jewish practice of anointing the heads and bodies of priests and kings with oil, and suggests divine appointment or ratification. (The rite conducted for crowning Solomon is outlined in the first chapter of 1 Kings, and is the basis of the anointing that occurs at the coronation of the monarch of the United Kingdom of Great Britain and Northern Ireland.) In the first century CE Jewish belief was various about a Messiah, a man who might be sent by Yahweh as a great king to restore the ancient state of Israel by defeating its enemies, in order to establish the reign of God on earth. Some segments of Judaism believed that this "end time" would involve the resurrection of the bodies of the righteous dead, who would then live in God's kingdom for a long time or perhaps forever. The enemy now was not one of the ancient foes of Israel recounted in the scriptures but the Roman imperium that controlled and taxed Yahweh's own people. To overthrow that oppression, it was clear, would require a superhuman force with a superhuman general, a new Moses to lead his people not to the promised land, which they already inhabited, but out of the talons of the Roman eagle. Thinking about the end of Roman rule blended into thinking about the end of time itself. Eschatology—concern about the last things, the conflagration, doomsday—was as bright as the sun on the Judean desert.

It had been diversely prophesized that the Messiah would be a descendent of David, "a son of God" or "one like the son of man." These ambiguous terms are theologically nebulous, but the Messiah's power would derive from God's nomination, not from himself. He would not be God, or an aspect of God, but a man lifted up by God. The letters of Paul, written in the decade of the 50s, make clear that early followers of Yeshua, both Jews and gentiles—Christians, we'd call them, though Paul never uses the term—held that Yeshua was the Messiah, a liberator or savior with a purpose that went beyond Jewish traditional expectations to a promise of eternal life for believers in his efficacy. By the time of the earliest gospel, written around 70 CE, the belief was secure enough for its writer to start with: "The beginning of the good message of Iesous the Anointed." Iesous Christos, Jesus Christ: those words mean Yeshua the Messiah.

In a probably hopeless attempt to break through centuries of overuse, in this book I call him Yeshua, except when translating directly from Greek, when I maintain the Greek form.

Calling him by his birth name, however, comes with its own translation trouble. It accents his identity as a Jew, an itinerant teacher of righteousness and a prophet of the end time, but by refusing the Greek translation it runs counter to history. It was in Greek and in the Hellenized Roman world, from Damascus and Antioch to Ephesus and Corinth, that the local Yeshua cult in Palestine spread abroad and gradually separated from Judaism. The farther the cult went westward, the less likely its gentile adherents were to understand Christos as anything other than an alternative or second name of Iesous. The traditional Jewish expectation of a Messiah began to become irrelevant. Judaism was already a Hellenized religion, but the Hellenization of the new sect increased in the decades of the 40s and 50s and turned a Galilean preacher into a general savior. In the gentile world the Yeshua cult became the Christos cult, and the expressly Jewish Messiah became the universal Christ.

The Jerusalem remnant, whose leaders were the Yeshua followers Simon Peter (Shimon Kifa) and John (Yochanan), together with James (Ya'akov) the brother of Yeshua, was for some years after the Crucifixion a kind of mother house to the Christos cult of the west, as we can see in Paul's visits to Jerusalem to pay his respects, pay his dues, and seek approval for his self-ordained mission. But after the leveling of Jerusalem and the destruction of the Temple in 70 CE, the original apostles, dispersed or executed, lost their claim of centrality and the focus shifted westward to Antioch and ultimately to Rome. Socially this meant that a small Jewish subset in Palestine, where Yeshua was understood to be a spiritual reformer of the established Judean order, moved to a collection of diaspora Jews and gentiles who, sometime in the second century, saw him as a radical break with Hebraic practice. The Galilean cult became a new religion of the uncircumcised, yet one that worshipped the deity of the circumcised, who was no longer called by the Hebrew proper name Yahweh but the general Greek word Theos. Because the new sect arose inside the Roman Empire, and because its language was the Greek of the Roman Empire, its increase was quicker and easier.

I am going to use the name Yeshua anyway. If nothing else, it should help to remind us that though all the Christian documents from the first century are in Greek, the words ascribed to Yeshua in the gospels were already translations of his Aramaic speech. That is also a help when reflecting on how later factions of Christianity fell to arguing over the meaning of his sayings, or when a textual scholar today must make a difficult choice among the variant readings in the Greek manuscripts that have come down to us. "This is my body": the phrase has caused a great deal of dissension over the meaning of "is" in Yeshua's words over the bread at the Last Supper. Was he saying I am in this bread actually, or metaphorically, or spiritually, or memorially? And always will be when you repeat the action? Or was he saying only that right now, at this moment, like bread I am consumed? The earliest recorded formulation is in Paul (1 Corinthians 11.24: *touto mou estin to soma*; word for word, "this of me is the body"). But in a Semitic language such as Aramaic, as John Barton points out, there would be no verb in the sentence at all, no equivalent of *estin*, just "this my body" or "my body this."[2] The arguments over meaning might remain, but they should not be about the word *is*.

---

2. Barton, *History of the Bible*, 155. Mark (14.22) uses the same words in a slightly different order; Matthew (26.26) and Luke (22.19) copy Mark.

I must make it clear, however, that by preferring his Hebrew/Aramaic name I do not hope to recapture the historical Yeshua or retrieve his original words or what he might have meant by them. As I explain below in a section on evidence, there is no path to the actual man behind the faith that followed in his wake. We have the texts of the New Testament, that's all. Calling him Yeshua is my way of defamiliarizing our use of the word *Jesus* while at the same time reminding us that he was a Jew.

A second category of translation familiarity sticks to the word *gospel*. It too has acquired derived meanings: a gospel sect, the gospel truth, the gospel tradition, gospel-sharp, gospel music, a gospel singer, the prosperity gospel, a gospel shop (a scornful eighteenth-century name for a Methodist chapel), and a delightful term for a puritan zealot, a hot gospeler. *Gospel* is very much an English word. It comes from Old English *god-spel*, meaning good word or good news, as translated from Latin *evangelium*, good news or, more precisely, good message. *Gospel* lost that meaning many centuries ago. It is unfortunate that it is still used, but it would be hard to replace: the Good Message would seem very awkward now as a descriptive noun for the four canonical gospels, though nothing prevents a translation from using it. Most European languages use some variant of *evangelium*, though those variants too have lost the original meaning, except in modern Greek. In English we have *evangelist* and *evangelize* and *evangelical*, but when we speak of the books themselves we call them gospels.

The word in Greek is *euaggelion* (εὐαγγέλιον; the double gamma γγ, or *gg* in Roman letters, is pronounced *ng*, explaining the Latin form of the word). *Euaggelion* and its variants appear often in the New Testament, particularly in Paul, who tends to refer less to specific proclamations of Yeshua and more to the entirety of his message, or to Yeshua as bearer of the good message. In classical Greek the word usually referred to a happy report, such as victory in a battle, or to the reward given to the messenger of the report. It appears in the Septuagint chiefly as a verb, meaning to proclaim the good news of rescue by God. As far as we know, however, Mark was the first to use the word to describe a book. "The beginning of the good message of Iesous the Anointed"—that is his Incipit or opening, the first line of a scroll that normally stood for a title. By "beginning" did he mean that this is the Incipit, or did he mean that this is the start of the good message? Or that Iesous the Anointed is the good message itself? Mark avoids the biographical background that so occupies Matthew and Luke, who go into detail about the genealogy and birth of Yeshua. Instead

Mark jumps to what he considered important, the start of Yeshua's ministry, suggesting that the good news consists not of the arrival of the Messiah on earth but of his mature activity on earth. Not the man but his words and deeds. In line with much scholarship, I think the phrase "son of God" that appears in some manuscripts at the end of the first verse is likely a later addition, what biblical scholars call "secondary." Mark is careful to show that Yahweh names Yeshua as his son at the moment of his baptism in the River Jordan. In Mark he did not exist from birth as the son of God as the gospel of Matthew has it, or from his miraculous conception as Luke has it, or as the word (*logos*) of God from all time as John has it. In Mark he was nominated or appointed by God at the moment his agency was authorized.[3]

The other evangelists do not use *euaggelion* to describe their books. In fact Matthew uses the noun only four times and Luke doesn't use it at all, though he does apply the verb form ten times, with the meaning of *evangelize*: "to proclaim the good message."[4] Perhaps Mark did not intend the word to mean a book, but it is a sign of his influence that *euaggelion* became the universal term in early Christianity to describe all the gospels, including the various noncanonical gospels written in the second century.

Though not of the same degree of importance, another New Testament translated word is also a complication for its readers: *church*. The Greek word *ekklesia* means an assembly or gathering of people; its root meaning is "to call out." It is rare in the gospels but is pervasive in Paul, Acts, and Revelation to describe the gatherings of early followers of Christos outside Palestine. To render the word as *church*, however, as almost all translations do, gives a misleading impression. After the establishment of Christianity as the state religion of the empire in the late fourth century, the significance of *ekklesia* was very different from what it had been in the first century. The model of the gatherings of the earliest diasporic Christians was the diasporic Jewish assembly called the synagogue, a place for reading the Hebrew scriptures, discussion, and prayer, independent of the Temple in Jerusalem. In neither the Jewish nor the Christian case did the gathering have anything like the implied

---

3. This position, which touches on the divinity of Yeshua, is discussed a number of times elsewhere in the book. I should note that it is possible that the entirety of the first verse of Mark is secondary, inserted later to explain the purpose of the gospel.

4. Painter, *Mark's Gospel*, 24.

authority that *church* achieved later and has today, whether referring to an organized sect of Christianity or to a building dedicated to worship.

Through Latin the Greek word eventually gave us such terms as *ecclesiastic*, increasing our modern sense of a historic and powerful institution. Such expansions of the first-century use of *ekklesia* imply an ordained practice that misunderstands what those first gatherings were: soft and private meetings of small groups in a house or hall in Antioch or Philippi or Rome, providing opportunity to discuss the effect of the Resurrection or the meaning of redemption and to celebrate an elementary rite centered around a meal, the earliest representation of the Last Supper.[5] Paul's first letter to the Corinthians is a corrective to improper ritual and moral practice, and reveals clearly that the *ekklesia* of Corinth was not an established organization but an informal gathering of like-minded people unsure of how the new faith was to be exercised.

Translating gospel. Beyond our numbed sense of those crucial translated words—*Jesus, Christ, gospel, church*—lies the larger field of translating the scriptures themselves into other languages. I've mentioned the Septuagint, the Greek version of the Hebrew bible made in Alexandria and Palestine in the third and second centuries BCE. In the legend of its origin, Ptolemy II Philadelphus commissioned seventy-two biblical scholars to prepare a translation so he could learn the history and philosophy of the Jews. Thus it became known as the Septuagint, from the Latin word for seventy, and is abbreviated by the Roman numeral LXX. That tale is mythical, but it is true that the Jews of Ptolemaic Egypt and elsewhere had over the centuries lost their Hebrew and needed a version in the common language.[6]

So it was with the new religion as well. By the end of the second century, translations of the New Testament had been made into Latin, Syriac, and Coptic. Other ancient translations include versions in Slavic, Germanic, and Aramaic languages, as well as Georgian, Armenian,

---

5. Adams treats the nature of the gatherings in *Earliest Christian Meeting Places*.

6. As with much of ancient literature, the story of the Greek Septuagint is complicated and contentious. The order of its books differs from the canonical Hebrew version (the Masoretic text), and certain books are included that are considered apocryphal in Talmudic Judaism. What is important for us is that all the New Testament writers quoted from it rather than from the Hebrew scriptures and adopted some of its language. As a result, certain Greek terms from the Septuagint became crucial to the New Testament and the development of Christianity, such as *christos, pneuma hagios* (sacred breath or holy spirit), and *hamartia* (mistake or sin), which I discuss later. A useful summary is provided by the article on the Septuagint by Emmanuel Tov in Coogan, *Oxford Encylopedia of the Books of the Bible*, 2:305–17.

Ethiopic, Persian, and Arabic. Many surviving non-Greek manuscripts are important to textual scholars because they sometimes contain alternative readings to the Greek manuscripts.[7] There is no need here to trace the history of New Testament translation because the overriding point is not where or when translations occurred but that so many did occur, and so readily. Christianity would not have become the world's largest religion had it not encouraged or allowed translations of its major writings and ritual practices. Unlike ancient Hebrew for Judaism, Koine Greek became neither the sole ceremonial language of Christianity nor the only official language of its documents. Since the words of Yeshua in the New Testament were already translations of his Aramaic speech, no superior or sacred quality was attached to Greek; the language was used as a convenience because it was widely understood in the regions where the new religion proliferated.

Outside Palestine the eucharistic rite began in Greek for a similar convenience, and like the gospels eventually was translated into the languages of other cities that contained Christian communities. Some of those languages have been preserved in ritual practices into the present, well after they ceased to be spoken as vernaculars. A notable example is Syriac, an Aramaic language close to Yeshua's own tongue, still used in two branches of Syriac Christianity. The Egyptian language called Coptic is the linguistic basis of an ancient Christian group that developed in Alexandria and that still has contemporary adherents in Egypt and West Asia. Like Syriac, Coptic was supplanted as a spoken language by Arabic after Islamic conquest but remained in the Christian liturgy. Meanwhile Greek was retained in areas of the eastern Mediterranean that continued to speak it, bolstered by Constantine's establishment of Constantinople as the capital of the Roman empire in 330 CE, and remains the ritual language of various branches of the Eastern (or Greek) Orthodox Church.

By far the most important example of a translated Christian language is Latin. Jerome's Latin Vulgate, completed around 400, included both testaments and became the principal version of the bible in the west and the official edition for the Roman church. A thousand years later the Vulgate's status was further elevated when it was chosen as the first book to be printed in Europe with movable type (the Gutenberg Bible, Mainz, 1455). The printing press was the most important technology

---

7. The standard introduction to textual matters is Metzger and Ehrman, *Text of the New Testament*. Their discussion of the importance of ancient witnesses, including early translations and patristic quotations, is contained on pp. 94–134.

behind the Reformation, and the Vulgate was often the basic text for early modern biblical translations into vernacular European languages. What was true of the bible was true of ceremonial Christianity as well. Latin was the universal language of the Roman rite around the world from the early middle ages to the late 1960s; it is still used in Rome and elsewhere, though the vast majority of Latin-rite Masses are now in local languages. The Mass retained a few Greek phrases—*Kyrie eleison* (Lord, have mercy) and *agios athanatos eleison imas* (holy deathless one, have mercy on us, in the Good Friday service)—but the language that came to dominate Christianity was Latin.

It serves us well to remember that this happened not because Latin had a privileged position in early Christianity—as we've seen, it was a latecomer to Greek, which had both priority and evangelic authenticity. It happened because the Roman empire, its imperial administration, its architecture, its priestly garments, its hierarchical social codes, and especially its Italic language, were appropriated by the center of Christian authority. Latin is still the official language of Roman Catholicism for law, communication, and doctrinal pronouncement. It achieved this status not because Yeshua spoke it, or even had it spoken to him, but because Rome spoke it. The rising Christian establishment subsumed the falling Roman empire. As if to solidify the notion after the fact, in the fifteenth century the Vatican chose a new title for the pope as head of the church: Pontifex Maximus or Supreme Pontiff, a designation borrowed directly from the title of the high priest of the pagan religion of ancient Rome. In the Roman imperial era, the Pontifex Maximus was the emperor himself.

I grew up in a Catholic world that accepted without question the concept of a monarchic papacy. The pope of my youth, Pius XII (Eugenio Pacelli, reigned 1939–1958), seemed to me then the very signal of sanctity and infallible righteousness. His otherness was complete: his clothing, his speech, his celibate appearance, his piecing dark eyes behind reflective round glasses—all of these increased the aura of his holy power, which was exercised with rigorous conviction. No one in my circle thought to question the absurd nature of his office, dispensing blessings and indulgences along with divisive theological doctrine, and pontificating with equal assurance on family, sexuality, medicine, evolution, capital punishment, and liturgical practice. During the Second World War he worked behind the scenes to help displaced people and the Allied cause but, living inside Mussolini's Italy and thinking his primary duty was to protect the prerogatives of the church, he failed to condemn outright the

Nazi persecution of the Jews at a time when papal censure might have had force. His reputation has been much tarnished by this diplomatic prevarication, but at the time it had little effect for ordinary Catholics like my parents.

Pius XII, so full of imperial proclamations, had as little to say about the gospels as most of his modern predecessors and successors. Of course there is a vast difference in space, time, and purpose between the organization of the twentieth-century Latin church and the first-century documents that were used to certify its belief system. But overlooking the gospels in favor of theorizing about the nature of God and his works, which we call theology, was already a Christian habit from the first formalizing of doctrine under Constantine, at the council of Nicaea in 325 CE. This intriguing circumstance is discussed in the next chapter. For now, I propose to look at the gospels as documents—what they were for, who they were for, what they set out to document—and why Mark, as the oldest of them, had the impact that it did.

Four gospels. The relationships among the four gospels have never been clear. At the outside limits they were written between 65 and 110 CE, or from thirty-five to eighty years after the Crucifixion of Yeshua, which occurred around 30 CE. The canonical gospels were accepted as genuine by the middle of the second century, when they had achieved wide circulation in the form of copied and recopied papyrus manuscripts. But dating them precisely, identifying their authors and places of composition, and making reasonable suppositions about their purposes and audiences—these matters are difficult and perhaps unresolvable.

> Matthew, Mark, Luke, and John,
> Bless the bed I lay upon.

The child's bedtime prayer orders the gospels in the traditional way, the way they appear in all the bibles you are likely to see, no matter the translation. This ordering dates from the second century, based on the notion that the apostle Matthew wrote the first gospel, in Hebrew. Though the idea of Hebrew (or Aramaic) composition lost favor, the order remained unchallenged; in the fifth century Augustine of Hippo solidified the notion that Matthew was first, that Mark prepared a summary of Matthew, and then Luke synthesized the two versions. John came later and reflected a different sense of Yeshua's significance than the first three. The traditional chronology remained standard. Because shorter and thought to derive from Matthew, Mark's gospel was never very important to the developed Christian church.

The Synoptic Problem. Readers had long recognized the similarities of the first three gospels, which were called *synoptic* because they could be "seen together" in the sense of laid side by side. Though the synoptics differ in length and emphasis, they tell the same story in the same narrative order and with the approximate same goal: Yeshua appears in Galilee, predicts the end of time and the arrival of the kingdom of God, teaches a new way of thinking about God and human interaction, effects cures of spiritual and physical evils, goes to Jerusalem to spread his message, is rejected by the Temple establishment, is tried and condemned, executed by the Roman forces on a cross, set in a tomb, and rises again. It is a simple yet extraordinary story, a biography of a reformer first honored then spurred, and its overplot is followed in all four gospels. Why then are there four instead of one? More particularly, why are the three synoptic gospels so closely related?

Addressing the problem through critical (or scientific) philology, a number of scholars over time proposed a change in the order of composition. It makes a good deal more sense, they held, to consider Mark as primary. He would have based his account on traditional stories and sayings of Yeshua that had been circulating in the various Christian assemblies in the empire, such as those Paul visited and wrote to. This material was predominantly oral and probably was first received from the apostles and disciples of Yeshua. In the nature of oral transmission, it varied in detail and emphasis from place to place. Matthew and Luke, in different locations and working independently of each other, used Mark as their primary source, often copying him directly, even when his Greek is more awkward than their more fluid styles. Each also added material that Mark did not have or chose not to use.

It is a reasonable supposition, but the theory solves only part of the problem. Of the non-Markan material, Matthew and Luke share a good portion but put what they share in different narrative sections of their texts. Does that mean that Luke copied Matthew as well as Mark? If so, why would Luke alter the placement, especially since the additions are not narrative but consist almost entirely of quotations ascribed to Yeshua? It makes more sense to think Matthew and Luke received the new material separately from a second common source, written rather than oral because the wording each uses is close, often identical. Scholars gave this putative document the title Q (for *Quelle*, German for source), and presumed it to be a list of the sayings of Yeshua compiled fairly early and later lost. Mark probably did not have it, though he may have had a shorter list of sayings. Q, itself a hypothesis, made possible a further idea, called the Two-Document Hypothesis (figure 1).

FIGURE 1

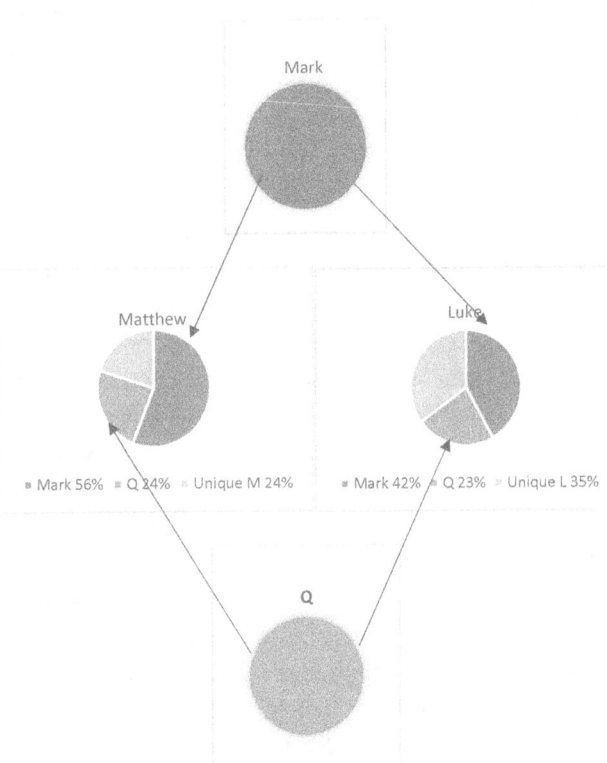

The Two-Document Hypothesis

The last piece of the synoptic puzzle was the problem of material that is specific to Matthew or specific to Luke (M and L in the diagram)—material not in Mark or the hypothetical Q document that must have come from other sources, including oral tradition known to the Christian communities of Matthew or Luke.

Figure 1 gives the percentages of source use. In rough terms, about half of both Matthew and Luke comes directly from Mark, including the outline and a good portion of the phrasing. About a quarter of each comes from Q, mostly sayings. The last quarter is "special material" (German

Sondergut) that appears only in Matthew or only in Luke and in no other gospel. Since Matthew and Luke are each twice as long as Mark, the percentages disguise the degree to which the others depend on him; only a very small portion of Mark is not found in one or both of the others.

It is a very neat theory, and the great majority of modern scholars accept it. There is only one trouble: no external evidence supports it, no historical records, no absolute dates—like many literary theories, it is a deduction that proceeds from analyzing the texts themselves. I think it is right because no other explanation fits the internal evidence as well; the alternative explanations are considerably less convincing.[8] In this book I assume what is known as Markan priority, though I recognize it cannot be absolutely proved. We simply cannot know with assurance the order of composition of the gospels, any more than we can know who Homer was, or even if he existed. Ancient texts generally do not lend themselves to that kind of certainty.

Lack of evidence. Even the most carefully documented biography is likely to distort some aspect of its subject's actual life. A life must be understood backward, Kierkegaard famously said, but can only be lived forward. Retrospection is the essential characteristic of life writing. If this is a biographical challenge for a contemporary figure, how much more difficult for someone who died two millennia ago. Whatever their subject, the historians in the Roman empire of the first century CE—Pliny, Tacitus, Suetonius, Plutarch—leave us longing for more detail, more evidence, more certainty. When we turn to the New Testament, the lack of external records is a major problem. It would be wonderful to find the historical Yeshua who is veiled behind the gospels, but all the rigors of historical scholarship have failed to uncover him. The quest for the historical Jesus, to use the title of Albert Schweitzer's famous book from 1906, has provided revealing contexts of first-century Judaism and useful insights into the social conditions of Galilee. But the quest is ultimately futile: there is no access to the actual Yeshua. What the gospels say, no

---

8. The history of the synoptic problem is another complex topic that is not very helpful in the context of this book. However, two alternatives to the Two-Document Hypothesis still attract some historians today. The earliest and least likely dates to Jakob Griesbach in the 1780s, revived by William Farmer in 1964; usually called the Two-Gospel Hypothesis, it proposes that Matthew was first, Luke drew on him, and finally Mark drew on both. The second, called the Farrer Hypothesis after an essay by Austin Farrer of 1955, claims Markan priority over Matthew but holds that Luke used both Mark and Matthew. Other scholars accept Markan priority but doubt the existence of Q, even though they recognize that leaves a hole in the theory. A useful general introduction is Goodacre's *Synoptic Problem*.

matter how much they may have been biased or corrupted, is what we have. While there are a few mentions of Christians in Roman sources, and references to a leader called Christus,[9] the hard truth is that everything of substance comes from the New Testament, written by those committed to the cause.

The books collected there were composed over a period of about a century by separate writers spread around the empire. They differ significantly in genre and purpose. Side by side in the last part of the complete Christian bible are letters of instruction to specific communities that contain indirect theology, more general letters of hope and correction, the biographical-eschatological works we call gospels, a history of the earliest proselytizing (Acts of the Apostles, presented as part two of the gospel of Luke), and a strange book of overwrought revelation or prophetic symbolism that is at best equivocal and at worst incomprehensible. Though everything in the New Testament comes out of belief in Yeshua as Messiah, it is impossible to draw from the totality an absolute sense of the history behind that belief. The gospels themselves, which claim authority as records of the life and death of a charismatic teacher, often contradict each other. I will have more to say about that later; for now it is important to acknowledge that to speak of the historical Yeshua is to speak of the remembered Yeshua, the man recalled in a variety of oral traditions that were written down and embellished two or three generations later.

We take for granted that important events will be documented, dated according to a recognized calendar, with a result available for some form of retrieval. Despite centuries of biblical scholarship, it is simply not possible to find such certainty with New Testament records. It is best to admit our ignorance and to acknowledge that Paul and the evangelists were interested in something other than modern historical accuracy. In fact, the notion that the events contained in the gospels could be analyzed systematically is foreign to the nature of their texts. We do not know even the most basic things, such as who the writers were, when they wrote, where they wrote, or for whom.

Who. It is understandable that the Christian church, once established, would want to secure the authenticity of the gospels by claiming apostolic authority. Justin Martyr, one of the earliest apologists, writing about 150 CE, called them the "memoirs" or "reminiscences" of the apostles. From an early stage the gospels of Matthew and John

---

9. For example, Josephus, *Antiquities of the Jews* 20.9 (c. 93–94 CE); Tacitus, *Annals* 15.44 (c. 118 CE).

were associated with the apostles of those names. Luke was assumed to be the sometime companion of Paul. Similarly, Mark was supposed to be the John Mark of Acts, another of Paul's companions. But there exists no evidence for any of this. Given their late dates, it is unlikely that the apostles Matthew or John wrote the gospels ascribed to them, or had them ghostwritten based on reminiscences. The only testimony for Luke's connection to Paul comes from the "we" passages of Acts (chapters 16, 20–21, 27–28), in which the writer suddenly shifts from the third person to the first person plural, implying that he was, for a time, part of Paul's entourage. Its opening verses claim that Acts was written by the evangelist of the gospel according to Luke for a man named Theophilus, though the author is not named in either book and Theophilus, which means "lover of God," might have been an imaginary or idealized audience.[10] Though Paul called himself an apostle of Christ, he never met the man Yeshua and could at best have secondhand information about his life, gathered from his meetings with Peter, James, and John in Jerusalem, or from other first-generation disciples.

There is no support at all for the association of Mark the evangelist with the John Mark of Acts. There is one piece of evidence, however, for connecting Mark to the apostle Peter. Eusebius, the bishop of Caesarea, wrote the first history of the church around 325 CE. In it he quoted Papias, the overseer of the Christians in Hierapolis in the early second century, to the effect that Mark was "Peter's interpreter" and wrote his gospel based on Peter's teaching, with details as the apostle remembered them.[11] Papias' work did not survive and there are serious doubts about the reliability of Eusebius as a historian. He was clearly an apologist bolstering the authority of the church, just after Emperor Constantine granted Christians the right to practice the religion openly.

We have to conclude that the gospels are anonymous. Were their authors Jews, Hellenized diaspora Jews, or gentiles? Were they pagan "God fearers" who had been attracted to Judaism and attended a synagogue to learn about the Jewish belief in a single God? We simply don't know. The

---

10. Loveday Alexander, who thinks Theophilus was an actual person, examines the possibilities in *Acts: The People's Bible Commentary*.

11. Eusebius, *History of the Church*, 39.15. In the translation by McGiffert (103): "Mark, having become the interpreter of Peter, wrote down accurately, though not in order, whatsoever he remembered of the things said or done by Christ. For he neither heard the Lord nor followed him, but afterward, as I said, he followed Peter, who adapted his teaching to the needs of his hearers, but with no intention of giving a connected account of the Lord's discourses, so that Mark committed no error while he thus wrote some things as he remembered them."

internal evidence can be read in a variety of ways. Of course there is no harm in continuing to identify them by their traditional names, so long as we understand that we are referring to texts rather than identifiable authors. It is better than calling them One, Two, Three, and Four.

When. Things are not much improved when we seek dates of composition. Part of the problem is historiographic, a problematic tendency to use one part of the New Testament to date another. For example, the letters of Paul must have been written between the late 40s and the early 60s, but any more precise dating depends on Paul's travels as related in Acts, which many commentators find questionable, and the writer of Acts, in a perfect circle, may well have used Paul's letters as his chronological basis. Dating the gospels is even harder, as we have seen with regard to the Synoptic Problem. All in all, the process of dating the New Testament is "like a line of drunks, propping each other up, with no fixed wall to lean on."[12] We can be reasonably confident that all of the gospels had been written by 110 CE, but beyond that we have to make assumptions. Using the same limited field of information, scholars often reach opposite conclusions.

Here's a classic case of how the gospels can contradict each other or historical dates regarding the birth of Yeshua. It is widely accepted that the date established in the sixth century as the beginning of the year AD 1 (Anno Domini, in the Year of the Lord) was based on a faulty calculation. Matthew in chapter 2 places the Nativity "during the time of King Herod." That is Herod the Great, who died in March or April of 4 BCE. Luke, on the other hand, in his chapter 2 says it occurred during an imperial census: "This was the first registration while Quirinius was governing Syria." Publius Sulpicius Quirinius was Roman Legate to the province of Syria (which included Palestine) from the year 6 CE, when he did organize a census, but that creates a difference from Matthew of at least ten years. Which is correct? Scholars have long worried this bone; Luke's Greek syntax is confusing and some conclude that the adjective "first" actually means "prior to," making it possible to use Matthew's template and setting the birth of Yeshua around 5 BCE.[13] (Yes, Christ was born Before Christ, another calendrical confusion.) My Greek is not good enough to judge the worth of that reading, but it looks to me like special pleading.

---

12. Barton, *History of the Bible*, 162.

13. For example, Harold W. Hoehner in Evans, *Encylopedia of the Historical Jesus*, 114. For a more complete discussion, see Hoehner's *Chronological Aspects*.

There is so much in Luke that is ornamented or fanciful that I am not inclined to take his chronology literally.

The dates of gospel composition are equally difficult and again there is wide disparity of opinion. We can't speak of a consensus, but most experts think that Mark was composed between 65 and 75 CE. If written for a persecuted community in Rome, as some scholars hold based on the Papias citation, an early date is likely, since Nero's supposed persecution of Christians would have taken place in the years immediately after the great fire of 64 CE. Others argue for a later date in Syria or Palestine, primarily based on Yeshua's prophesy of the destruction of the Temple in Mark 13.2. Jerusalem and the Temple were in fact razed by the army of Titus in July and August of the year 70, but we need not conclude that Mark gave his Yeshua the prophesy after the fact; Judea had been ripe for a rebellion for some years, and the First Jewish War against Roman forces had begun in 66. Given Rome's habit with insurrections, many people could have foreseen the likely conclusion in Jerusalem. Furthermore, one of the gospel's major themes is the prediction of the end time with the imminent arrival of God's kingdom. Mark presents Yeshua as a teacher and healer but primarily as an eschatological prophet who, in the rest of chapter 13, foresees the end of the corrupt Temple-state together with the end of "this adulterous and mistaken [or sinful] generation" (8.38).

I lean strongly toward composition soon after the destruction, but the safest course is to strike an average and assume a date of about 70 for Mark. Since Matthew and Luke rely on Mark's work and include what appear to be later traditions, they are likely to be some ten years after Mark. John, which clearly comes out of a different tradition than the synoptics, perhaps one directly connected to Jerusalem as the end of his gospel implies (21.24), is best dated around the close of the century. Figure 2 gives my approximations.

FIGURE 2

Paul's letters	50–60
Mark	70
Matthew	80–85
Luke	80–90
John	90–110

Conjectured dates: Paul and the evangelists

I have left out Acts of the Apostles, the non-Pauline letters, and Revelation; there is too much controversy over their dates to make useful estimates, though probably all are later than Luke and some later than John. Conjectures about Acts, for instance, range from 80 to 120 CE, while the second letter ascribed to Peter might be as late 150 CE.[14] There is considerable controversy over the dates in figure 2, sometimes based on differing evaluations of the evidence, sometimes on predetermined notions of what should be the case. In his sensible history of the bible, John Barton notes that the differences often involve a writer's attitude to scriptural authority. Those who accept the bible as divinely inspired allow the gospels early dates, on the presumption that the oral tradition on which they are based would have been less corrupted in the first generation after the Crucifixion. Those who approach the New Testament more historically tend to admit the possibility of later dates, placing John, Acts, and some of the general letters well into the second century.[15] In such a contested arena the best we can hope for is balance. Complete objectivity is as beyond reach as absolute chronology, because the record is insufficient and always will be.

Where and for whom. These related questions must be left unanswered, even though there are plenty of guesses. Mark, as we saw, might have been written in Rome, Syria, or Palestine but, all peace to Papias, the argument for any location is guesswork based on internal evidence. Among the signals: Mark's rather basic Greek, suggesting to some commentators that he was not a native speaker; his occasionally inexact geography of Palestine; his imprecise sense of Temple and legal practice. For every argument in favor of one location, at least one is against. Some sections of Mark are clearly addressed to non-Jews, such as the explanation of ritual washing practices at the beginning of chapter 7. Scholars for some time insisted that each gospel was directed to a specific Christian assembly, which may be true but becomes almost irrelevant when we consider that they all were circulating by the second century, just as Paul's letters were, copied and recopied as useful guides for other communities.

What. Trying to determine the genre of the gospels is not as simple as it might seem. Genre is determined not only by an author's intention and chosen form but also by comparison with works of a parallel nature, and as far as the gospels are concerned there really are none. Mark's Good

---

14. Telford, *New Testament*, 82.
15. Barton, *History of the Bible*, 163.

Message has similarities to a number of classical and Hebrew genres, but the combining of them is unique. It is closest to classical biographies (*bios* is the term, anticipating the modern abbreviation), which were normally about a great man's life as a model of behavior for others.[16] We are most familiar with this type through Plutarch's *Lives of the Noble Greeks and Romans*, which was the source for Shakespeare's Roman plays. Plutarch, born near Delphi about 46 CE, wrote in Greek around the turn of the second century. Mark could not have known his work, but Plutarch followed a well-established biographical tradition in Hellenistic culture. He presents in parallel the lives of extraordinary Greeks and Romans who changed the world, such as Pericles, Alexander, Demosthenes, Brutus, Pompey, Julius Caesar, and Mark Antony, movers and shakers of lesser mortals. As Cassius bitterly says of Julius Caesar in Shakespeare's play:

> Why, man, he doth bestride the narrow world
> Like a Colossus, and we petty men
> Walk under his huge legs, and peep about
> To find ourselves dishonorable graves.

Mark too presents the public life of an extraordinary man, not a high figure who moved and shook the earth but one who changed minds by what he spoke. Strangely, Mark is less concerned with what Yeshua taught than with the *effect* of his teaching, which tends to emphasize him as an exceptional being in the eyes of his hearers, somewhat like the Hebrew prophets in the age of revelation and without parallel in his own age. He is singled out by God. Though Mark's Yeshua never claims he is God, it is clear that he is surrounded by divinity, approved by it, infused by it.

At the same time, the book is apocalyptic. The authority of Yeshua is steeped in a sense of the promised end of evil and the establishment of a new reign, secured by God and open to the righteous and repentant. As Adela Yarbo Collins notes in her commentary on Mark, the gospel might be seen as a new type of biography that departed from the Greek and Roman tradition. She calls it an "Eschatological Historical Monograph";[17] i.e., a history of the era that precedes the end of time. That would make its genre almost an anti-biography in the classical sense, an exemplary life story that anticipates, in the very near future, the end of the need for exemplary life stories.

---

16. Bryan outlines the features Mark shares with Hellenistic biographies in *Preface to Mark*, 22–64.

17. Collins, *Mark*, 42, 94.

Collins admits that this is not a sufficient explanation because Mark is also similar to wisdom books and disquisitions on the Torah, collections of miracles, parable stories, and the writings of the Hebrew prophets. As we will see in chapter 7, the gospel has relationships to Greek tragedy and the Homeric epics as well. Mark's Yeshua, a prophet, a lawyer, a spiritual guide, a miracle worker and exorcist, is also a social reformer. He is a feeder of the hungry, a healer of the sick, an advocate for the poor and oppressed. And beyond those aspects he is presented, at first secretly, and then explicitly, as an extraordinary man anointed by God to proclaim the imminent arrival of a new world.

But Mark is more than the sum of its parts. If we accept the Two-Document Hypothesis, as most scholars do, Mark is the primary and central record of the Yeshua tradition. What had been remembered of Yeshua as episodes transmitted by word of mouth and passed on again, possibly altered in the telling, became for the first time fixed in black characters on a scroll of papyrus. The retold memories of the closest disciples, the first generation of followers who were contemporaries of Yeshua, had by the next generation spread farther than they had a right to expect. It is apparent from Paul's early letters, written twenty to thirty years after the Crucifixion, that the main elements of belief were established even earlier, probably within a few years of Yeshua's death. The earliest record comes from Paul's first letter to the Corinthians (15.3–5), most likely written by 55 CE:

> For I handed on to you the most important thing that I also received:
> *That the Anointed [Christos] died for our sins according to the scriptures;*
> *and that he was buried;*
> *and that he was raised on the third day according to the scriptures;*
> *and that he appeared to Cephas, then to the Twelve.*

(Cephas or Kifa is Aramaic for Rock; Petros in Greek, Peter in English, it is the nickname Yeshua gave to Simon, the first apostle.) Many commentators have remarked that the language and phrasing of these verses are not typical of Paul. He seems to be quoting a well-established rubric, an elementary creed articulated as litany or mantra, perhaps a chant or hymn. It expressed in a clear mnemonic formula the essential belief of the apostles and earliest followers who accepted the Resurrection as fact.[18]

---

18. Of the many treatments of this passage as expressing the article or rule of faith,

The practice of the eucharist, though not fixed in ritual form and no doubt variously exercised, had also been recognized in broad outline, as Paul notes in the same letter (11.23–26). It and the article of faith were central to the Christos cult well before Mark. But the stories that backed them up—that is, the traditions about the life and death of Yeshua—were isolated bits, pieces of memory, open to misunderstanding. Paul wrote to the believers in Corinth in part to correct essential truths and practices they had confused or misunderstood. The tradition being passed to the second generation of followers was subject not only to mistake and variation but also ran the risk of oblivion.

Paul's letters say very little about the man he proposes as transformer of the world, and between Paul and Mark no documents about Yeshua, including the sayings source, the hypothetical Q, have survived. By writing down the narrative of his life, Mark set in train a process with enormous implications for history. Copies could be made and distributed in material form to be used by others to repeat or enlarge or preach from, giving context to the article of faith, and incarnating the story of the life of Yeshua.

Of course it is possible, even likely, that Mark changed things to suit the needs of his immediate audience, whoever they might have been. He could have invented episodes as well. We know from Matthew's and Luke's additions that Mark disregarded parts of the Yeshua tradition that were circulating elsewhere, or did not know about them, though it is just as possible that some of those addenda were invented. This is a subject for chapter 5, as is the connection between Mark's writing and the oral tradition on which it is based. Here I need to emphasize that the other synoptic gospels expand and elaborate what Mark gave them: a basic narrative and a general rationale for the life of the subject of the gospels, from his adoption as the son of God to the discovery of the empty tomb.[19] As I have said, John comes out of a literary and memorial tradition distinct from the synoptics, and scholars disagree over whether he used any of

---

two of the clearest are contained in Mack, *A Myth of Innocence*, 104, and Ehrman, *How Jesus Became God*, 136–43.

19. Adoptionism, a non-Trinitarian theological position that holds that Yeshua had only a single nature, that of an ordinary human, can be seen by implication in some of Paul's letters as well as in Mark. The belief seemed to exist in early Christianity simultaneously with the belief that he was both human and divine, and was ultimately overtaken by the doctrine of the Trinity. In *How Jesus Became God*, Ehrman traces the development of "high" and "low" Christologies from the New Testament to the Council of Nicaea.

them. But John's basic story remains as Mark outlined it, and his wording often follows Mark's.

All of which adds up to this: as the earliest record of the life of Yeshua, the Good Message According to Mark is one of the most influential books of all time.

2

Reading Mark

Mark you this, Bassanio?
The devil can cite Scripture for his purpose.

—Shakespeare, *The Merchant of Venice*

I F   I T   I S   T R U E that the Good Message of Mark is so central, why has it not been recognized more widely as a preeminent work of western literature and world culture? In one sense it has been, in the realm of biblical scholarship. There are many books on Mark, ranging from verse-by-verse commentary to complete reevaluations of the nature of Christianity. I can report that some of these are decent, some are confined by devotion, and a few are remarkable works of research and textual understanding. Yet their appreciation of the rarity of a work such as Mark, not just its influence but its inherent quality, has not been generally realized by ordinary people, whether pious Christians or those who, like me, are interested in culture and history.

Part of the difficulty applies to the gospels as a whole—and those words give away my meaning. Since the four gospels cover the same ground, we tend to think of them *as a whole* rather than as individual texts. No doubt there are devotional groups who read the New Testament book by book but most people encounter it in selections, even in individual verses. And of course many people never encounter it at all. Those who do tend to read passages as they occur, perhaps in a random kind of divination: open the book, see where your finger falls. Or they read in what are versions of lectionaries: books that order biblical passages according to a specific theme for daily use. These have become popular in some Christian denominations and for private consultation or psychological assistance. Here is a selection of results from Amazon.com when I searched just now for books under "bible readings": *The One Year Bible, Truth for Life: 365 Daily Devotions, The Bible in a Year, The Married Couple's Bible Study, Reading the Bible for Change, The Bible in 52 Weeks*... you get the point.

That is how I learned the little I knew about the New Testament as a child: through the recitation of passages from the altar, selected to conform to the liturgical calendar or that never-ending stream of Requiem Masses. If the day at hand was, say, one of the feasts of Mary, and if Matthew had the most appropriate section, Matthew provided the reading. Or Mary at the foot of the cross: then it had to be John. Though the author was identified, the important thing was not which gospel was being read but that it was *the* gospel, all considered equal, with differences or variations among them ignored, all *verbum dei*, the word of God.

There are two aspects of this long-standing habit, a practice that survives in most churches today. Taken together, they have been the foundation of the selective approach of established Christianity to the New Testament. I call them Reading Backward and Reading Sideways.

Reading Backward. However great the break Christianity eventually made with Judaism, in the first century it was essential to accentuate their intertwined or progressive relationship. Paul was a Jew, a Pharisee opposed to Yeshua's followers in the early 30s until his miraculous conversion on the way to Damascus, yet he became the principal proclaimer of the Good Message to the west, spreading the Christos cult in Greek to the gentile world. Nonetheless he was careful to maintain the Jewish traditions, or so the Acts of the Apostles claims (21.26), such as observing the festivals and performing the purification rite in the Temple. At the same occasion he gave a speech to in Jerusalem proclaiming his conversion to the new way—in Aramaic, not Greek. To his assemblies of diaspora Jews and gentile Christians he explained that Yeshua's salvation was effected through the old religion of Israel, by the one God of the Jews. He followed the model of the Septuagint and called him Theos, not Yahweh or Elohim; all the same, he is the God who made a pact with Abraham long ago and now has sent his anointed representative to change the nature of time. The prophets projected it, and now it has come to pass. He never suggested that Jews who chose to follow Christos were freed from circumcision and the Law. He insisted only that gentiles could become believers without first becoming Jews. This is one of the main themes of his letter to the Romans, which became a crucial document in the development of early Christian theology.

Again according to Acts (28.23), when Paul was under arrest in Rome he tried to convince the Jewish community of he truth of his message, drawing on passages "both from the law of Moses and the prophets." When some of the Roman Jews remained unconvinced, he chastised their dull hearts by quoting from chapter 6 of Isaiah; he could use the scriptures both as argument and as condemnation. As John Barton sees it, Paul made the Hebrew bible "a story of disaster calling out for rescue," contradicting the Jewish understanding that the sacred books are the story of Israel's contract with Yahweh. In the Christian view Adam is the main character, his sin of disobedience requiring rescue by the new Adam in the figure of Christos; for Judaism the main character is Abraham as founder of the nation.[1] Supersessionism was a later concept, an idea that Christianity was a Jewish sect that superseded Judaism, but can be seen as already implicit in Paul. Not all scholars would accept that as fact, but there is no doubt that Paul draws on the Hebrew scriptures often to establish his case with a great sense of urgency. He believed that the world might end in his own lifetime, that he had very few years left to spread the word. His work was pressing and his mission overwhelming. Yeshua would return with the new kingdom so soon that theological squabbling was irrelevant. Time was about to end. Evil would be destroyed. The dead would rise, the righteous would be rewarded, and peace would reign.

Fifteen or twenty years later, Mark was more interested in exactly how the new related to the old. The kingdom had not arrived, Paul was dead, Rome and its evil still controlled the world, but the Yeshua that Mark presents is as eschatological as Paul's. To credit Yeshua's authenticity, the earliest evangelist used a careful parallel between the past and the present, stabilizing the tactic of detecting how the Messiah's arrival was predicted in the Hebrew scriptures. For Mark as for Paul, the fulfillment of prophesy is proof of Yeshua's appointment.

Mark jumps right to it. After the Incipit, he calls on the prophets to secure the validity of John the Baptizer as precursor to the Messiah. "As it was written in Isaiah the prophet," he writes, then quotes:

---

1. Barton, *History of the Bible*, 313–14.

> *See now, I send my messenger before your face*
> *who will lay the road for you.*
> *The voice of one shouting in the wasteland,*
> *Prepare the way of the Lord, straighten his paths.*

Mark continues with "Then John came, baptizing in the wasteland," assured that the ancient prophesy will clinch his point without the need for further argument. John the Baptizer was sent to prepare the way for Yeshua; God's prophets forecast it, therefore it must be true. Mark identifies the verses as from Isaiah but actually only the second two lines are from that book (40.3). The first two are from Malachi (3.1), and you have to widen their context and meaning to understand the passages as forecasts of the Baptizer. That doesn't matter to Mark, who was probably quoting from memory; what matters is the connection he can make between the Hebrew scriptures and Yeshua as the Anointed, linking the ancient to the now. That is reading backward, justifying the present by the past.

It was the custom in Judaism, of course. Jewish ritual practice and the rule of daily life were based on the Tanakh, the collection of miscellaneous writings that make up the Hebrew bible. The first five books of that bible, the Torah or the Law, were ascribed to Moses as dictated by God. (They are called the Pentateuch in Christianity, from a Greek word meaning "five scrolls.") The scrolls of the Torah certified the contract, a covenant between Yahweh and Israel. The scrolls themselves were revered, and are still paraded during synagogue services. As Werner Kelber notes, the Jewish veneration of scrolls "is without parallel in classical antiquity."[2] But many cultures appeal to a founding myth or document, often from the distant past, as a guide or justification for contemporary circumstance. Whether the Bhagavad Gita, King John's Magna Carta, or the American constitution, it is useful to be free to interpret or reinterpret a sacred charter in order to explain or sustain a new condition. If the scroll needs to be stretched to make the accommodation, אָמֵן, *ahmain*, so be it.

In Mark there are numerous appeals to scripture, about twenty in all, and most are put into the mouth of Yeshua. His teaching is imbued with quotations from or references to the Torah, and he often cites the prophets to proclaim that the scripture has now been fulfilled or soon will be with his death. Here are some examples of Mark's approach.

---

2. Kelber, *Oral and Written Gospel*, 16.

- And he said to them, "Isaiah prophesied correctly about you dissemblers, as it is written: *This people reveres me with their lips but their heart is kept far away from me; they worship me in vain, pronouncing doctrines that are the edicts of men.* Neglecting God's commandment, you keep up the traditions of men" (7.6–8).

- Then he lectured them, saying, "Was it not written that *My house will be called a house of prayer for all the nations*? But you have made it a cave of bandits" (11.17).

- "Regarding the dead rising, have you not read in the book of Moses about the bush, how God spoke to him, saying: *I am the God of Abraham and the God of Isaac and the God of Jacob*? He is not God of the dead but of the living" (12.26–27).

- Iesous said to them, "Am I a bandit, that you come out with swords and clubs to capture me? I was with you every day teaching in the Temple and you did not arrest me. But the scriptures must be fulfilled" (14.48–49).

- Iesous said to them, "You will all desert me, for it is written: *I will strike the shepherd and the sheep will be scattered.* But when I am raised I will walk ahead of you to Galilee" (14.27–28).

Given what Christianity became, it is easy to forget how thoroughly the synoptics see Yeshua as a Jewish prophet. Though Mark vilifies the Temple authorities for rejecting the Messiah, his gospel ties Yeshua inextricably to observant practice. Citing authorizing passages from the ancient scriptures, and interpreting them with new understanding, caused Yeshua to stand out as a teacher in Galilee and be condemned in Jerusalem. Despite his scriptural evidence, official Judaism rebuffed the emancipator it allegedly expected. Mark saw the irony implicit in the Yeshua story and made it central to his telling. Mark's narrator and Mark's Yeshua do not hesitate to take a line or two of the Hebrew scriptures out of context in order to make a point about that irony.

With such a backdrop it is not surprising that the early church did something similar with the New Testament. The First Council of Nicaea in 325, called by Emperor Constantine to regularize certain principles of the faith, was the key occasion for separating doctrine from the gospels. Now that Christianity was permitted in the Roman empire, Constantine wanted disagreements about fundamentals resolved. The council, made up of more than three hundred bishops, chiefly from the eastern empire, focused on the most pressing issue of Christology: how the Messiah as Son of God was linked to the divinity and oneness of the Father. The first version of the Nicene Creed was written then; it insisted that there was only one God, yet held that Iesous was God too, begotten by the Father from before time and of the same substance as the Father. (The Greek word used was *homoousion*, meaning consubstantial. The position of the Holy Spirit was left undefined until the creed was altered and expanded at a second council, in Constantinople in 381.)

A leading reason for calling the Council of Nicaea was the popularity of an opposing position taken by Arius of Alexandria. Arius held that the Son had to have been made by the Father, was not consubstantial with him, and logically was subordinate to him. The teaching may have represented a widespread belief that Arius expressed in philosophic terms; we know he had adherents in Alexandria and elsewhere and that his popularity incensed his bishop, Athanasius. After assessing the arguments the council condemned Arianism as heretical. So began the long history of the church establishing doctrine negatively, reaching consensus by rejecting what was considered outside the bounds of acceptable belief. Paul had anticipated this method in his instructions to the assembly in Corinth around 55 CE: "It is necessary for there to be factions among you, so that what is acceptable should become evident to you" (1 Corinthians 11.19). Constantine, who thought himself Pontifex Maximus of Christianity, acted as arbiter or president of the council. He took the anti-Arian position and it was he who insisted on inserting *consubstantial* into the creed. Why he did this is not known; perhaps he sensed it was a majority opinion of the bishops and the easiest course. Thus one of the most challenging concepts in the history of Christianity, that Yeshua was the Son of the Father yet coexisted with him from all time, was a political rather than a theological decision.[3]

For us the significance of the debate lies in the fact that neither the Nicene nor the Arian position about Yeshua's relationship to the divine Father is expressed in the New Testament. The two sides at Nicaea used selected verses, especially from the gospel of John, to support their views. Both took for granted the great leap, that the man Yeshua was God in

---

3. Eusebius, the bishop of Caesarea, writing to his church about the creed after the council: ". . . but our most pious emperor, before any one else, testified that it was most orthodox. He confessed, moreover, that such were his own sentiments; and he advised all present to agree to it, and to subscribe its articles and assent to them, with the insertion of the single word Consubstantial . . ." (Quoted from Stevenson, *A New Eusebius*, 345.) I treat the "son of God" question in more detail in chapter 4.

reality, and argued only over whether he was always so or was made so, whether he was equal to the Father or dependent on him. John can be seen to imply both positions. Mark implies neither. "Son of God" is as close as Mark gets to claiming any form of divinity for Yeshua, but Mark's context for the term implies adoption, as I have said before, or at the most an elevation or exaltation to a higher level.

Even before Nicaea it was habitual practice to use selective reading of the New Testament to support theological positions. A tradition of *testimonia* had developed, in which lists of passages in the Hebrew scriptures—now called the Old Testament from the Christian perspective—were interpreted as pointing to the arrival of Yeshua as Messiah. The custom found its ultimate expression in the middle ages in the practice of typology, a form of reading that saw Old Testament figures as types or previews of New Testament antitypes, who replaced or apotheosized them. Thus Adam = Christ, Eve = Mary, Moses as liberator = Christ as savior, Isaac about to be sacrificed by his father = Christ sacrificed by his Father, Jonah in the belly of the big fish = Christ in the tomb, and so on in many imaginative allegorical or anagogic representations.

The doctrine of the Trinity is an important example of reshaping scripture for theological intent. There is only one expression of the Trinity in the gospels (Matthew 28.19, a textually contentious verse), yet the concept became central to Christian understanding of the godhead. The idea confuses most believers and has caused others, including followers of Islam, to claim that Christianity never entirely freed itself from the pagan polytheism of the Hellenistic world. How this happened is complicated and we needn't get bogged down here in theological subtleties. The point is that the belief in the Trinity is theology, not gospel. The same is true of the Nicene Creed, which became the required profession of faith and still is so, with a few additions and variations, in the Roman, Eastern, and major reformed churches. It is a philosophic expression of what the Christian community came to believe, or wanted to believe, or felt necessary to believe. Though it contains articles about Yeshua's birth, death, and resurrection, it uses the founding texts selectively, reading backward to find what bolsters a predetermined intention.

The original version (figure 3) was a reaction against the belief about Yeshua as son of God that tended toward a "low" Christology position. Arianism was not adoptionism, but in proclaiming that the Son had been made by the Father, Arius thought he was holding to the traditional view. The majority of bishops at the council chose a "high" Christology, which seemed necessary if the three persons of the Trinity were to be counted as equal in being and status. (The comments in square brackets are notes made by various members of the council on the meaning of crucial phrases of the creed. The longer final note specifically rejects forms of Arianism that claimed that Yeshua was not consubstantial with the Father.)[4]

FIGURE 3

We believe in one God, the omnipotent father,
maker of all things visible and invisible.
And in one lord Iesous Christos, the son of God
[the only-begotten; that is, of the essence of the father, God of God],
light of light, true God of true God,
begotten, not made, being of one substance with the father
by whom all things were made [both in heaven and on earth],
who for us men and our salvation came down and was incarnate and made man.
He suffered, and on the third day he rose again, ascended into heaven,
from where he shall come to judge the living and the dead.
And in the holy spirit.
[But those who say, there was a time when he was not,
or he was not before he was made, or he is of another substance or essence,
or the son of God is created, or changeable or alterable,
they are condemned by the holy universal and apostolic church.]

The Nicene Creed of 325

Certain Hebraic terms found in the gospels—such as the Father, Messiah (Christos), son of God, holy spirit—had become detached from their Jewish contexts. This probably started to occur in the second century and

---

4. There was no published original text from Nicaea; this version is pieced together from references to the council, especially the letter from Eusebius mentioned in the previous note. In *Nicaea and Its Legacy*, Ayres thinks it unlikely that minutes were kept at all since the delegates did not expect that their deliberations would stand "as a binding and universal formula of Christian faith" (85, 88). It is likely that the original formula incorporated parts of one or several baptismal creeds dating from as early as the second century, with the more philosophic anti-Arian clauses interpolated. Most bishops in the fourth century probably thought their local creeds sufficient for catechumens seeking baptism and saw no need for the anti-Arian statements from Nicaea.

increased thereafter, so that gentile Christians west of Palestine tended to take the terms literally as they understood them, and concluded that the Yahweh of the Jews must be made of three parts or persons: triune is the word, three in one. It's worth repeating that the argument that prompted the council was not about the divinity of Yeshua, only about whether he was begotten by the Father or made by the Father, and therefore whether he existed eternally with the Father or subsequent to the Father.

This preliminary text was revised at a second council, in Constantinople in 381, when an expanded form of the creed was determined. It is the version, with minor modifications, that most Christian sects still subscribe to. The most significant change was the addition of final clauses about the Holy Spirit and the resurrection of the dead (figure 4).[5]

FIGURE 4

And [we believe] in the holy spirit, the lord and life-giver,
who proceeds from the father,
who is worshipped and glorified together with the father and
 the son,
who spoke by the prophets;
and in one holy universal and apostolic church;
we acknowledge one baptism for the forgiveness of sins;
we wait for the resurrection of the dead and the life of the
 coming age.

Ending of the Constantinopolitan Creed of 381

You would find it hard to discover texts in the New Testament that clearly state some of the main articles in either version. Composed in the enthusiasm of Christianity's new status as the official religion of the Roman empire,[6] and in opposition to the continuing appeal of Arianism,

---

5. The exact text of the Constantinople version of 381 CE is also uncertain; the section I quote is from Ayres, *Nicaea and Its Legacy*, 255, slightly modified. Sometime in the sixth century a new phrase was inserted in the creed as a result of the controversy over *filioque* (Latin for "and the son"), asserting that the Holy Spirit "proceeds from the Father and the Son." Advocated by Augustine of Hippo among others, *filioque* was accepted by most Western churches but never by Eastern Orthodoxy.

6. The Edict of Milan, issued by Constantine and his co-emperor Licinius in 313, ended the Diocletian persecution of Christians and granted freedom of religion. It was not until the Edict of Thessalonica, issued by Emperor Theodosius in 380, that Christianity became the state religion, confirming its Nicene form in the Constantinople council of 381.

the Constantinople revision of the Nicene Creed placed a tradition of belief above the ambiguities of the gospels. In so doing it showed the way for the medieval church to deal with scripture. Once fully established, the church preferred to proclaim its bible in selections, as I encountered them in Mass. By picking and choosing passages for a specific devotional or theological purpose, the texts could be shaped to the desired meaning by their liturgical or calendar placement without altering their words. Difficult or theologically ambiguous sections could be ignored. The readings of the epistle and gospel at Mass could be made parallel in content. The meaning of a gospel did not lie in its narrative cohesion but in its quotability.

The Shakespearean epigraph for this chapter is spoken by Antonio, the merchant of Venice in the play of that title. He's referring to the Jew Shylock, who has used a story about Jacob and Laban's sheep, from chapter 30 of Genesis, to justify lending money at interest. Antonio insists that Shylock is diabolically twisting the meaning of the passage. Reading the bible backward can achieve notorious and contradictory results, but it became the custom of Christianity. Made up of a random collection of very different genres of writing, the New Testament is an opportunity for creative and disparate interpretation. Along the way the gospels lost their literary integrity and became storehouses for ecclesiastic raids.

Reading sideways. As I've indicated before, one of the curiosities of the New Testament is that we have four gospels relating the same story, each written with its own style and emphasis, especially with regard to the appointment and divinity of Yeshua. Though Matthew and Luke depend on Mark, they seem designed to replace Mark, and perhaps John was designed to replace them in turn. It is fair to say that each gospel was written to be *the* gospel. But that is not what happened. For reasons that are not clear, all four survived and became authorized, whereas those written in the second century did not enter the canon.[7]

When I say "survived," we must remember that keeping a text alive in antiquity meant something material and deliberate: it had to be copied by hand, a tedious and costly process in the care of trained scribes who worked slowly with a reed or quill pen on papyrus, a plant material manufactured by other craftsmen who processed the scroll until it was receptive to ink. A text had to be distributed by hand, kept secure from

---

7. The non-canonical gospels and other second-century apocrypha are treated by Ehrman in *Lost Christianities*. The surviving texts are contained in multilingual form in Ehrman and Plese, *The Apocryphal Gospels*.

damp and insects and dust and smoke and fire; most important, it had to be recopied if any of those agents damaged the scroll, which might have a lifetime of less than a century. (Almost all of the most ancient papyri manuscripts surviving into the present have been discovered, usually by accident, in exceptionally dry conditions in Egypt, or in caves near the Dead Sea in Israel.) Preservation of any text meant work, expense, and determination. Considering that the literacy rate in the Roman empire in the first century was between three and ten percent, and at the lower end of that range in Palestine, someone had to have a good reason to maintain and duplicate each of the gospels. It would have been very easy for one to have been lost, simply forgotten in a house or library until it faded to dust.

This may be one of the reasons why early Christians preferred the codex to the scroll. A codex is a manuscript with cut leaves bound into a book, the same technology we are familiar with. It makes reading easier than working with a long scroll, which must be wound at each end, usually on a stick or holder, and requires two hands to keep open. A codex is especially well adapted to reading aloud in public. It also facilitates back-and-forth reference simply by turning pages, so much easier than unrolling a scroll.[8] As the scroll was replaced by the codex, so papyrus was gradually replaced by parchment, which is made from the skin of sheep, calves, or goats and is considerably more durable. The two most important early examples of the Christian bible in Greek, Old and New Testaments, are fourth-century codices on vellum, a fine grade of parchment: the great Codex Sinaiticus and the Codex Vaticanus.[9]

A more or less complete Christian bible encouraged reading backward, looking for how the Old Testament predicts the events of the New. Having all four gospels in a single bound book encouraged something

---

8. Kermode, *Genesis of Secrecy*, 88, discusses the significance of the codex as a form of biblical reference book. Barton, *History of the Bible*, 243–6, treats the possible reasons for Christian preference of the codex, as well as what he calls the "tolerance" of all four gospels.

9. Codex Sinaiticus (now in the British Library) is from the middle of the fourth century. Its origin is uncertain; it was uncovered in the mid-nineteenth century in Saint Catherine's Monastery in Sinai by the biblical scholar Constantin von Tischendorf. Some of its Old Testament has perished but the New Testament is entire. Intriguingly, it includes a noncanonical book of the late second century called *The Shepherd of Hermas*. Codex Vaticanus (in the Vatican Library) is similarly dated and also uncertain in origin; it has been known since 1475 and contains both testaments (with some lacunae) and most of the Apocrypha. These and other significant early copies are reviewed by Metzger and Ehrman, *Text of the New Testament*, 52–94.

else as well. What I call reading sideways refers to the tendency, very much still alive, to think of the gospels as a single unit rather than individually. In this sense, reading sideways is another habit that attacks the literary integrity of the individual works.

An example: Yeshua changes water into wine at the wedding feast at Cana only in John (chapter 2). This miracle is out of keeping with the synoptics, especially Mark, where the wonders serve to show Yeshua's power but, more important, are socially directed: toward healing, feeding the hungry, aiding the distressed. Water to wine does nothing except save the wedding host embarrassment, and is accomplished only because Yeshua's mother requests it. It hardly seems in tune with Yeshua's purpose in Galilee. In Mark (3.31–35), the mother of Yeshua is presented as drastically different. Far from loving and supporting him, twice she tries to stop his itinerant preaching and miracle working, thinking he's lost his mind. He refuses to speak with her when she and his siblings arrive at a house where he is eating, and leaves them outside the door. John's story is emotive, Mark's is harsh, but John's version of the mother is one that Christianity took to heart and remembers.

Barton has an example of a different type. In children's Christmas pageants it is regular practice to portray scenes of the angels appearing to shepherds on the hillside and the arrival of the wise men at Herod's court and the stable in Bethlehem. Shepherds and magi are always included in statuary scenes of the Christmas crèche, and are as much a part of Noël as no room at the inn, the manger as cradle, and the donkey to Egypt.[10] That the shepherds are only in Luke, the wise men only in Matthew, and neither in Mark, shows how deeply ingrained reading sideways became in the Christian mind and memory. Since the gospels differ in detail, why not put them all together? That is how the popular notion of Yeshua was constructed.

It can help to understand Mark's distinct and spare approach to list those parts of the usual Christian story that are not in his gospel. If we had only Mark we would have none of the following (figure 5). Note how many of these scenes have been regularly depicted in the European tradition of painting, sculpture, and music from the Middle Ages.

---

10. Barton, *History of the Bible*, 191–92. Ehrman makes this point in a different way in *Misquoting Jesus*, 213–15.

40 CREATING JESUS

FIGURE 5

Genealogy of Yeshua	Annunciation/Magnificat	Joseph
Bethlehem/Nativity	Shepherds	Wise men
King Herod	Flight to Egypt	Slaughter of innocents
Angels in dreams	Circumcision	Loving virgin mother
Child Yeshua in Temple	Wedding at Cana	Lord's Prayer
Sermon on the Mount	Peter walking on water	Raising Lazarus
Yeshua weeping	Foot washing	Pilate's wife
Pilate washing hands	Ecce Homo	Thirty pieces of silver
Suicide of Judas	Six of the sayings on cross	Deposition (Pietà)
Guards at tomb	Noli me tangere	Journey to Emmaus
Resurrection appearances	Doubting Thomas	Ascension

Not in Mark

In addition, we would be missing some twenty or so parables, including the hidden treasure, the lost sheep, the wedding feast, the talents, the prodigal son, the good Samaritan, the wise and foolish virgins, and the workers in the vineyard. Most shocking of all, I suppose, we would have no Christmas.

Perhaps that is why the early Christians held on to all four gospels: none was sufficient. In fact, reading sideways was a very early practice. We know of a Christian apologist named Tatian (or Tatianus), an Assyrian who flourished about 170 CE. Tatian harmonized the gospels in a work now called the *Diatessaron*, a Latinized word of Greek origin meaning "made out of four." Tatian patiently took words and phrases from the four gospels and stitched them together in a seamless continuity, changing the narrative location of an incident or saying to fit his purpose. The four evangelists became one. The *Diatessaron* was a popular way of reading the gospel story and in fact replaced the individual gospels in Syriac liturgy up to the fourth century.[11]

A harmonization is the ultimate example of reading the gospels sideways. But what I mean by the term is more of a habit of mind, of *thinking* of the gospels sideways. Consider it a slanted view, a pattern of looking over the shoulder of one evangelist to see another. I cannot argue that it has harmed the Christian religion to follow the practice, which might

11. Metzger and Ehrman, *Text of the New Testament*, 131–34.

have been inevitable given the diverse approaches of the evangelists. I do think, however, that something important was lost in the process. My main objection I have already stated, that reading backward and reading sideways have together distorted our ability to see a particular gospel as it is, for its distinctive or unique qualities as a literary work and social or historical document. That this is especially true in the case of the gospel of Mark is the theme of the rest of this book.

Records. People I talk to about the New Testament often wonder why we have no narrative account of Yeshua's life before 70 CE. If the oral tradition was so active, why did no one write it down? They also wonder why Paul did not write anything for at least fifteen years after his conversion, or anything important enough to be preserved. The questions are understandable but upside down. The real question is: why do we have so much? Yeshua, after all, was a nobody from a nowhere in a distant corner of the empire who was stirring up trouble at a difficult time, a situation the Romans were used to handling with swift and permanent retribution. Objections to Roman rule in Palestine were growing around the year 30, and the collusion of the Temple establishment with the occupiers was painful for pious Jews to witness. The annual festival of Passover brought hundreds or thousands of pilgrims to Jerusalem to celebrate their deliverance from an earlier oppressor in Egypt. The money changers in the Temple served a regular function, to convert other currencies to Roman or Herodian coin so pilgrims could make gifts to the Temple. The dove sellers were essential to the animal-sacrifice rituals. The bother Yeshua made was enough to infuriate the Sadducees and his insults made the senior priests fume, even if, as Mark holds, they acted out of envy.

Pontius Pilatus had been Prefect of Judea for some four years. He might have been shallow and corrupt but he was not stupid. He saw a danger and acted. Starting with Mark, the gospels spin the responsibility for the Crucifixion toward the Jews, a theme that proved disastrous in the history of antisemitism, but Yeshua was summarily executed by the Roman provincial authority because he was a threat to peace and order. "Are you the king of the Jews?" Pilate asks, and Yeshua gives an ambiguous reply, *sy legeis*, literally "You say" (Mark 15.2). It can be rendered as "So you say" or "You said it" or even "Your words." Burton Mack offers the useful suggestion that the answer implies: yes, that's what you as a Roman official would call me.[12] However meant, it was enough for Pilate.

---

12. Mack, *Myth of Innocence*, 295. For a view that claims Yeshua was executed because the Romans thought he was dangerously insane, see Meggitt, "The Madness of King Jesus."

Anyone claiming to be king of the Judeans was automatically in revolt against Rome. For a Roman official, Messiah and King of the Jews were equivalent titles, and both were treasonous. Though the "aggravated" penalty of crucifixion was normally reserved for slaves and outcasts, Yeshua had forfeited whatever protection he enjoyed as a freeman when he was judged an insurgent.[13] He was hanging on a cross with two other criminals at the place called Skull a few hours after dawn: an ordinary morning in the empire. All three were set there as ordinary Roman warnings of the terrible death awaiting slaves and thieves and rebels who disturbed the peace. Maybe some secretary employed by Pilate recorded the sentence, maybe not. Why bother? It was a regular occurrence.

Yeshua was not a writer. As I mentioned before, we can't be sure he was fully literate. That actually does not matter, since most teaching of the Hebrew scriptures was done orally, as teaching was done all over the ancient world. Yeshua fit the pattern: he was Jewish teacher who schooled his students by lecturing. He spoke, he entreated, he conversed, he debated, he quoted the scriptures from memory. Perhaps he taught in the classical and Jewish fashion by having his students memorize his words, an interesting possibility that would lend support to the accuracy of the oral tradition before Mark.[14] His companions were mostly workers and fishermen, maybe artisans or craftsmen like himself.[15] Perhaps some could read, perhaps not; there are degrees of literacy, after all, ranging from the simple ability to work with numbers to comprehension of written Greek or Hebrew. Even if they could read, his companions were not writers and probably did not have the financial means to hire secretaries. Money was short in the small Yeshua set, even if its members—and

---

13. Writing about Roman torture in general, Coleman notes that in the imperial period it grew more common to apply torture to the classes above slaves when "the security of the state, embodied by the emperor, was threatened" ("The Fragility of Evidence," 117).

14. This and parallel ideas are invoked by Rodríguez, *Oral Tradition*, 34. I deal with the oral tradition in chapter 5.

15. On the question of the economic class of Yeshua and his companions, it is worth mentioning that artisans in Palestine were probably a step above the rural peasantry in income and status. Fishermen like Peter and Zebedee, the father of James and John, likely belonged to collectives in the very large fishing industry in Galilee that included processed food (e.g., dried fish and *garum*, the fermented fish sauce loved by Romans). Cooperative associations were a common way for small family enterprises to buy or lease boats, hire helpers, negotiate fishing leases, sell their catch, and facilitate tax payments. See Hanson and Oakman, *Palestine in the Time of Jesus*, 107; and the entry on "Fishing, Nets" in Rousseau and Arav, *Jesus and His World*, 93–97.

perhaps its leader—continued to work their trades as Paul did. Why write the message down? The world was going to end within their lifetimes, so their teacher predicted. All they had to do was remember what he said.

After his death, when they had visions of his resurrected body and spoke to him as if he were alive, or believed that they did, their job was to proclaim his message, to convince other Jews in Judea and Galilee, and eventually farther afield, that his words were true. That was to be done the way the teacher did it, face to face, in small groups in small houses or in larger groups on the lakeshore or hillside—by speech, not writing.

In antiquity there was nothing unusual about preferring the spoken word. The vast majority of people were illiterate and regularly received information and entertainment through their ears. Teachers, reformers, religious leaders, all used their voices to pass along knowledge and wisdom. Siddhartha Gautama, known as the Buddha, an itinerant spiritual teacher five centuries before Yeshua, altered the thought of much of South, Southeast, and East Asia in the way that Yeshua's influence altered the thought of West Asia and Europe. Yet there are no surviving written documents about the Buddha earlier than two centuries after his death. Much later, six centuries after Yeshua, Mohammed received divine revelations orally over a period of twenty-three years, dictated to him, we are told, by the archangel Gabriel. Mohammed was illiterate. He memorized the verses and recited them to others; *Qur'an* means The Recitation. Only after his death was the full Recitation written down and a canonical text formulated.

In the Athens of the fourth century BCE, Socrates too was not a writer and relied on his best student to record his life and thought. Yeshua had no Plato taking down his words. As a writer of Greek Paul did not reach the level of Plato, but in any case Paul was not recording a life and thus is a different case from the evangelists. Paul was an educated Hellenized Jew from the diaspora; most likely Greek was his mother tongue. He tilted the other way from the synoptics. He stressed the philosophic and theological implications of the Good Message, extending it to everyone by emphasizing the importance of belief in the resurrected Yeshua. Paul was not writing an organized account, but addressing specific assemblies of believers who were new to the Christos cult and needed instruction. When he dictated his first letter he had no idea he was beginning the New Testament and would have been shocked at the thought. He was not writing for the ages, which he believed were about to end; he was writing for the moment. He would have been equally stunned, even horrified, that his letters became sacred scripture, and are still so considered twenty centuries later.

When we think about the forces behind the writing of the earliest gospel, some two decades after Paul's first letter, we should bear in mind that Mark was intended as a compendium of what was known about Yeshua's mission for the use of believers, some of whom still expected the kingdom of God to arrive any day. It was not meant to convert new devotees but to reinforce knowledge and belief for second-generation Christians. It was a way to preserve the oral tradition that was circulating and continued to circulate into a third generation. We can imagine Mark in a study with scrolls around his desk, gathering individual episodes and sayings attributed to Yeshua, holding conversations with fellow believers and travelers, taking notes, then laying them out in a reasonable chronological order, editing them, and stitching them together: a cut-and-paste job at first, then a list, then a narrative.

But this is a modern idea, influenced by print culture. As Eric Eve points out, first-century writers did not use desks, which would be too awkward for a long scroll of papyrus, and they relied more on memory than on notes.[16] Since writing in the technical sense of inscribing letters on a roll was a skilled business, it is just as likely that Mark dictated his words to a professional scribe, who would be sitting on the floor or a low stool with the scroll draped over a leg. This is how Paul composed his letters, by dictation. When he wrote a personal comment at the end of a message, he would remark on it. "See what large letters I wrote to you with my own hand," he notes in the conclusion of Galatians (6.11).

However Mark may have worked, he was recording ephemera, like Plato recording Socratic dialogues after the fact, and no doubt improving them. In Mark's case it was the ephemera of Yeshua's spoken words and actions as remembered by its witnesses, who passed on the information orally to other hearers who became rememberers. In the end Mark created a paradoxical work of literature, a long-lasting record of disappearing speech. That this work survived, and became the basis of similar works at the root of a new religion, sometimes seems like mere chance.

Now and then as I worked on this book on a tired afternoon, when the Dublin sky was winter dull and I felt the quantity of scholarship behind my back overwhelming, I walked from Trinity College up Dame Street to the Chester Beatty Library on the grounds of Dublin Castle.

---

16. Eve, *Writing the Gospels*, 11.

There I stared at the display of a leaf from a manuscript designated P[45] (the *P* stands for papyrus). Behind heavy glass and dimly lit for the sake of preservation, the page is difficult to read—it is displayed more as an art object than a document, as if it were a sacred icon. P[45] and the other pages on display *are* art objects now, though they were once precious parts of a believing community of readers and listeners. The remains of P[45] are thirty leaves from a papyrus codex dated to about 300 CE, one of the earliest surviving examples of a partial New Testament, containing significant portions of the four gospels and Acts. It was discovered in Egypt in the 1930s and bought by Chester Beatty (1875–1968), a New York mining engineer and avid antiquities collector, who moved to London in 1913, then to Dublin in 1950, where he built a library to house his manuscript collection. Later the Irish state constructed the current premises at Dublin Castle. Although there are extant fragments of papyrus manuscripts of the New Testament scattered around the world that predate P[45], most are many hundreds of years later.

Christian manuscript procurement is a relic of the acquisitional side of colonialism. It is parallel to looting ancient monuments and objects, if not as offensive; its goal is the preservation and study of ancient pages that are not in use and would otherwise be lost. Beatty's finds depended on dealers who were various in their honesty, and his collection is emblematic of the random and sometimes larcenous nature of the discoveries of ancient documents from the nineteenth century to the present. Yet there exist many more Greek manuscripts of the New Testament than of any other ancient Greek texts; something close to 6,000 have been catalogued. If we add to the Greek examples those in Latin and the other ancient languages of Christendom, we get a total of something like 25,000 manuscripts of New Testament texts. They are dated from about 300 to about 1600 and range from small torn fragments to complete copies of the bible. The reason is clear enough: the establishment of monasteries in late antiquity and the early middle ages, where the conservation of the canon eventually became a principal activity. The problem for the preservation of the first-century texts was getting past the era of the cult's isolation and oppression to the year 313, when Constantine ended the Diocletian persecutions and liberated religion from state control. At that point professional scribes took over the copying of Christian manuscripts. Until then there was no universal church institution, just an individual *ekklesia* with *presbyteros*, an assembly with elders in various cities, sometimes with a supervising *episkopos*, an "overseer" whose role evolved into the figure we now call a bishop. We know the Christians of the second to fourth centuries used the gospels and other texts in liturgies and sermons, but we know very little about how the manuscripts were recopied, distributed, and preserved. It is possible that much was lost. The amazing thing is how much was not.

Translating Mark. In the translation that follows, I have tried to be as faithful to Mark as common sense in English allows. "Literal" has many meanings in translation theory; I mean accurate to Mark's style and language as I understand them, without elaboration or subjective influence. Overexposure has made it difficult for a modern reader to grasp the innovative and sometimes shocking qualities of this work, so I have tried to create a fresh quality to the text to counter its familiarity.

One method I followed is to provide alternative renderings of some words and phrases that later became part of Christian theology and achieved a meaning they do not actually have in Mark's Greek. (They have *potential* for those later understandings, but that is a separate matter.) A few of these I discussed in the previous chapter: *euaggelion* I give in its original sense as "good message" and *Christos* as "anointed." I would like to call Jesus by his Hebrew and Aramaic name Yeshua, as I do in the commentary, but that would be unfaithful to the Greek; to defamiliarize the word I have kept it in the Romanized Greek form of *Iesous*. Despite the inconsistency, I have used the standard English equivalent for the names of other characters in the gospel to avoid unnecessary confusion.

Some less common phrases deserve explanation. *Hamartia*, normally translated in the gospels as "sin," in Greek holds a number of different senses around the implication of error; I have usually rendered it as "mistake." The Greek *aggelos* (angel) is the standard form of Hebrew *mal'akh*, which means "messenger." More controversial is my turning *pneuma hagios* into "sacred breath" instead of the traditional "holy spirit." Judaism had been vigorously monotheistic since at least the third century BCE and holy spirit was the regular term for the action of God on earth. It described a function of Yahweh, not a separate being or person of the godhead. Because a later Christian doctrine made the Holy Spirit (or Holy Ghost) into the Third Person of the Trinity, it is difficult to disestablish that meaning from how Mark uses it. These and other unusual translations are explained in the Textual Notes that immediately follow the translation.

Scholars often note that Mark's Greek is rough. It is true that the text is not "literary" in the artistic sense when compared to Luke, for example, who is a much better writer of Greek and more elaborate in detail and characterization. But we should remember that a better writer can also mean a better inventor, and in Luke we are often faced with material that seems legendary or even bizarre. The roughness of Mark, perhaps a bit like the simple sentences of Ernest Hemingway or the poetic diction of Bertolt Brecht, conveys a different sense of the literary, simple, direct, seemingly honest. Some translations smooth out that quality. Take the word *euthus*, for example. It means "immediately" or "soon" or "at once" or "instantly" or "directly," and it is fair to convey its sense with a few other phrases, such as "right away" or "right then." It is one of Mark's favorite words, repeated forty times. For the sake of variety, some versions rely on the thesaurus, sometimes using one word, sometimes another. It is true that Mark's repetition can feel clunky and unbalanced, but he uses the word as a conjunction, often preceded by "and," to convey a sense of hurry: hurry to the end of the story, hurry to believe in the good message, hurry to the end of the world. For that reason I have maintained the evangelist's usage and rendered it always as "immediately."

The Greek text. The many surviving ancient manuscripts of Mark contain various readings, sometimes of controversial passages. It is in the nature of works dependent on repeated hand copying that errors or deliberate changes and additions will occur. Every modern biblical editor or translator must make choices among the variants, leaving the others behind or relegating them to tiny-print notes that are easily ignored by readers. I have indicated when I have omitted a verse or passage that the best scholarship thinks is secondary, but have placed all the explanatory textual notes at the end of the gospel in a more readable format.

The Greek text of the New Testament has been subject to high-level critical scholarship for two hundred years. It now differs in important regards from the Textus Receptus, or "received text," which was based on a Greek text established by Erasmus in 1516. Erasmus's work was revolutionary in that it applied critical methods, but the Greek manuscripts available to him were not always the best or the most ancient, and subsequent study has revised his text considerably. Unfortunately the Textus Receptus dominated translation for centuries, especially in the Protestant tradition. It was the basis of the great English versions of the sixteenth century including that by William Tyndale, which in turn was the bedrock for the King James Version of 1611.

With regard to Mark, the most notable departure from the Textus Receptus is the rejection of the longer ending of the gospel, which summarizes the Resurrection appearances of Yeshua and his charge to proclaim the good news throughout the world. This is almost universally recognized as secondary and in most modern bibles is marked as inauthentic. Textual scholarship aside, any close reading, even in a translation, will discover that the language and style of narration of the longer ending is out of key with the rest of Mark. In the earliest recoverable reading, Mark leaves us in shock at the empty tomb at the end of verse 8 of chapter 16. Adela Yarbo Collins holds that at the time of Mark "the tradition about the appearances of Jesus did not seem to be a part of the story of Jesus." The evangelist did not need to include those scenes since his audience already knew the belief that the risen Yeshua materialized before the women and apostles; it was enough to allude to them through the prediction of the Young Man who presents the news of the Resurrection to the women in the tomb.[17] Though this is not a complete justification—and we might as well say that Mark did not *choose* to include the appearances—Collins's position does highlight the powerful strangeness of the text as Mark probably wrote it. It is also understandable why some later scribe or adherent would want to add those scenes, especially as the gospels composed after Mark detail them. For the sake of completeness, I give the longer ending in the textual notes, and discuss it in detail in chapter 7.

Many people agree that the standard chapter and verse numbers in the bible interfere with reading; they stand on the page like endless footnote indicators to nowhere, a form of numerical terrorism that makes the strangeness of the text even more distant. It is important to note that the current numbers are editorial insertions dating from the middle ages; the ancient Greek manuscripts do not have verse numbers. Nor are the words separated from each other—like all writing in classical antiquity, the text runs on without spaces or punctuation in what is called *scriptio continua*. It was up to the reader to discover each word from its surrounding texture. This is easier to do with an inflected language such as Greek or Latin, in which word endings change according to grammatical position. Especially when reading aloud, or silently mouthing the words, the endings can make the boundaries clearer. Here is an example in modern type of how the last verse of Mark (16.8) would have been copied out in an ancient manuscript:

---

17. Collins, *Mark*, 801. She details the complications of the longer ending, and a separate shorter addition that occurs in a single Old Latin version, 802–18.

καιεξελθουσαιεφυγοναποτουμνημειουειχενγαραυταςτρομοςκα
ιεκστασιςκαιουδενιουδενειπονεφοβουντογαρ

It looks impossible—no spaces, no punctuation, no help. It is quite difficult for me, but for a practiced reader the words make themselves known. I suppose they would make themselves known in English also, given patience and time:

theyleftandranawayfromthetombseizedbytremblingandconfu
siontheysaidnothingtoanonebecausetheywereafraid

Fortunately modern editors divide the words and add the diacritical marks that later became standard for Greek, and I am very grateful for their first aid.

Despite my dislike of those biblical numbers, some division is highly useful for reading to a group, and fairly early various kinds of headings or breathing marks appeared in manuscripts of the New Testament, particularly in lectionaries. In the end I have felt compelled to retain chapter and verse numbers, chiefly because they are necessary for reference and comparison with other versions.

How to read Mark. The Good Message of Mark is above all a story. Whether read privately or aloud, whether considered religious or secular, liturgical or historical, a poem or an epic, an act of veneration or an experience of literature, the ideal is to go through the text in one sitting. It is half the length of the other gospels, spare, and direct. It takes about an hour or so to read silently, depending on your speed and whether you stop to contemplate. If that's not possible, reading in two sittings will do as well; there is a natural break about halfway through, after chapter 9. But of course readers are free to do as they like.

Set your preconceptions aside. Read it for what it is: a narrative about an extraordinary man told for others to learn from and appreciate. It draws together what one writer knew about the man a generation after he died, and suggests along the way the importance of his life and death.

3

The Good Message According to Mark

A literal translation

1

The beginning of the good message of Iesous the Anointed.

²As it was written in Isaiah the prophet:

> *See now, I send my messenger before your face*
> *who will lay the road for you.*
> ³*The voice of one shouting in the wasteland,*
> *Prepare the way of the Lord, straighten his paths.*

⁴Then John came, baptizing in the wasteland and urging a baptism of contrition that pardoned mistakes. ⁵People went out from the entire district of Judea and all of Jerusalem and were baptized by him in the River Jordan, acknowledging their mistakes. ⁶John dressed in a skin of camel hair with a leather belt around his waist and ate locusts and wild honey. ⁷And he preached that "Someone stronger is coming after me; I am not fit to bend down and loosen the thong of his sandals. ⁸I baptized you with water, but he will baptize you with the sacred breath."

⁹It was then that Iesous came from Nazareth in Galilee and was baptized by John in the Jordan. ¹⁰And immediately as he rose from the water, he saw the sky split open and a breath like a dove descend on him. ¹¹And a voice came from the sky, "You are my treasured son, and I am pleased

with you." ¹²Immediately the breath drove him out into the wasteland. ¹³He was in the wasteland forty days, tested by the Adversary. He lived among the wild beasts, attended by the Messengers.

¹⁴After John was arrested, Iesous walked to Galilee, preaching God's good message, ¹⁵saying, "The time has come, the reign of God is near; reconsider your life and put your trust in the good message." ¹⁶And walking by the Sea of Galilee he saw Simon and his brother Andrew, fishermen casting into the water. ¹⁷Iesous said to them, "Walk along with me and I will make you fishers of men." ¹⁸And immediately they left their nets and followed him. ¹⁹Passing on a little, he saw James, the son of Zebedee, and his brother John, who were in a boat preparing their nets. ²⁰Immediately he called them, and they left their father Zebedee in the boat with his hired hands, and fell in after him.

²¹Then they walked to Capernaum and immediately on the Sabbath he taught in the synagogue. ²²They were astonished at his words because he was teaching them as someone with authority, not as the scribes did. ²³Immediately a man with an impure spirit appeared in their synagogue, and he cried out, ²⁴"What do you want with us, Iesous of Nazareth? Did you come to destroy us? I know who you are, the holy one of God." ²⁵Iesous restrained him, saying, "Do not speak, and come out of him." ²⁶The impure spirit threw the man into spasms, shouted in a loud voice, and came out of him. ²⁷Everybody was astonished again, and they asked themselves, "What is this new teaching? He has such authority that even the demons obey his commands." ²⁸The news spread fast and immediately he was a celebrity in all the districts of Galilee.

²⁹They left the assembly immediately and went into the house of Simon and Andrew, along with James and John. ³⁰They found Simon's mother-in-law in bed, sweating with a fever. They told him about her immediately. ³¹He went to her, raised her up, and took her by the hand. The fever disappeared and she began to look after them. ³²After sunset that evening, they brought to him all those who were sick or infected by demons. ³³The entire city had crowded at the door. ³⁴He healed many who were sick with different diseases, and expelled many demons. He did not allow the demons to speak because they knew who he was.

³⁵He rose very early, while it was still dark, and went to a deserted place to pray. ³⁶Simon and the others searched for him, ³⁷and when they found him said, "Everyone is looking for you." ³⁸But he said, "Let us go another way to the nearby towns so that I can teach there as well—that is why I have come out." ³⁹So he went on, preaching in the synagogues in all of Galilee and expelling demons.

⁴⁰And a leper came up to him, pleading and falling on his knees, and said, "If you wish it, you can make me clean." ⁴¹He was moved by compassion, stretched out his hand, touched him, and said, "I do wish it; you are clean." ⁴²The skin disease fell from him immediately and he was cleansed. ⁴³He sent him away immediately and warned him in strong terms, ⁴⁴"Say nothing to anyone, but show yourself to the priest and make the cleansing offering as commanded by Moses as proof for them." ⁴⁵But when the man left he could not keep it secret and talked about the event everywhere, so that he could no longer go into a city openly. Again he sought out deserted places because people were coming to him from all sides.

2

After a few days he went back to Capernaum. When the news spread that he was at home, ²so many people came to see him there was no room left, not even at the door. He was announcing the word to them ³when four others arrived carrying a paralyzed man. ⁴They could not get near him because of the crowd, so they took off the roof above him and when they had gouged out a hole, they lowered the paralytic on his mat. ⁵When Iesous saw their trust, he said to the paralyzed man, "Child, you are freed from your sins." ⁶A few of the scribes were sitting there, considering this in their hearts: ⁷"Why does the man speak like this? It is blasphemy. Only God can forgive sins." ⁸Iesous sensed immediately what they were thinking and said, "Why are you questioning this within yourselves? ⁹Which is easier, to say to the paralytic, Your mistakes are forgiven, or to say, Get up, pick up your mat and walk? ¹⁰So you can know that the son of man has the authority to forgive sins on earth"—he said to the paralytic, ¹¹"To you I say, get up, pick up your mat, and go home." ¹²He rose immediately, picked up the mat, and went out in view of everybody. All were amazed and praised God, saying, "We have never seen anything like this."

¹³He went out again along the sea with the crowd around him and he taught them. ¹⁴Walking on, he saw Alphaeus' son Levi sitting at his tax booth and he said, "Come along with me." He stood up and joined him. ¹⁵Later he was at dinner in his house, reclining at table with many tax collectors and sinners who were eating with Iesous and the many disciples who followed him. ¹⁶The scribes of the Pharisees noticed he was eating with sinners and tax collectors and said to the disciples, "Why does he eat with tax collectors and sinners?" ¹⁷Iesous overheard and said to them, "The healthy do not need a doctor, only the sick. I did not come to invite the righteous, but sinners."

¹⁸The disciples of John and the Pharisees fasted. Some people said to him, "Why is it that the disciples of John and the disciples of the Pharisees fast, but your disciples do not?" ¹⁹Iesous said to them, "Wedding guests do not fast while they are with the bridegroom, do they? As long as they are with the bridegroom they are not able to fast. ²⁰But the days will come when the bridegroom is taken away from them, then they will fast on that day. ²¹No one sews a patch of unshrunk cloth on an old cloak because the patch will tear away, the new from the old, and make the tear worse. ²²And no one puts new wine into old wineskins because the wine will burst the wineskins and the wine will be lost and the skins as well. No, new wine goes into new wineskins."

²³Once on the Sabbath he was passing through grainfields and his disciples, in pushing their way through, began to pluck off the heads of grain. ²⁴The Pharisees said to him, "Look here, why are they violating the Sabbath?" ²⁵He replied, "Did you never read what David did when he and his companions were hungry and in need? ²⁶How he went into the house of God when Abiathar was high priest and ate the bread of the Presence, which is not lawful to eat except by the priests, and gave the bread to his followers as well?" ²⁷Then he said to them, "The Sabbath exists for man, not man for the Sabbath, ²⁸so the son of man is master even of the Sabbath."

3

He went to the synagogue again and found a man with a shriveled hand. ²They were watching to see whether he would heal him on the Sabbath, so that they could bring a charge against him. ³He said to the man with the deformed hand, "Stand up here in the middle." ⁴Then he said to them, "Is it permitted on the Sabbath to do good or to do evil, to save a life or to kill it?" No one answered. ⁵He looked around with anger and felt sorrow at the hardness of their hearts, and said to the man, "Stretch out your hand." He put out his hand and it was restored. ⁶The Pharisees left and immediately colluded with the Herodians about how they might destroy him.

⁷But Iesous and his followers retreated to the sea, followed by another great crowd of people from Galilee and Judea, ⁸and from Jerusalem and Idumea and beyond the Jordan, and Tyre and Sidon. This huge number came to see him after hearing about all he had been doing. ⁹He told his disciples to have a small boat always ready, so that the crowd would not crush him. ¹⁰He had healed so many that the crowd pressed on him and everyone in pain or distress wanted to touch him. ¹¹Whenever they saw him, even the unclean spirits prostrated before him and cried out, "You are the son of God." ¹²But he reprimanded them and barred them from making this known.

¹³Then he went up the mountain to call those he wanted around him, and they joined him. ¹⁴He selected twelve to be with him, and called them apostles so that he could send them to proclaim ¹⁵and with the authority to expel demons. ¹⁶He appointed the Twelve. To Simon he added the name Rock [Peter], ¹⁷and James the son of Zebedee and John the brother of James, and added the name Boanerges, which is Sons of Thunder, ¹⁸and Andrew and Philip and Bartholomew and Matthew and Thomas and James the son of Alphaeus and Thaddaeus and Simon the Canaanite ¹⁹and Judas Iscariot, who also betrayed him.

²⁰Then he went into a house, but the press of people was so great it was not even possible to eat. ²¹When his family heard, they set out to hold him back, saying he had lost his wits. ²²The scribes arrived from Jerusalem claiming, "He has Beelzeboul inside him and by the power of the chief of demons he expels demons." ²³He called them together and spoke to them by analogies, "How can the Adversary expel the Adversary? ²⁴If a kingdom is divided against itself it cannot stand. ²⁵And if a house is divided against itself the house cannot stand. ²⁶And if the Adversary rises up against himself and has been divided, he cannot stand but comes

to an end. ²⁷No one can break into the house of a strong man to rob his belongings, unless he first ties up the strong man. Then he can plunder the house. ²⁸Listen, I am telling you the truth: all people, all the sons of men, will be forgiven their mistakes and slanders, no matter how many they have vilified. ²⁹But whoever blasphemes against the sacred breath will never gain forgiveness but be guilty of everlasting sin." ³⁰Because they had been saying he harbored an unclean spirit.

³¹Then his mother and brothers arrived and stood outside, and sent someone to call him. ³²A large group was sitting around him and they said, "Look, your mother and brothers and sister are all outside asking for you." ³³He answered, "Who are my mother and brothers?" ³⁴He glanced at everybody sitting in a circle around him and said, "See, here are my mother and brothers. ³⁵Anyone who does the will of God is my brother and sister and mother."

4

He started to teach again beside the sea, but the throng was so large that he had to climb into a boat and sat down in it on the sea, with the crowd on the shore facing the water. ²He began teaching them numerous things in comparison stories, and his teaching was like this. ³"Listen. A sower went out to sow. ⁴As he sowed, one seed fell on the pathway and birds came and ate it. ⁵Another fell on rocky ground where the soil was shallow. It sprang up immediately ⁶but when the sun rose it burned it and it shriveled. ⁷Yet another fell among the thornbushes and the thornbushes grew up and choked it so it could not bear fruit. ⁸But others landed on good soil, grew well and matured and yielded a crop thirty times the sowing, or sixty times or a hundred." ⁹Then he said, "If you have ears to hear, then hear."

¹⁰When he was alone with his companions and the Twelve, they asked him about the story. ¹¹He said, "The secret about the reign of God has been revealed to you, but to people who are outside all must be conveyed in similarities,

> ¹²*so that seeing, they might see but not perceive, and hearing, they might hear but not understand, lest they repent and be forgiven."*

[13]He continued, "Do you not understand this comparison? How will you understand all the other parables? [14]The sower is sowing the word. [15]These are those along the road where the word is sown, and when they hear, the Adversary comes and immediately takes away the word sown in them. [16]Similarly these are those sown on rocky ground and when they hear the word they accept it with joy immediately, [17]but they have no root inside, it is temporary only, and when distress or persecution comes because of the word, they fall away immediately. [18]These are those sown among the thorns, they have heard the word [19]but the cares of the times and delusions about wealth or other desires choke the word and it cannot bear fruit. [20]And these are those sown in good soil, people who hear the word and accept it and bear fruit, one thirty times, one sixty, and one a hundred."

[21]He said to them, "Is a lamp brought in order to be put under a basket or under the bed? Or is it not put on the lampstand? [22]Because there is nothing hidden that will not be made known, and nothing secret that will not come to light. [23]If anyone has ears to hear, let him hear." [24]And he said, "Mind what you hear: what measure you measure will be measured to you, and more will be added to you. [25]Whoever has will be given more, and whoever does not have, even what he has will be taken away from him." [26]And he said, "The reign of God is like this, as if a man puts seed in the soil, [27]and he sleeps and rises night and day, and the seed sprouts and grows, how he does not know. [28]The soil brings fruit by itself, first green, then a head, then the full grain in the head. [29]When the fruit is there, he immediately sends for the gathering hook because the harvest has come." [30]And he said, "To what can we liken the reign of God, or in what analogy can we set it? [31]As a mustard seed, when planted in the earth, is the smallest of seeds on the earth, [32]yet when sown grows taller than all the garden plants and makes branches big enough for the birds of the sky to nest in its shadow."

[33]He often spoke the word to them in many similar parables, to the extent they were able to hear. [34]In fact he did not speak to them without such parables. To his disciples in private, however, he explained it all.

[35]And he said to them that day, when evening arrived, "Let us cross over to the other side." [36]They sent the crowd away and took him in the boat,

just as he was, and other boats were with him. ³⁷A violent windstorm rose up and the waves were breaking over the boat so that the boat was rapidly filling up. ³⁸And he was in the stern, sleeping on the cushion. They woke him and said, "Teacher, do you not realize we are about to perish?" ³⁹He woke up and admonished the wind and said to the sea, "Silence, be still." The wind died down and there was a great calm. ⁴⁰He said to them, "Why are you fearful? You still do not have trust?" ⁴¹They were frightened and in great awe, and said to one another, "Then who is this, that even the wind and the sea obey him?"

5

And they arrived at the other side of the sea, in the region of the Gerasenes. ² When he stepped out of the boat, he was immediately met by a man with an unclean spirit coming out of the tombs, ³a man who lived in the tombs. No one could bind him, not even with chains, ⁴because he had been put in shackles and manacles many times but the chains had been torn in two and the shackles shattered, and no one could restrain him. ⁵Throughout the night and day he cried out in the tombs and in the mountains and cut himself with stones. ⁶When he saw Iesous in the distance, he ran and prostrated himself in front of him. ⁷He cried out in a loud voice, "What do you have to do with me, Iesous, son of the most high God? Swear to me by God, do not torment me." ⁸Because he was saying to him, "Come out of this man, you unclean spirit." ⁹Then he asked him, "What is your name?" And he answered, "Legion is my name, for we are many." ¹⁰And he begged him many times not to send them out of the region.

¹¹It happened that a large herd of pigs was foraging on the mountain, ¹²and they begged him, saying, "Send us into the pigs so we can infest them." ¹³He allowed them, and the unclean spirits went out and entered the pigs and the herd plunged down the cliff into the sea, about two thousand of them, and were drowned in the sea. ¹⁴The herdsmen ran off to report to city and hamlet these strange events, and they went out to see what had happened. ¹⁵They came to Iesous and saw the man infested by demons sitting, clothed and sober-minded, the same person who had had the legion, and they grew alarmed. ¹⁶Those who had seen it described what happened to the demoniac and the pigs, ¹⁷and they began to implore him to leave their district. ¹⁸He got into the boat, and

the man who had been infested by demons begged that he might go with him. ¹⁹But he would not permit it and said to him, "Go home to your family and tell them how much the Lord did for you and had mercy on you." ²⁰He left and began to proclaim in the Decapolis how much Iesous had done for him, and all were amazed.

²¹When Iesous crossed back to the other side in the boat, a large crowd gathered around him by the sea. ²²One of the leaders of the synagogue, who was named Jairus, came and saw him, fell at his feet, ²³and begged him in these words: "My little daughter is near the end. Come, lay your hands on her, cure her, let her live." ²⁴He went with him but the crowd followed and pressed upon him.

²⁵A woman had a flow of blood for twelve years ²⁶and had suffered greatly under many physicians. She had spent everything without benefit; in fact she grew worse. ²⁷She had heard about Iesous and came up behind him in the crowd and touched his cloak, ²⁸thinking, "If I just touch his clothes, I will be cured." ²⁹The bleeding dried up immediately and she knew in her body that she had been cured of the affliction. ³⁰And immediately Iesous sensed that a power had left him, and he turned to the crowd and said, "Who touched my cloak?" ³¹The disciples said, "Look at this crowd pressing on you, and you ask who touched me?" ³²As he searched around to see who had done it, ³³the woman, knowing what had been done for her, approached him shaking with fear, fell down and told the truth. ³⁴He said to her, "Daughter, your trust has healed you. Go in peace and remain free of your affliction."

³⁵While he was speaking, they came from the synagogue leader's house and said, "Your daughter has died. Why do you still bother the Teacher?" ³⁶Iesous overheard what they said and said to the leader, "Do not be afraid, only trust." ³⁷He would not allow anyone to go with him except Peter and James and his brother John. ³⁸They arrived at the house of the synagogue leader and he found an uproar of weeping and wailing. ³⁹He went in and said: "Why do you make this commotion and weep so? The child is not dead but asleep." ⁴⁰They ridiculed him, but he pushed them out and brought the girl's father and mother into her room, along with those with him. ⁴¹He took the child's hand and said to her, "Talitha koum," which translated is, "Little girl, wake up." ⁴²Immediately the girl stood up and began walking; for she was twelve years old. And they were

amazed, greatly amazed. ⁴³But he admonished them strictly that no one should know this, and asked that she be fed.

6

And he went out from that place and came to his home town, and his disciples accompanied him. ²And when the Sabbath came he started to teach in the synagogue and many of those listening were astonished, saying, "Where does he get these things that come to him and what is the wisdom given to him, so that he can accomplish so many powerful acts? ³Is this not the builder, Mary's son, the brother of James and Joses and Judas and Simon? Are not his sisters here with us?" And they were scandalized by him. ⁴And Iesous said to them, "A prophet is not without honor except in his own town and among his relatives and in his own house." ⁵And he was not able to do any powerful work there, though he did lay hands on a few people who were sick and healed them. ⁶He was stunned by their distrust, and he left for the villages all around, to teach there.

⁷He called the Twelve together and began to send them out two by two, and gave them authority over unclean spirits, ⁸and instructed them to take nothing but a staff for the journey, no bread, no bag, no money in the belt, ⁹just the sandals on their feet, and not to put on two tunics. ¹⁰He would say to them, "When you enter a house, stay there until you leave the place. ¹¹If the place does not want you or listen to you, when you leave you should shake off the dust under your feet, as a rebuke to them." ¹²And they dispersed and preached that people should repent. ¹³They expelled many demons, and anointed with oil many of the sick and relieved them.

¹⁴King Herod then heard of him, given that his name had become known, and some were saying that John the Baptizer had risen from the dead, that was the reason the miraculous powers operated in him. ¹⁵But others said he was Elijah, and others said he was a prophet like one of the prophets. ¹⁶But when Herod heard, he said, "John, the one I beheaded, is risen."

¹⁷Herod himself had John seized and locked in prison over the matter of Herodias, his brother Philip's wife, because he had married her. ¹⁸John

had said to Herod, "It is not lawful for you to take your brother's wife." ¹⁹Herodias held it against him and wanted to kill him, but did not have the power ²⁰because Herod revered John and knew him to be a righteous and holy man, so kept him safe. He had listened to him and felt disturbed, but still listened with pleasure. ²¹A festive day came when on his birthday Herod gave a dinner for his chief ministers and military tribunes and the leading men of Galilee. ²²The daughter of Herodias came in and danced and so pleased Herod and those reclining at table with him that the king said to the girl, "You can ask me for whatever you want and I will give it to you." ²³And he swore to her, "Whatever you might ask me I will give you, up to half my kingdom." ²⁴She went out and said to her mother, "What should I ask for?" And she said, "The head of John the Baptizer." ²⁵She hurried to the king immediately and said, "I want you to give me right now the head of John the Baptizer on a plate." ²⁶This filled the king with sorrow, but he was not willing to refuse her because of his oaths and those reclining at table. ²⁷So the king immediately sent for the executioner and commanded that his head be brought. He left and beheaded him in the prison, ²⁸and brought his head on a plate and gave it to the girl and the girl gave it to her mother. ²⁹ When his disciples heard, they arrived, took up the corpse, and set it in a tomb.

³⁰And the apostles gathered around Iesous and told him all the things they did and what they had taught. ³¹He said to them, "Come away on your own to a secluded place and rest a while." Since many people had been coming and going, they had no chance even to eat. ³²And they went away in the boat to a secluded place by themselves. ³³But many saw them leaving and recognized them, and rushed on foot from all the cities and got there before them. ³⁴On stepping out he saw a great crowd and felt compassion toward them because they were like sheep without a shepherd, and he began to teach them many things. ³⁵The hour was late when the disciples said to him, "This place is desolate and the hour is already late. ³⁶Send them away so that they can go to the nearby farms and villages and buy something to eat." ³⁷He answered them with, "You can give them something to eat." And they said to him, "Do you mean that we should go and buy two hundred denarii worth of bread to feed them?" ³⁸He said to them, "How many loaves do you have? Go and look." They checked and said, "Five, and two fish." ³⁹Then he asked them to make them all recline in groups on the green grass, ⁴⁰and they leaned back in groups of hundreds and fifties. ⁴¹He took the five loaves and the two fish,

looked up to the sky, blessed and broke the loaves, and continued to pass them to the disciples to set before the people. He also divided the two fish among all. ⁴²They all ate and were satisfied. ⁴³And they collected twelve baskets of broken pieces of bread and fish. ⁴⁴Those who had eaten the loaves numbered five thousand men. ⁴⁵Immediately he urged his disciples to board the boat and go ahead to the other side, to Bethsaida, while he sent the crowd away. ⁴⁶He took leave of them, and went to the mountain to pray.

⁴⁷When evening came, the boat was in the middle of the sea and he was by himself on land. ⁴⁸He saw them struggling to row, because the wind was against them. About the fourth watch of the night he came to them, walking on the sea, intending to pass them by. ⁴⁹Seeing him walking on the sea, they thought it was a phantom and they shouted out; ⁵⁰they all had seen him and were shaken. But immediately he spoke to them and said, "Have courage, I am here, do not be afraid." ⁵¹He stepped into the boat with them and the wind died down. But they were deeply shocked inside; ⁵²they did not understand the incident of the loaves because their hearts had hardened. ⁵³They crossed over to the land and moored at Gennesaret. ⁵⁴When they disembarked he was recognized immediately, ⁵⁵and people ran around the countryside and began to carry the sick on mats to wherever they heard he was. ⁵⁶Wherever he went, in villages, cities, or farms, they laid down the ailing in marketplaces and begged that they might touch only the fringe of his cloak. And as many as touched him were healed.

7

Pharisees and some scribes from Jerusalem congregated around him. ²They had seen a few of his disciples eating bread with impure hands, that is, unwashed hands, ³because the Pharisees and all the Jews do not eat without washing their hands as far as the elbow, according to the tradition of the elders, ⁴and coming from the marketplace they do not eat until they wash. There are many other things which they inherited and observe: washing drinking cups and vessels and copper pots and dining couches. ⁵So the Pharisees and the scribes questioned him, "Why do your disciples not walk in the tradition of the elders, but eat bread with unwashed hands?" ⁶And he said to them, "Isaiah prophesied correctly about you dissemblers, as it is written:

> *This people reveres me with their lips but their heart is kept far away from me;* ⁷*they worship me in vain, pronouncing doctrines that are the edicts of men.*

⁸Neglecting God's commandment, you keep up the traditions of men." ⁹And he said to them, "You actually set aside God's commandment in order to guard your tradition. ¹⁰For Moses said, *Honor your father and your mother* and *Anyone who abuses father or mother must die.* ¹¹But you say that if a man says to his father or mother, Whatever I had for your benefit is now Korban—that is, a gift—¹²you no longer allow him to do anything for the father or mother, ¹³invalidating the word of God for the sake of the tradition you have carried on. And you do many things like this."

¹⁴Then he called the crowd together again and said to them, "Listen to me, all of you, and understand. ¹⁵Nothing from outside that comes into a man can defile him, but things coming out of a man can defile him." ¹⁷When he went into the house away from the crowd, the disciples asked him about the riddle. ¹⁸He said to them, "Are you so slow to understand as well? Do you not realize that anything from outside that goes into a man cannot pollute him ¹⁹because it does not go into the heart but into the belly, and passes out into the latrine," purifying all foods. ²⁰And he said further, "What comes out of a man makes him unclean. ²¹Evil thoughts come from within the heart, fornication, thefts, murders, adulteries, ²²avarice, depravity, deceit, promiscuity, the evil eye, slander, pride, foolishness, ²³all these evils come from within and they defile the man."

²⁴He rose up from there and went away to the borderlands of Tyre. He went into a house, hoping no one would know, but it was not possible for him to remain private. ²⁵Immediately a woman heard about him, a woman whose young daughter had an unclean spirit, and she came and fell at his feet. ²⁶Now the woman was a Greek, a Syro-Phoenician by birth, and she implored him to force the demon out of her daughter. ²⁷He said to her, "First let the children be fed; it is not good to take bread from the children and throw it to the dogs." ²⁸She replied, "Yes, sir, but even the dogs under the table eat the crumbs the children drop." ²⁹And he said to her, "Because of your words, go; the demon has left your daughter." ³⁰When she went home she found the child in bed, and the demon was gone.

³¹Again he left the region of Tyre and came across Sidon to the Sea of Galilee to the center of the region of the Decapolis. ³²And they brought to him a deaf man with a speech impediment, and begged him to lay a hand on him. ³³He took him aside from the crowd in private and put his fingers into his ears and then spat and touched his tongue. ³⁴He looked up to the sky, murmured, and said to him, "Ephphatha," that is, "Be opened." ³⁵And his ears were opened and the shackle on his tongue released, and he began to speak plainly. ³⁶He demanded they tell no one, but the more he demanded, the more they proclaimed. For they were struck with boundless astonishment and said, "He has done all things well. He makes the deaf hear and the mute speak."

8

In those days a great crowd was gathered again, and with nothing to eat. He called the disciples and said to them, ²"I feel sympathy for the crowd because they have been with me for three days already and have nothing to eat. ³If I send them home hungry, they will faint on the road, since some have come from far away." ⁴The disciples answered, "But where could anyone find bread to feed them in this deserted place?" ⁵He asked them, "How many loaves do you have?" And they said, "Seven." ⁶Then he told the crowd to recline on the ground. He took the seven loaves, gave thanks, broke them and passed them to his disciples so that they could set them out, and they set them before the crowd. ⁷They also had a few small fish. Having blessed them, he ordered that these be set out too. ⁸They ate and were satisfied, and they collected seven baskets of leftover pieces. ⁹This time there were about four thousand people. Then he sent them away.

¹⁰Immediately he stepped into the boat with his disciples and went to the district of Dalmanoutha. ¹¹And the Pharisees came out and began to argue with him, asking him for a sign from heaven, testing him. ¹²He sighed from the depth of his soul and said, "Why does this generation look for a sign? The truth is, no sign will be given to this generation." ¹³He left them, embarked again, and traveled to the other side. ¹⁴But they had neglected to get bread and had only one loaf with them in the boat. ¹⁵He warned them, saying, "You must watch out for the leaven of the Pharisees and the leaven of Herod." ¹⁶They were arguing with one

another over the bread. ¹⁷He understood and said, "Why do you argue because you have no bread? You still do not perceive or understand. ¹⁸Have you hardened your hearts? You have eyes but do not see, and ears but do not hear. Do you not remember, ¹⁹when I broke the five loaves for the five thousand, how many full baskets of pieces you collected?" They said to him, "Twelve." ²⁰"And when seven fed the four thousand, how many full baskets did you collect?" They said, "Seven." ²¹He said to them, "And still you do not understand?"

²²They arrived at Bethsaida, where they brought a blind man to him and asked him to touch him. ²³He took the blind man's hand and led him out of the village. He spat on his eyes and laid hands on him, and asked him, "Do you see anything?" ²⁴Having looked up, he said, "I see men as I see trees, but walking." ²⁵He laid his hands on the eyes again, and he opened his eyes and was cured and began to see everything clearly. ²⁶He sent him home, saying, "Do not go into the village."

²⁷Iesous and his disciples went into the villages around Caesarea Philippi. On the way he asked them, "Who do people say I am?" ²⁸They answered him, "John the Baptizer, and others, Elijah, and still others, one of the prophets." ²⁹And he asked, "But you, who do you say I am?" Peter answered him, "You are the Anointed One." ³⁰Then he warned them not to say that about him to anyone. ³¹He began to teach them that it was necessary for the son of man to suffer greatly and be repudiated by the elders and the chief priests and the scribes, and be killed, and after three days to rise. ³²He was speaking the word openly, and Peter took him aside and began to reprimand him. ³³He turned and looked at his disciples, and reprimanded Peter, saying, "Get out of my sight, Adversary, for you are not thinking of the concerns of God but of the concerns of men." ³⁴Then he called the crowd together with his disciples and said to them, "If anyone wants to come after me, let him take up his cross and follow me. ³⁵Because whoever wants to save his life will lose it, but whoever will lose his life because of me and the good message will save it. ³⁶For what advantage does a man have if he gains the whole world and loses his life? ³⁷What can a man give in exchange for his life? ³⁸Whoever might be ashamed of me and my words in this adulterous and mistaken generation, the son of man will in turn be ashamed of him when he shall come in the glory of his Father with the sacred Messengers." ⁹·¹And he said to

them, "I speak the truth when I say to you that there are some standing here who will not taste death before they see the reign of God arrive in power."

9

²After six days Iesous took Peter and James and John and brought them up a high mountain, alone by themselves. And he was transformed in front of them, ³so that his clothes became so shining white that no launderer on earth could make them so white. ⁴Then Elijah appeared to them with Moses, and they were talking with Iesous. ⁵Peter responded and said to Iesous, "Rabbi, it is good that we are here. Let us build three huts, one for you, one for Moses, and one for Elijah." ⁶He did not know what to say, because they were terrified. ⁷Then a cloud came, overshadowing them, and voice came out of the cloud: "This is my beloved son, listen to him." ⁸Suddenly they looked around and saw no one any longer, except Iesous alone with them. ⁹Coming down from the mountain, he warned them to tell no one what they had seen until the son of man had risen from the dead. ¹⁰They kept that word to themselves, debating what it is to rise from the dead. ¹¹And they asked him, saying, "Why do the scribes say that Elijah must come first?" ¹²He said to them, "Elijah indeed comes first and restores everything, and yet how has it been written of the son of man that he should suffer greatly and be despised? ¹³But I say to you that Elijah has come already, and they did to him whatever they wanted, as it was written about him."

¹⁴Coming back to the disciples, they saw a great crowd around them and scribes arguing with them. ¹⁵When the crowd saw him they were very surprised and immediately ran and welcomed him. ¹⁶And he asked them, "What are you discussing with one another?" ¹⁷One of the crowd answered him, "Teacher, I brought my son to you because he has a silent spirit in him, ¹⁸and whenever it seizes him it throws him down, and he foams at the mouth and grates his teeth and is wasting away. I asked your disciples to expel it, but they did not have the strength." ¹⁹Responding, he said, "O untrusting generation, how much longer will I be with you and bear with you? Bring him to me." ²⁰They brought him to him, and seeing him, the spirit immediately threw him into convulsions. He fell upon the ground and began to roll around, foaming at the mouth. ²¹And he asked his father, "How long has this been with him?" And he said, "From

childhood, ²²and it has often thrown him into both fire and water, so that it might destroy him. If you are able to do anything, help us, have pity on us." ²³Iesous said to him, "If you are able? Everything is possible for someone who trusts." ²⁴The father of the child immediately shouted, "I do trust; help my distrust." ²⁵When Iesous saw that the crowd was rushing together, he admonished the unclean spirit, saying to it, "Silent and deaf spirit, I charge you to come out of him and never enter him again." ²⁶It shrieked, threw him into desperate convulsions, then came out. He looked like a corpse, and many said he was dead. ²⁷Then Iesous took him by the hand, woke him, and he stood up. ²⁸When he was in the house the disciples asked him in private, "Why could we not expel it?" ²⁹He said to them, "Nothing can expel one of this nature, except prayer."

³⁰They left from there and were traveling through Galilee, and he did not want anyone to know, ³¹because he was teaching his disciples. He said to them, "The son of man will be surrendered into the hands of men and they will kill him, and when killed, after three days he will arise." ³²But they did not understand his words and were afraid to ask him.

³³They went to Capernaum, and when at home he asked them, "What were you discussing along the road?" ³⁴They were silent, because on the road they had been debating with one another who was the greatest. ³⁵He sat down and called the Twelve and said to them, "If anyone would like to be first, he will be last of all and servant of all." He picked a child, set him in the middle, gathered him in his arms, and said to them, ³⁷"Whoever accepts one of the little children like this in my name, accepts me; and whoever accepts me, accepts not me but the one who sent me." ³⁸John answered him, "Teacher, we saw someone expelling demons in your name and we prevented him, because he does not walk with us." ³⁹Iesous said, "Do not prevent him, since no one who does powerful work in my name is likely to abuse me. ⁴⁰Whoever is not against us is for us. ⁴¹Whoever might give you a cup of water to drink in the name of the Anointed, in truth he will not lose his reward. ⁴²But whoever entices to sin one of these little ones who trust me, it would be better to hang a heavy millstone around his neck and throw him into the sea. ⁴³If your hand causes you to sin, cut it off; it is better for you to go into life crippled than to go into Gehenna with two hands, into the unquenchable fire. ⁴⁵And if your foot causes you to sin, cut it off; it is better for you to go into life lame than

be thrown into Gehenna with two feet. ⁴⁷And if your eye causes you to sin, pluck it out; it is better for you to enter the reign of God with one eye than with two eyes be thrown into Gehenna, ⁴⁸*where the worm does not die and the fire is not quenched.* ⁴⁹For everyone will be salted with fire. ⁵⁰Salt is good, but if salt becomes flat, what will you season it with? Have salt within yourselves, and be at peace with each other."

10

And he left there and went into the region of Judea and across the Jordan. Crowds gathered around him again and he taught them again, as was his habit. ²The Pharisees asked him if it is lawful for a husband to divorce his wife, testing him. ³He answered them, "What did Moses command you?" ⁴They said, "Moses permitted him to write a roll of divorce and send her away." ⁵Iesous said to them, "Your hardness of heart caused him to write this law for you. ⁶But from the beginning of creation, male and female he made them, ⁷and because of this a man will leave his father and mother and be joined to his wife ⁸and the two will be one body, which means they are no longer two, but one body. ⁹Therefore what God has conjoined man must not divide." ¹⁰In a house again, the disciples asked him about this. ¹¹He said to them, "Anyone who divorces his wife and marries another, commits adultery against her, ¹²and if she divorces her husband and marries another, she commits adultery."

¹³Then they were bringing little children to him, so that he might touch them, but the disciples reprimanded them. ¹⁴Iesous saw it and was indignant and said to them, "Let the little children come to me, do not stop them, because the reign of God belongs to them. ¹⁵I tell you the truth, whoever does not accept the reign of God as a child, shall never enter it." ¹⁶Then he took them in his arms, blessed them, and laid his hands on them.

¹⁷As he started out on the road, someone rushed up and knelt to him, asking, "Good teacher, what should I do to inherit age-long life?" ¹⁸Iesous said to him, "Why do you call me good? No one is good except God alone. ¹⁹You know the laws: do not murder, do not commit adultery, do not steal, do not testify falsely, do not defraud, honor your father and mother." ²⁰And he said to him, "Teacher, I have obeyed all these since my youth." ²¹Iesous looked at him and admired him and said to him, "You

lack one thing: Go, sell everything you have and give to the poor, and you will have wealth in heaven. Then come, walk with me." ²²But his face grew somber at the words and he went away saddened, because he was a man with a great estate. ²³Looking around, Iesous said to his disciples, "How difficult it will be for the rich to come into the reign of God." The disciples stood stupefied at his words. ²⁴But Iesous said to them again, "Children, it is difficult to come into the reign of God. ²⁵It is easier for a camel to thread a needle's eye than for a rich man to enter into the reign of God." They were astonished, saying among themselves, "Then who could be saved?" ²⁷Iesous looked closely at them and said, "For men, it is impossible, but not for God. With God, everything is possible." ²⁸Peter began to say to him, "Look, we have left everything and walked with you." ²⁹Iesous said, "I tell you the truth, there is no one who has left house or brothers or sisters or mother or father or children or fields because of me and because of the good message, ³⁰who will not have a hundred times now, in this time, houses and brothers and sisters and mothers and children and fields with persecutions, and in the age which is coming, age-long life. ³¹Because many first will be last, and the last first."

³²Then they were on the road going up to Jerusalem with Iesous leading them, and they were amazed, and those walking behind were afraid. Bringing the Twelve near again, he began to tell them what was about to happen to him: ³³"Look now, we are going up to Jerusalem and the son of man will be handed over to the chief priests and the scribes and they will condemn him to death and will hand him over to the foreigners. ³⁴They will ridicule him and spit on him and flog him and kill him, and after three days he will rise." ³⁵Then James and John, the two sons of Zebedee, approached and said to him, "Teacher, our wish is that whatever we ask you, you would do for us." ³⁶He said to them, "What do you want me to do for you?" ³⁷And they said to him, "Let us sit, one of us at your right hand and one at the left, in your glory." ³⁸Iesous said to them, "You do not know what you ask. Can you drink the cup that I drink or be baptized with the baptism I will be baptized with?" ³⁹They said to him, "We can." Iesous said to them, "The cup I drink you will drink, and the baptism I am baptized with you will be baptized with, ⁴⁰but to sit at my right hand or left is not in my gift, because it has been reserved for others." ⁴¹Hearing this, the ten grew angry with James and John. ⁴²Iesous called them near and said to them, "You know that those called the leaders of the gentile nations do rule them, and their great ones lord it over them.

⁴³But it is not so with you. Whoever wants to become great among you will be your servant, ⁴⁴and whoever wants to be first among you will be the slave of all. ⁴⁵For the son of man came not to be served but to serve, and to give his life as ransom for many."

⁴⁶Then they went to Jericho. As he was leaving Jericho with his disciples and a large crowd, the son of Timaeus, Bartimaeus, a blind beggar, was sitting by the road. ⁴⁷Having heard that it was Iesous of Nazareth, he cried out and said, "Son of David, Iesous, have pity on me." ⁴⁸Many people admonished him and hushed him, but he cried out all the more, "Son of David, have pity on me." ⁴⁹Iesous stopped and asked that he be brought. They called the blind man and said, "Have courage, stand up, he is calling you." ⁵⁰He tossed off his cloak, stood up, and went to Iesous. ⁵¹In answer Iesous said to him, "What do you want me to do for you?" And the blind man said, "Rabbouni, that I might recover my sight." ⁵²Iesous said, "Go, your trust has healed you." And immediately he recovered his sight and began to walk with him on the road.

11

When they approached Jerusalem, at Bethphage and Bethany at the Hill of Olives, he sent two of his disciples ²and said to them, "Go into the village in front of you, and immediately as you enter it you will find a colt tied up that no one has ever sat on. Untie it and bring it. ³And if anyone says to you, Why are you doing this? say, Its master needs it and will send it back here immediately." ⁴They left and found the colt tied outside a door on the street and untied it. ⁵Some people standing there said to them, "What are you doing, untying that colt?" ⁶They answered as Iesous had instructed, and they permitted them. ⁷So they brought the colt to Iesous, laid their cloaks on its back, and he sat on it. ⁸And many people spread their cloaks on the road, and others laid down branches cut from the fields. ⁹Both those walking ahead and behind cried out:

> *Hosanna!*
> *Blessed is the one coming in the name of the Lord!*
> ¹⁰*Blessed is the coming reign of our father David!*
> *Highest hosanna!*

¹¹Then he entered Jerusalem and the Temple, and looked around at everything, but the hour was already late and he went to Bethany with the Twelve.

¹²Leaving Bethany the next day, he was hungry. ¹³He saw a fig tree in leaf in the distance and went to see if he could find anything on it, but he found nothing apart from leaves because it was not fig season. ¹⁴And he said to it, "May no one ever eat fruit from you again." And his disciples heard it.

¹⁵They arrived in Jerusalem. He entered the Temple and began to push out all those buying and selling in the Temple, and overturned the tables of the money changers and the benches of the dove sellers, ¹⁶and would not permit anyone to carry a vessel through the Temple. ¹⁷Then he lectured them, saying, "Was it not written that *My house will be called a house of prayer for all the nations*? But you have made it a cave of bandits." ¹⁸The chief priests and the scribes heard this and began to plot a way to destroy him. They feared him because all the crowd were in awe of his teaching. ¹⁹When evening came, he left the city.

²⁰Passing by in the morning, they saw that the fig tree was withered from the roots. ²¹Peter remembered and said, "Rabbi, look, the fig tree you cursed has withered." ²²Iesous said, "Trust in God. ²³I speak the truth, if someone says to a mountain, Lift yourself up and throw yourself into the sea, and does not doubt in his heart but trusts that what he says will happen, it will be done for him. ²⁴That is why I say to you, no matter what you pray or ask for, trust you will receive it and it will be yours. ²⁵And when you stand praying, let go of anything you hold against anyone, so that your Father in the heavens might overlook your own transgressions."

²⁷They went back to Jerusalem. As he was walking in the Temple, the chief priests and the scribes and the elders approached ²⁸and said to him, "By what authority are you doing these things? Who gave you the authority to do this?" ²⁹Iesous said to them, "I will ask you one question. Answer me and I will tell by what authority I do this. ³⁰Did John's baptism come from heaven or from men? Tell me that." ³¹They debated with each other, saying, "How should we answer? If we say from heaven, he will demand, Then why did you not trust in him? ³²But if we say from

men"—in that case they feared the people because they all thought John was a true prophet. ³³So they answered Iesous by saying, "We do not know." Iesous said to them, "Then neither will I say by what authority I am doing these things."

12

Then he began to speak to them in parables. "A man planted a vineyard and set a wall around it, dug out a wine vat, and built a watchtower. He rented it to farmers and traveled abroad. ²At the proper time he sent a servant to the tenant farmers, so that he might collect from them some of the fruit of the vineyard, ³but they grabbed him, beat him, and sent him away empty-handed. ⁴Then he sent another servant to them, and they hit him on the head and treated him disgracefully. ⁵And so he sent another, but they killed him, and then many others, some they beat, some they killed. ⁶He had one more, a much-loved son, and he sent him last to them, saying, They will have respect for my son. ⁷But the tenants said to each other, This is the heir—come on, let us kill him and we will get the inheritance. ⁸And they snatched him and killed him and threw him outside the vineyard. ⁹What will the owner of the vineyard do now? He will come and destroy the tenants and give the vineyard to others. Have you not read the scripture?

> ¹¹*The stone the builders rejected has become the cornerstone.*
> *The Lord did this and it is wonderful in our eyes.*

¹²Then they looked for a way to arrest him but they worried about the crowd. They understood he had told the parable against them, but they left him and went away.

¹³Then they sent some of the Pharisees and Herodians to him, trying to catch him through his own words. ¹⁴They came and said to him, "Teacher, we know you are true and are not influenced by others. You disregard a person's status and teach the way of God in harmony with the truth. Does it accord with our Law to pay taxes to Caesar or not? Should we pay or not pay?" ¹⁵Knowing their hypocrisy, he said to them, "Why do you test me like this? Bring me a denarius, so I can look at it." ¹⁶They brought it and he said, "Whose likeness is this, and whose title?" They said to him, "Caesar's." ¹⁷Iesous said to them, "What is Caesar's give back to Caesar, and what is God's to God." And they were amazed at him.

¹⁸Then Sadducees, who say there is no resurrection, came to question him, saying, ¹⁹"Teacher, Moses wrote for us that if a man's brother dies and leaves behind a wife but no offspring, the man should take his brother's wife and have children for his brother. ¹²There were seven brothers, and the first took a wife and died without a child. ²¹And the second took her and died without a child, and the third exactly the same, ²²and so on through the seven, all without offspring. Finally the woman died as well. ²³At the resurrection, when they rise, whose wife will she be? Because all seven had her as a wife." ²⁴Iesous said to them, "Are you not mistaken? It seems you do not know the scriptures or the power of God. ²⁵When they rise from the dead they do not marry nor are they given in marriage, but are like the Messengers in the heavens. ²⁶Regarding the dead rising, have you not read in the book of Moses about the bush, how God spoke to him, saying:

> *I am the God of Abraham and the God of Isaac and the God of Jacob?*

²⁷He is not God of the dead but of the living. You are highly mistaken."

²⁸One of the scribes had arrived and heard them debating. Seeing that he answered them well, he asked him, "Which commandment is the first of all?" ²⁹Iesous answered, "The first is:

> *Hear, O Israel, the Lord our God, the Lord is one,* ³⁰*and you shall love the Lord your God with all of your heart and all of your life and with all of your mind and with all of your strength.*

³¹Second is this:

> *You shall love your neighbor as yourself.*

There is no greater commandment than these." ³²The scribe said to him, "Correct, Teacher, you speak the truth that he is one and there is no other beside him, ³³and to love him with all heart and with all understanding and strength, and to love one's neighbor as oneself, those are more important than all burnt offerings and sacrifices." ³⁴Iesous saw that he had answered wisely and said to him, "You are not far from the reign of God." Then no one dared to question him any longer.

³⁵Teaching in the Temple, Iesous said, "How can the scribes hold that the Anointed is the son of David? ³⁶David himself said, speaking by the sacred breath,

The lord said to my lord:
Sit at my right hand
until I set your enemies under your feet.

³⁷If David himself calls him lord, how can he be his son?" The great crowd heard him with pleasure. ³⁸As he continued teaching, he said, "Watch out for the scribes, who want to walk around in long robes and accept greetings in the marketplaces, ³⁹and have the distinguished seats in synagogues and the highest places at dinners, ⁴⁰but devour widows' houses and pray at length just for the look of it. They will receive harsh judgment."

⁴¹He sat down opposite the treasury and watched how the crowd put money into the treasury. Many wealthy people put in large sums. ⁴²Then a poor widow arrived and threw in two of the smallest coins, worth very little. ⁴³He called his disciples and said to them, "To tell the truth, this poor widow has put in more than all of those donating to the treasury. ⁴⁴They all gave out of their riches, but in her poverty she gave as much as she had, all of her livelihood."

13

As he was leaving the Temple one of his disciples said to him, "Look, Teacher, what stones and what buildings!" ²Iesous said to him, "You see these great buildings? Not one stone upon stone will be left here, all will be demolished."

³Sitting on the Hill of Olives, opposite the Temple, Peter and James and John and Andrew asked him in private, ⁴"Tell us when these things will take place. And what will be the sign that they are about to occur?" ⁵Iesous said to them, "Be careful that no one misleads you. ⁶Many will come in my name, saying I am the one, and will mislead many others. ⁷When you hear of wars and rumors of wars, do not be alarmed. That must happen, but it is not yet the end. ⁸For nation will rise up against nation and kingdom against kingdom. There will be earthquakes throughout the lands and famines. These are the start of the birth pangs. ⁹Look out for yourselves. They will hand you over to councils and you will be beaten in synagogues, and you will stand before governors and kings because of me, to give testimony to them. ¹⁰But first the good message must be proclaimed to all the nations. ¹¹And when they take you away and hand

you over, do not be anxious beforehand about what you should say, but say whatever comes to you in that hour, because it is not you speaking but the sacred breath. ¹²Brother will betray brother to death and father, child. Children will rebel against parents and put them to death. ¹³And you will be detested by all because of my name, but the one who endures to the end will be rescued.

¹⁴"When you see *the abomination that makes desolation* standing where it should not be—the one reading, let him understand—then let those in Judea escape to the mountains, ¹⁵let no one on the roof come down or go in to take anything out of his house, ¹⁶and let no one in the field return to get his cloak. ¹⁷It will be miserable in those days for women who are pregnant or nursing. ¹⁸Pray that it will not be winter, ¹⁹because those days will see suffering never before endured, since the beginning of God's creation until now, and never will occur again. ²⁰If the Lord had not shortened those days, nobody would survive, but for the sake of the elect he has chosen, he has shortened the days. ²¹Then if anyone says to you, Look, here is the Anointed, look there. Do not trust it. ²²Because some false Anointed and false prophets will appear and perform signs and wonders, trying to lead the chosen astray if they can. Be careful, then—I have predicted everything for you.

²⁴"But in those days, after all that suffering,

> *The sun will darken*
> *and the moon will not give its light;*
> ²⁵*the stars will fall from the sky*
> *and the powers in the heavens will topple.*

²⁶Then they will see the son of man coming in clouds with great power and glory, ²⁷and he will send the Messengers and bring together his chosen from the four winds, from the end of the earth to the end of the sky.

²⁸"Now learn from a story of the fig tree. When a branch becomes tender and sends out its leaves, you know that summer is near. ²⁹So you too, when you see these things happening, you know that it is near, at the door. ³⁰I tell you the truth, this generation will not pass away until all these things take place. ³¹Heaven and earth will pass away, but my words will never pass away.

³²"No one knows about that day or the hour, not even the Messengers in the sky, not the son, but only the Father. ³³Stay alert, be on guard, because you do not know when the time is. ³⁴It is like a man going abroad who has left his house and delegated tasks to each of his servants, and told the watchman to be vigilant. ³⁵So stay awake, because you do not know when the master of the house will return, at evening, or midnight, or at cockcrow, or dawn. ³⁶He might come suddenly and find you sleeping. ³⁷What I say to you now I say to all: keep awake."

14

Because the feast of Passover and Unleavened Bread would begin in two days, the chief priests and scribes tried to find a way to arrest him through a trick, and kill him. ²They said it should not be during the festival because the people would riot.

³He was in Bethany at the house of Simon, called the Leper. While he was reclining at table, a woman arrived with a stone flask of very expensive fragrant oil made from pure nard. She broke open the flask and poured it on his head. ⁴Some of those present grew indignant and reproved her, saying, "Why waste such fragrant oil? ⁵It could have been sold for more than three hundred denarii and the money distributed to the poor." ⁶Iesous said, "Leave her alone. Why do you make trouble for her? She has done something good for me. ⁷You always have the poor with you, and you can help them whenever you want, but you do not always have me. ⁸She did what she could. She has anointed my body in advance for burial. ⁹In truth, wherever the good message is preached in the whole world, what she has done will be remembered."

¹⁰Then Judas Iscariot, one of the Twelve, went to the chief priests in order to betray him to them. ¹¹They listened to him with delight and promised him silver, so he sought out an opportune way to hand him over.

¹²On the first day of Unleavened Bread, when the Passover lamb is to be sacrificed, his disciples said to him, "Where do you wish us to go to prepare, so that you can eat the Passover feast?" ¹³He sent two of his disciples and said to them, "Go into the city and you will meet a man carrying a jug of water. Follow him, ¹⁴and wherever he enters, say to the owner of the house that the teacher says, Where is my guestroom where

I can eat the Passover with my disciples? ¹⁵He will show you a large upper room, furnished and ready. Prepare for us there." ¹⁶His disciples left for the city, found things as he had described, and they prepared for the Passover.

¹⁷When evening fell he went there with the Twelve. ¹⁸While they reclined and ate, Iesous said, "What I am about to say is true: one of you eating with me will betray me." ¹⁹They were much perplexed and said to him one by one, "Surely not I?" ²⁰He said to them, "It is one of the Twelve, one dipping in the bowl with me. ²¹Indeed the son of man will depart as it was written about him. But woe to the man who hands over the son of man. Better for him not to have been born."

²²While they were eating, Iesous took bread, gave praise, broke it, and gave it to them, saying, "Take, this is my body." ²³And holding a cup, he gave thanks and offered it to them, and they all drank from it. ²⁴Then he said to them, "This is my blood of the covenant which is poured out for many. ²⁵In all truth I say to you, I will not drink the fruit of the vine again until that day when I drink it for the first time in the reign of God." ²⁶After they sang a hymn, they went out to the Hill of Olives.

²⁷Iesous said to them, "You will all desert me, for it is written:

> *I will strike the shepherd and the sheep will be scattered.*

²⁸But when I am raised I will walk ahead of you to Galilee." ²⁹Then Peter said to him, "Even if all fall away, I will not." ³⁰Iesous said to him, "I speak the truth that today, this very night, before the cock crows twice, you will deny me three times." ³¹But Peter insisted with great emphasis, "I will die with you if necessary, but will not deny you." And the others all spoke in the same way.

³²They came to a place called Gethsemane and he said to his disciples, "Sit here while I pray." ³³He took Peter and James and John with him, and he began to be deeply uneasy, gravely distressed. ³⁴He said to them, "My spirit is very sorrowful, to the point of death. Stay here and keep watch." ³⁵He went a little further and fell on the ground and prayed that if it were possible, the hour might pass him by. ³⁶He said, "Abba, Father, all things are possible for you. Take this cup away from me. But not what I want, but what you want." ³⁷He returned to find them sleeping and said

to Peter, "Simon, are you asleep? You could not stay awake for one hour? ³⁸Watch and pray so you do not fall into temptation. The spirit is always willing but the flesh is weak." ³⁹He left again and prayed in the same words. ⁴⁰Returning once more, he found them sleeping. Their eyes were heavy and they did not know what to say to him. ⁴¹Coming back a third time, he said to them, "Are you still sleeping and resting? Enough now, the hour has come. Look on as the son of man is turned over to the hand of sinners. ⁴²Get up, let us go. See, my betrayer approaches."

⁴³And immediately as he was speaking Judas arrived, one of the Twelve, and with him a mob with swords and clubs from the chief priests and scribes and elders. ⁴⁴The betrayer had arranged a sign for them, saying, "The man I will kiss is the one. Secure him and take him away." ⁴⁵He went up to him immediately and said, "Rabbi," and kissed him. ⁴⁶And they laid hands on him and arrested him. ⁴⁷A certain man standing near drew his sword, struck the servant of the high priest, and cut off his ear. ⁴⁸Iesous said to them, "Am I a bandit, that you come out with swords and clubs to capture me? ⁴⁹I was with you every day teaching in Temple and you did not arrest me. But the scriptures must be fulfilled." ⁵⁰Then they all left him and ran away. ⁵¹A certain young man was with him, wearing just a linen cloth. ⁵²They seized him, but he dropped the cloth and escaped naked.

⁵³They then led Iesous to the high priest, and all the chief priests and scribes and elders assembled. ⁵⁴Peter followed him at a distance, all the way to the courtyard of the high priest, where he sat with the attendants, warming himself at the fire. ⁵⁵The chief priests and the council known as the Sanhedrin were looking for testimony against Iesous so they could put him to death, but they could not find any. ⁵⁶Though many gave false witness against him, their testimonies did not agree. ⁵⁷Some others stood up to deliver misleading declarations such as, ⁵⁸"We heard him say: I will destroy this Temple made by hands and in three days I will build another not made by hands." But again the testimony was inconsistent. ⁶⁰Then the high priest stood in the middle to question Iesous, saying, "You have no answer to what these people allege against you?" ⁶¹But he was silent and answered nothing. The high priest questioned him again, saying to him, "Are you the Anointed, the son of the Blessed One?" ⁶²Iesous said, "I am. And you will see the son of man sitting at the right hand of power, coming on the clouds of heaven." ⁶³The high priest tore his clothes and

said, "Why do we need more witnesses? ⁶⁴You heard the blasphemy. How does it appear to you?" And they all condemned him as deserving death. ⁶⁵Then some began to spit on him. They blindfolded him, hit him and said, "Prophesy!" And the attendants slapped him on the face.

⁶⁶While Peter was below in the courtyard, one of the high priest's servant girls came out. ⁶⁷When she saw Peter warming himself, she studied him and said, "You were with the Nazarene Iesous as well." ⁶⁸But he denied it. "I do not know or understand what you are saying," he said, and went out to the entrance hall, and a cock crowed. ⁶⁹The servant girl saw him and said again to the people standing around, "He is one of them." ⁷⁰But again he denied it. A moment later, those standing there said to Peter, "Really, you are one of them, because you also are a Galilean." ⁷¹He began to curse and swear, "I do not know this man you are talking about." ⁷²And immediately the cock crowed for the second time. Then Peter remembered what Iesous had said to him: "Before the cock crows twice, you will deny me three times." And he broke down and wept.

15

And immediately in the morning the chief priests, in council with the elders and scribes and all of the Sanhedrin, bound Iesous, took him away, and delivered him to Pilate. ²Pilate asked him, "Are you the king of the Jews?" In answer he said, "So you say." ³Then the chief priests accused him of many things. ⁴Pilate questioned him again, saying, "You have no answer? Look at how many things they charge you with." ⁵But Iesous still said nothing, and this made Pilate wonder.

⁶At the festival he used to free one prisoner they requested. ⁷It so happened that a man called Barabbas was jailed with the rebels who had committed murder during the insurrection. ⁸The crowd came up and cried out, demanding that he follow this custom for them. ⁹Pilate answered them, "Do you want me to release to you the king of the Jews?" ¹⁰He was well aware that the chief priests had turned him over out of envy. ¹¹But the chief priests stirred up the crowd so that he would release Barabbas to them instead. ¹²Pilate answered, "Then what do you want me to do to him, the man you call the king of the Jews?" ¹³They cried out, "Crucify him!" Pilate said, "What evil has he done?" ¹⁴But they shouted all the

more, "Crucify him!" ¹⁵So Pilate, wanting to satisfy the crowd, released Barabbas to them and handed Iesous over to be flogged and crucified.

¹⁶The soldiers took him away to the palace, that is, the Praetorium, and called the whole cohort together. ¹⁷They put a purple cloak on him and twisted together a crown of thorns and set it on him, ¹⁸and saluted him with "Hail, king of the Jews." ¹⁹They repeatedly struck his head with a rod, spat on him, and bending their knees, paid homage to him. ²⁰After they mocked him, they took off the purple robe and put his own clothes on him. Then they led him out to crucify him.

²¹A man passing by, Simon of Cyrene, the father of Alexander and Rufus, was coming in from the country, and they forced him to carry his crossbeam. ²²They led him to Golgotha, which translated is the place called Skull. ²³They offered him wine laced with myrrh, but he did not take it. ²⁴Then they crucified him and divided his clothes, throwing lots to decide who should have what. ²⁵It was the third hour when they crucified him. ²⁶The inscription of the accusation against him was written as: the king of the Jews. ²⁷They crucified two bandits with him, one at his right hand and one at his left.

²⁹People passing by reviled him, shaking their heads and saying, "Ha, the man destroying the Temple and building it in three days, ³⁰save yourself, come down from the cross." ³¹In the same way the chief priests also mocked him among themselves, along with the scribes, saying, "He saved others but cannot save himself. ³²The Anointed, the king of Israel, let him come down from the cross now, so we can see and trust." Those crucified with him also reviled him.

³³When the sixth hour arrived, darkness came over the whole land until the ninth hour. ³⁴And at the ninth hour Iesous cried out in a loud voice:

Eloi, Eloi, lema sabachthani?

which translated is, "My God, my God, why have you forgotten me?" ³⁵Some of those standing by heard him and said, "Look, he is calling Elijah." ³⁶One man then ran, filled a sponge with sour wine, put it on a reed staff, offered it to him to drink, and said, "Let him be. Let us see if Elijah comes to take him down." ³⁷But Iesous uttered a loud cry and breathed his last. ³⁸The curtain in the Temple was torn in two from top to bottom.

³⁹When the centurion standing in front of him saw how he died, he said, "Truly, this man was God's son."

⁴⁰Now there were also women watching from the distance, including Mary of Magdala, and Mary the mother of James the younger and Joses, and Salome. ⁴¹They had followed him when he was in Galilee and had served him, along with many others who had come up with him to Jerusalem. ⁴²When it was already evening, since it was the day of Preparation, that is, the day before the Sabbath, ⁴³Joseph from Arimathea, a prominent member of the council, who was himself also waiting for the reign of God, boldly went to Pilate and requested the body of Iesous. ⁴⁴But Pilate wondered how he could be dead so soon and called the centurion to ask if he were already dead. ⁴⁵When he learned from the centurion it was so, he gave the corpse to Joseph. ⁴⁶He bought a linen cloth, took him down, wrapped him in the cloth, and set him in a tomb cut out of rock. Then he rolled a stone over the entrance to the tomb. ⁴⁷Mary of Magdala and Mary the mother of Joses watched where he was laid.

16

When the Sabbath was over, Mary of Magdala, and Mary the mother of James, and Salome bought perfumes so they could go and anoint him. ²Very early on the first day of the week they went to the tomb after sunrise. ³They said to one another, "Who will roll away the stone from the entrance of the tomb for us?" ⁴They looked up and saw that the stone had been rolled away, though it was very large. ⁵Entering the tomb, they saw a young man sitting on the right, clothed in a white robe, and they were greatly astonished. ⁶He said to them, "Do not be alarmed. You are looking for Iesous of Nazareth, who was crucified. He is risen, he is not here. See, there is the place where they laid him. ⁷But go, tell his disciples and Peter that he is going ahead of you into Galilee. You will see him there, as he told you." ⁸They left and ran away from the tomb, seized by trembling and confusion. They said nothing to anyone, because they were afraid.

Textual Notes

This translation is based on the latest edition of the Greek text of Nestle, *Novum Testamentum Graece*. For alternative manuscript readings I have also referred to Collins, *Mark: A Commentary*. Some of the information in these notes is treated more completely elsewhere in the book.

Title/ Titles were used inconsistently in ancient scrolls and may have been added by owners or readers rather than authors. Some reliable manuscripts read only *kata markon*, "According to Mark."

1.1/ The good message: Greek *euaggelion* (pronounced *euanghelion*) means good message or good news. Old English *god-spel* or *gospel* (good words, good news) was carried into Reformation and modern use despite losing its original meaning.

/ Iesous: Greek for the Hebrew *Yehosshua* or *Yeshua*. In the New Testament tradition, the customary translation is Jesus. Outside New Testament Greek, the standard English equivalent is Joshua.

/ the Anointed: Greek *xristos* (Christos) means "anointed" and is a direct translation of Hebrew *mashiah* (Messiah), implying divine appointment or ratification.

/ Some manuscripts add *huiou theou* (son of God) at the end of the verse, most likely a later (secondary) insertion.

1.2/ Malachi 3.1; Isaiah 40.3. The New Testament writers quote the scriptures not from Hebrew but from the Greek version, the Septuagint, made in the third and second centuries BCE.

1.4/ pardoned mistakes: *eis aphesin hamartion* is usually rendered "for the forgiveness of sins," but *hamartia* has a range of meanings centered around loss, failure, or fault; it literally means "missing the mark," as in archery.

1.8/ with the sacred breath: *pneumati hagio* is usually rendered "with the holy spirit." In Judaic use the holy spirit referred to the actions of God on earth.

1.10/ immediately: the word *euthus* is used repeatedly in Mark as a connective.

1.13/ Adversary: Greek *satanas*, based on Hebrew *satan*, adversary or devil.

/ Messengers: or angels; *aggelos* is Greek for Hebrew *mal'akh*, messenger.

1.16/ Pharisees: a devout Jewish group of the Second Temple period stressing strict ritual purity and separation from Hellenistic influence.

1.22/ scribes: Greek *grammateis*, the interpreters of the Mosaic Law contained in the Torah, the first five books of the Hebrew scriptures (in Greek, the Pentateuch, "five scrolls").

1.34/ they knew who he was: some manuscripts add *xriston einai* to make the reading "they knew him to be the Anointed" (or the Messiah).

2.15/ his house: Levi's house.

2.25–26/ an adaptation of the story in 1 Samuel 21.1–6.

3.6/ Herodians: economic vassals of Herod Antipas in Galilee. See 6.14.

3.14/ and called them apostles: not all manuscripts have this phrase. *Apostolous* means delegates or ambassadors.

3.16/ Rock: *Petros* in Greek normally means stone or small rock. *Kifa* in Aramaic, it appears in Greek as *Kefas* (or *Cephas*) in the parallel scene in John 1.42 and in six places in Paul (1 Corinthians and Galatians).

3.20/ Simon the Canaanite: *kananaion* can also be translated "the zealous."

4.2/ in comparison stories: or in parables (*en parabolais*).

4.12/ Isaiah 6.9–10.

5.1/ Gerasenes: some manuscripts have Gadarenes, probably a scribal revision to conform to Matthew 8.28. Gerasenes is the best reading but is problematic because Gerasa (modern Jerash in Jordan) is some distance from the Sea of Galilee. Mark seems to use the word to mean people from the district of Gerasa.

5.20/ Decapolis: "Ten Cities," a region of Hellenized gentile communities east of the River Jordan.

5.41/ Talitha koum: transliteration of Aramaic.

6.1/ home town: *patrida* (fatherland or native place); in Mark Iesous adopts Capernaum as his base.

6.3/ builder: *tekton* means any kind of artisan or craftsman, including carpenter, mason, or metalworker.

/ Joses: a variant of Hebrew Yosef (Joseph).

6.11/ Under influence of Matthew 10.15, some manuscripts add "I say to you in truth, it will be more endurable for Sodom or Gomorrah on the day of judgment than for that city."

6.14/ King Herod: Herod Antipas (dates uncertain; reigned 4 BCE–39 CE) was not a king but the Jewish tetrarch of Galilee and Perea under

Roman rule. He was the son of Herod the Great (c. 72–4 BCE), client king of Judea.

6.22/ daughter of Herodias: unnamed in Mark and Matthew; identified as Salome by Josephus in *Antiquities of the Jews.*

6.36/ two hundred denarii: one Roman denarius was the daily pay for legionnaires and most workers.

6.45/ Bethsaida: ancient village probably on the north shore of the Sea of Galilee.

6.48/ fourth watch: in the Roman supremacy the night was divided into four quasi-military watches starting at sunset, the last from about 03.00 to 06.00 hours. They were roughly equivalent to Iesous' words in 13.35: "at evening, or midnight, or at cockcrow, or dawn."

7.6/ Isaiah 29.13.

7.10/ These commandments are variously in Exodus 20.12 and 21.17, Deuteronomy 5.16, and Leviticus 20.9.

7.11/ Korban: any sacrificial offering in the Temple; in this case, money.

7.16/ Absent in most manuscripts ("If anyone has ears to hear, let him hear").

7.19/ The Greek is difficult to parse but most textual scholars think "purifying all foods" is an editorial comment on the meaning of Iesous' statement, not part of his statement.

7.24/ Some manuscripts read "Tyre and Sindon."

7.26/ a Greek: a gentile.

/ Syro-Phoenician: Canaanite.

7.34/ Ephphatha: another transliterated Aramaic word.

8.10/ Dalmanoutha: unknown location, probably an error. The parallel in Matthew (15.39) reads "the borders of Magadan" (Magdala in some manuscripts).

8.27/ Caesarea Philippi: Banias, ancient site in the Golan Heights in northeast Galilee, reestablished as a city by the tetrarch Philip II in 3 BCE.

8.35–37/ life: Greek *psyche* is the innermost being of a person and can mean breath, life, or soul.

9.1/ Clearly belongs to the last section of chapter 8.

9.5/ Rabbi: Hebrew term of respect for a teacher. It did not acquire the meaning of an ordained religious leader until the Talmudic period, well after the destruction of the Temple in 70 CE.

9.11–13/ Elijah: an allusion to Malachi 4.5–6, where God promises to send the prophet Elijah "before the great and awesome day of the Lord comes," which the apostles connect to the resurrection of the dead. Iesous implies Elijah has come in the person of John the Baptizer.

9.43/ Gehenna: Greek for the Valley of Hinnom, west and southwest of Jerusalem. Condemned by Jeremiah (7.31) as Tophet, the site of sacrifice of children to a pagan god, in the Second-Temple period the valley was sometimes seen as a place where the unrighteous would be punished before their destruction.

9.44, 46/ Repetitions in the Textus Receptus of verse 48.

9.48/ Isaiah 66.24.

10.6-7/ Allusions to Genesis 1.27 and 2.24.

10.33/ foreigners: *ethnos* here means any people or nation other than Israel and could be translated "gentiles"; the reference is clearly to the occupying Romans.

10.51/ Rabbouni: a heightened variant of Rabbi.

11.1/ Bethphage and Bethany: on the road from Jericho, on or near the Hill of Olives east of Jerusalem.

11.9/ Adapted from Psalm 118.26.

11.17/ Isaiah 56.7.

11.26/ Absent in the best manuscripts ("But if you do not forgive, your Father in the heavens will not forgive your own transgressions").

12.11/ Psalm 118.22–23.

12.18/ Sadducees: a high-ranking Hellenized group, mostly priests, active from the second century BCE, with responsibility for maintaining the Temple.

12.26/ Exodus 3.6.

12.30/ Deuteronomy 6.4–5.

12.31/ Leviticus 19.18.

12.36/ Psalm 110.1.

12.42/ smallest coins: the Greek reads "two lepta, which is a quadrans." The copper lepton was the smallest Greek denomination. A quadrans (*kodrantes*) was a quarter of a Roman *as*, itself worth one-sixteenth of a silver denarius. Roman and Herodian coins were in mixed circulation in Judea.

13.14/ Daniel 9.27, 11.31, 12.11. The nature of the abomination (or sacrilege) is not clear.

/ the one reading, let him understand or "let the reader understand": likely an aside directed to someone reading the text aloud to a group. It is repeated in the parallel place in Matthew 24.15.

13.24–25/ Isaiah 13.10, 34.4.

14.5/ more than three hundred denarii: about a year's wages for a worker.

14.26/ sang a hymn: probably one of the praise psalms customary after the Passover meal (Psalms 115–118).

14.27/ Zechariah 13.7.

14.32/ Gethsemane: from Aramaic, "oil press."

14.55/ Sanhedrin: the judicial council of elders of the Temple.

14.62/ And you will see the son of man: Daniel 7.13.

15.1/ Pilate: Pontius Pilatus (dates unknown) was the Roman Prefect (Praefectus) of Judea 26–36 CE, with civil and military authority under the Legate of Syria and, ultimately, Emperor Tiberius.

15.2/ So you say: Greek *sy legeis* (literally "you say") can hold different meanings: e.g., you are right in what you say; those are your words; you said it; if you say so.

15.13/ Crucify him: Greek *stauronson auton* literally means "stake him" or "pin him."

15.25/ third hour: in springtime, about 09.00 hours.

15.28/ A secondary interpolation: "And the scripture was fulfilled that says, *He was counted with the outlaws*," Isaiah 52.12.

15.34/ Psalm 22.1, in Aramaic.

16.9–20/ The best early manuscripts stop after verse 8. While some scholars argue that Mark did not intend to end at this point, almost all agree it is the earliest recoverable reading. The longer ending in the Textus Receptus was added, probably in the second century, under the influence of the other gospels, to smooth Mark's abrupt conclusion and relate the Resurrection appearances. A shorter additional ending from a single Old Latin manuscript (the Codex Bobiensis, fourth or fifth century) probably dates from a Greek original also of the second century. One or both additions are included in most modern bibles, customarily marked as questionable. For the sake of completeness, both additions are given below; the longer ending is discussed in chapter 7.

The shorter additional ending:

[[Then they reported all these instructions promptly to those with Peter. After that Iesous himself sent out through them, from east to west, the holy and incorruptible proclamation of eternal salvation.]]

The longer additional ending:

[[⁹Now having risen early on the first day of the week, he appeared first to Mary of Magdala, from whom he had cast out seven demons. ¹⁰She made her way and spoke to those who had been with him, who had been mourning and weeping. ¹¹But they, hearing that he was alive and seen by her, distrusted it. ¹²After that he appeared in another form to two of them, as they were walking in the country. ¹³Going back, they spoke to the rest, but they did not trust them either. ¹⁴Last he appeared to the eleven as they were reclining at table and rebuked their distrust and hardness of heart because they had not trusted those who had seen him risen from the dead. ¹⁵And he said to them, "Make your way into all the world and proclaim the good message to all creation. ¹⁶The one who trusts and is baptized will be rescued; but the one who does not trust will be condemned. ¹⁷Now these signs will follow those who have trusted: they will cast out demons in my name, they will speak in new languages, ¹⁸they will take up serpents in their hands, and if they drink any deadly thing it will not harm them. They will lay hands upon the sick and they will be made well." ¹⁹After speaking to them, then the Lord Iesous was raised up into the heavens and sat at the right hand of God. ²⁰And they went out and preached everywhere, the Lord working together with them and confirming the word with attending signs.]]

4

Mark as Literary Object

Surely some revelation is at hand;
Surely the Second Coming is at hand.
   —W. B. Yeats, "The Second Coming"

Whoever Mark was, we can assume he was not a customary writer. It is often pointed out that his Greek is awkward, his word choice repetitive, and his transitions abrupt. Commentators sometimes make too much of these supposed limitations; as we will see in the next chapter, in several circumstances his diction and his brevity had advantages. Certainly Mark was not a writer of sovereign power like Isaiah or the singers of the Psalms, nor does his work have the sweep, depth, or grandeur of the classical Greek writers. Of his approximate contemporaries around the Roman empire, he shows none of the grace of Virgil, the wit of Ovid, or the historical understanding of Tacitus or Plutarch. Yet his task was large and his work became as influential as any of those more accomplished authors, if for different reasons. One does not have to be a great writer to achieve high result; sometimes the subject does it, sometimes the moment does it. Nor must one be an experienced author to write a great work. By trade Paul was a tent maker who turned out to be a profound thinker and wrote, offhand and in a great hurry, some deathless prose.

If Mark was not a regular writer, what did he think he was doing when he began his book? Was he, like a gossip columnist, simply recording what he had heard? Clearly it was more than that, since he devised a structure and a plot to contain the incidents and sayings he inherited and attempted to give them comprehensive significance. But his method is not straightforward. Mark's themes are elusive, and his characterization surprisingly sophisticated. Narrative, character, and themes work together, sometimes in tension, sometimes in concord, to make a book that is as subtle as its language is direct.

To speak of a sacred work as a literary object does not deny its sacred purpose. Treating the bible as literature is a well-established practice for a simple reason: whatever else it may be, the bible is literature. Of course, any writing is literature in the etymological sense, and certain books of both testaments are more self-consciously literary than others. Some follow established genres and norms, such as the prophets and Paul's letters; some employ poetic or highly metaphorical language, such as the Psalms and Revelation; some are openly narrative, such as Genesis and the gospels. In this chapter I will lay out some of the distinctive qualities of Mark and show why his formula could be followed by the other evangelists.

Structure. At first glance the structure of the narrative is simple, following the protagonist from appearance to disappearance. The life cycle is the natural vector, and the one generally followed in the pattern of classical *bios*, though it is not the only one possible. In their "corrections" of Mark, both Matthew and Luke spend considerable time with Yeshua's background and birth to establish him as the offspring of David, born in David's town, his nativity announced by magi or angels. Matthew traces his ancestry back to Abraham, Luke back to Adam, and adds details about his childhood. Mark's story is sparer, and notable for starting with Yeshua's actions rather than his inherited legitimacy.

The narrative is also notable for its speed. Luke (3.23) says that Yeshua was "about thirty years old" when his ministry began, and according to John's itemizing of the Passovers it lasted for three years. But in Mark it appears to be much shorter. Though it is not possible to establish a chronology from the text, in reading the gospel through it feels as if everything occurs in less than a single year. The brevity of the work contributes to its sense of speed, as if the author had to fit in all the material he had in a headlong rush. The most important event in Christianity, the Resurrection, according to the earliest recoverable reading, is treated in a mere eight verses.

Despite the linear plot, Mark has a carefully organized structure based on parallel episodes. The gospel begins with a double promise: John the Baptizer is promised by the Hebrew scriptures, then in turn he promises that "someone stronger is coming after me." Yeshua then appears for baptism, the beginning of a rising action that carries through his ministry in Galilee. He gathers followers, performs miracles of a social and medical nature, gets the better of representatives of the Temple establishment in debate, predicts the end of time, and becomes famous throughout Galilee for his interpretation of the scriptures. The rising action climaxes halfway through the book. First, on a high mountain before his three major apostles, he is transformed (*metamorphou*, changed) in a shining revelation called the Transfiguration; then he enters Jerusalem on a colt to shouts of hosanna. After those high points the action starts to fall quickly as he encounters opposition from the Temple authorities, leading to his arrest, trials before the Sanhedrin and Pilate, crucifixion, death, and burial. The final chapter at the empty tomb contains a new promise, that the resurrected Yeshua will meet the apostles in Galilee.

Each major element of the rising action is mirrored by a major element in the falling action: promise of coming against promise of return, Baptism against Crucifixion, elevation in Galilee against debasement in Jerusalem. A triangular graph of the structure looks like figure 6.

FIGURE 6

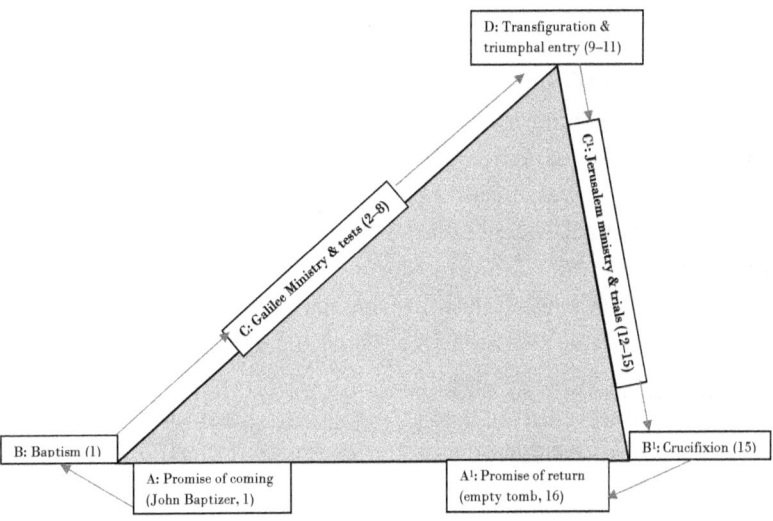

Structure of Mark (with chapters)

The Galilee ministry (C) is longer in time and length of text than that in Jerusalem (C^1). Though Mark does not say so explicitly, Yeshua and the apostles have come up to the capital for Passover, arriving about a week in advance as was usual for pilgrimage festivals. Despite the unequal timing of the two segments, their consequence is comparable and the greater intensity of the events in Jerusalem tends to balance them.[1]

It is significant that the climax of the rising action involves two events with echoes of the scriptures. The Transfiguration, an apocalyptic vision with the aura of dream, includes Elijah and Moses, establishing Yeshua's godly authorization and connection to or fulfilment of the original covenant. It leaves the apostles in awe. The triumphal entry to Jerusalem, with words adapted from Psalm 118.26, includes shouts of "our father David" along with the hosannas, and the colt Yeshua rides is an echo of the moment when Solomon mounts David's mule on the way to his anointing as king of Israel (1 Kings 1.33–40).[2]

The structure of the narrative is framed by promise: Yeshua arrives as predicted, and will return as predicted. Unlike the other gospels, his postmortem appearance is not narrated in Mark; we are left with an expectation. Yet returning is crucial to the structure of the gospel, which sees Yeshua as a fulfillment of a promise, and a promise of a future.

Yeshua as social character. In making the earliest gospel Mark also made the first written account of its protagonist's character. If we accept, along with practically all New Testament scholars, that the oral tradition about the life of Yeshua came in pieces, episodes relating his action and speech in discrete segments, it is still reasonable to think that some overall narrative was implied. The calling of the apostles has to come early, the journey to Jerusalem late. (Some commentators have insisted that the Passion story was already a complete narrative before Mark, though there is no external evidence for the assertion.) In the Galilee section, the order of the miracles and the order of the controversies do not matter much; what does matter is how the character develops as a result of their sequence. We can also assume that divergences in the tradition worked

---

1. The pattern of opposites described here, where event A opposes or prefigures A^1, B opposes B^1, and so on, is usually called a chiastic structure, from the Greek letter X (*chi*). It is a common mnemonic device in oral literature such as the Homeric epics, and some scholars see it in sections of the book of Genesis. In classical studies the device is also called a circle or ring structure: the story winds forward to a central point of clarification, then unwinds to the end, completing the circle. Though Mark's structure could be called circular, my triangle analysis permits the incorporation of his rhythmic pattern as well.

2. Matthew's treatment of the scene (21.5) has a different scriptural reference. He quotes Zechariah 9.9, imagining a future king: "Look, your king comes to you, humble and mounted on a donkey, upon a colt, the foal of a beast of burden."

their way into the persona of Yeshua as Mark presents him, partially explaining why the character does not appear fully unified, at least in the modern psychological sense. But, shocking as it sounds, Mark created Yeshua.

"Wait!" I hear someone shout. "Surely the character of Jesus Christ was created by God!"

By God or genetics, yes, and by his upbringing in a large artisan family and as a devout northern Jew under a Jewish ruler who was under Roman control. But I am not talking about the historical Yeshua. I am talking about the character as portrayed in the earliest gospel, a Yeshua remembered by eyewitnesses who passed on recollections that eventually found their way to the evangelist. Mark's Yeshua differs from the figure portrayed in the other gospels, not only in what he does and says but in how he responds to characters and their actions, and in what contexts he performs his own actions. He is more Davidic and regal in Matthew, and sometimes harsher ("I come not to bring peace but a sword," 10.34). He is more godlike and gnomic in Luke, full of difficult parables. In John he is a different character altogether, the incarnation of the word rather than a conveyor of it. Each of these Yeshuas, whether thought of as man, god, or man-god, is a literary artifact. Their resemblance to the historical Yeshua is a matter of speculation that is mostly pointless.

In Mark's version the character's journey is from an almost vacant condition to a blinding point of self-recognition and acceptance of his terrible fate. His literal travels on the road, always by foot except for the entry to Jerusalem, are a physical manifestation or shadow of his life journey: an itinerant prophet with an itinerary toward exaltation and death. His abrupt appearance at the beginning is a bit like the popping up of a comic-book superhero, arriving when called. The absence of information about background, parentage, birth, childhood, education, and occupation is striking for a biography; in the first chapter we are given only his name and that he "came from Nazareth in Galilee." Everything before is a blank. (The crucial years between ages twelve and thirty are a blank in all the gospels, presumably because the oral tradition, originating with the apostles, knew nothing of them or cared nothing for them.) In Mark the man enters fully mature, is baptized in the Jordan in Judea, is authorized by God's voice, is sent into the desert for forty days to prepare, walks back to Galilee, and begins his ministry—all within six short verses. It is the sketchiest of introductions.

Thereafter Yeshua's character is defined by two related social activities, preaching and healing. He has come to announce the imminent end of time and the arrival of a new reign of Yahweh on earth, in fulfillment of a number of prophesies in the scriptures. That is the Good Message he delivers and, he insists, all people—or all Jews, at any rate—must repent their misdeeds or they will not enter the new kingdom. He does not say publicly that he is the Messiah, and he certainly does not lead David's army to overthrow the Roman giant, but his basic theme is eschatological, and twice the heavens proclaim him to be Yahweh's son. As if to give a foretaste of the enormous change about to occur, and incidentally to support his claim of authority, he cures some of the bitterness of the world, specifically the bitterness of life in the promised land of the Jews under the Roman yoke.

The preaching and the cures go together, equal partners in his mission. In his first public showing, in the synagogue in Capernaum on the sabbath, he impresses with his teaching and purges a member of the assembly who is infected by an impure spirit. Mark narrates four exorcisms and eight medical cures, and says "many" more of both were performed. People flock to Yeshua for relief of body and soul, so many that on occasion he is in danger of being crushed. His understandings of scripture and morality go hand in hand with his mastery of physical and spiritual disease, and he is accepted as a prophet with superior powers.

Miracles are a problem for the rational mind, and exorcisms require a belief in malign spirits. What Yeshua's contemporaries accepted as signs from heaven a modern skeptic dismisses as superstitious credulity. Ernest Renan published his wildly popular (and anti-Semitic) *Life of Jesus* in 1863; I remember a Jesuit theologian at university still attacking Renan's rationalism a hundred years later. Renan disdained the miracles. "For vulgar audiences," he wrote, "the miracle proves the doctrine; for us the doctrine makes us forget the miracle."[3] He spoke as if the miracles could be ignored despite remaining in the text. They cannot be dismissed, no matter how much Renan wanted to forget them, and I have no rational explanation of them. They might be historical or they might be invented. The fact that the miracles are rarely mentioned in the New Testament outside the gospels could lead us to conclude that they are one of Mark's literary devices, but the ancient world provided many examples of miracle men, and there are surviving references to other Jewish wonder workers

---

3. Quoted in Carrère, *Kingdom*, 250.

around the time of Yeshua.⁴ Mark never claims that Yeshua's power over the body and the natural world was unique, only that he was exceptionally successful in exercising it.

We can nonetheless make a distinction between the healings in Mark and the outright wonders such as calming storms, walking on water, and the feedings of thousands with a few loaves and fishes. Those spectacular stories, shaped by related passages in the Hebrew scriptures,⁵ are designed above all to impress. The healings are also presented as miraculous, yet their meaning is not confined to supernaturalism. They exist simultaneously on two levels, one with the magical property of extraordinary remedy and one with the metaphorical property of alleviating evil. They are social as well as medicinal and they are performed primarily—though not always—for Yeshua's own people. In the terms used by Teresa Morgan in a comparison of Roman and Christian faith, Yeshua is acting as a patron of the poor and the sick, asking them to have trust (Greek *pistis*) in him as the representative of God.⁶ Yeshua proposes a pre-Freudian talking cure: proclaim your trust that the impossible can be done and it will be done. The cure is a by-product of the trust.

The nature of the illnesses reinforces the collective compact that Yeshua offers. As Ched Myers puts it, "In the symbolic order of Judaism, illness was associated with impurity or sin, a state that meant exclusion from full status in the body politic."⁷ All of the exorcisms and most of the medical cures are of disabilities that exclude the sufferer from society. They encompass disfiguring skin disease (at the time, all skin diseases were called leprosy), paralysis, a withered hand, deafness paired with speech impediment, blindness, insane behavior, rampant epilepsy, and a woman who has had "a flow of blood for twelve years." By curing those diseases Yeshua returns the victims to tribal cohesion, makes them whole in society as well as in body. It is significant that he tells the healed leper that he must now follow the ritual form outlined in the Torah and prove to a priest that he may rejoin the union of Jews.

---

4. A number of Jewish healers from the approximate period are discussed by Evans, *Jesus and His Contemporaries*, 213–44.

5. Eve, *Writing the Gospels*, 48.

6. Morgan, *Roman Faith and Christian Faith*. I discuss this issue more completely in chapter 6.

7. Myers, *Binding the Strong Man*, 145. The nature and significance of the miracles are discussed by Brown, *Miracles and the Critical Mind*.

Messiah. He also forbids the leper from speaking to anyone about the cure. That injunction at the end of the first chapter begins a theme of secrecy and withholding that has a number of implications for the character of Yeshua. Usually called the "messianic secret," the common interpretation is that he is the Anointed One, the Messiah, and knows he is, but does not want his identity spread about because his purpose will be misunderstood. His message is not combative but peaceful, and his function on earth cannot be valued until after the Resurrection. He will not bring about Israel's restoration by himself; God will create the new reign, and in God's good time. Since that is not what most Jews expected from a Messiah, Mark's Yeshua thinks it better to restrain talk about his powers and miraculous actions until the time is right.[8] The text is contradictory in this regard because the major thrust of the Galilee section is that he gains more and more celebrity and cannot go anywhere without being recognized, even in the regions of the gentiles such as the land of the Gerasenes (the incident of the pigs in chapter 5) or the area around Tyre (the Syro-Phoenician woman in chapter 7). Yet he continues to tell his supplicants not to discuss their remedies, and they continue to ignore his prohibition.

The textual contradiction also applies to the demons he expels, who know his identity and are frightened of his power. In those scenes we would expect the other characters to react to the revelations since the demons identify him with unambiguous words: "the holy one of God" (1.24), "the son of God" (3.11), and "son of the most high God" (5.7). But no one else reacts to those utterances or even seems to hear them. It is as if the demons and Yeshua were communicating telepathically or through a code known only to them, while the other characters stand mute in a freeze frame, disregarded in the text.

Yeshua's mother and siblings think he has lost his mind and try to stop his work. Again and again the apostles do not understand what he means, and they run away in fear when he is arrested. Yeshua acknowledges that the world, even the small world of Galilee, is not ready for his message. Explaining the parable of the sower, he says to the apostles, "The

---

8. "Messianic secret" is a term introduced by William Wrede in *Das Messiasgeheimnis in den Evangelien* (1901). Wrede's position has been challenged by a number of commentators, most recently by Adam Wright, *Of Conflict and Concealment*, 125. Wright notes that the term is actually a misnomer since the theme of withholding in Mark is not always related to Yeshua as Messiah but to his identity in a more general sense. An excellent treatment of secrecy in Mark from a literary perspective is Kermode, *Genesis of Secrecy*.

secret about the reign of God has been revealed to you, but to people who are outside all must be conveyed in similarities" (4.11). He quotes a cryptic passage from Isaiah about the need to withhold the complete truth from those who cannot comprehend it.

Another way to interpret the motif of messianic secrecy in Mark is one I find more psychologically convincing: Yeshua does not know he is the Messiah, or is not sure he is, or does not at first understand himself as the Messiah. In that case his journey of self-discovery is a gradual awakening to his calling. He begins with God proclaiming him as his "treasured son." Though the meaning of the title is imprecise, at his baptism he learns he is marked by God. It does not surprise him that he can heal the sick, quiet the storm, walk on water, or divide bread and fish to superabundance, but he attributes all these wonders to his trust in God. As he gains followers he gains confidence and, I suggest, begins to recognize that he is the Anointed in a distinct way. Contrary to the conventional image of the submissive or suffering Christ, he is not a passive player in the drama. His provocations in the synagogues and the Temple are deliberate, designed to gain the enmity of the scribes, the Pharisees, and ultimately the Temple establishment, and lead directly to the Crucifixion. Finally he accepts that his mission is to sacrifice himself to free his people, even though it is not clear what that liberation will mean.

The change is noticeable in chapter 8 in the section set around Caesarea Philippi. Yeshua asks the disciples, "Who do people say I am?" They answer that some think he is John the Baptizer, or Elijah, or one of the prophets, but Peter says, "You are the Anointed One." It is the first declaration that he is the Messiah, and he warns them not to reveal it to anyone. He then teaches them "that it was necessary for the son of man to suffer greatly and be repudiated by the elders and the chief priests and the scribes, and be killed, and after three days to rise." Peter, expecting a different type of deliverer, is so shocked that he upbraids Yeshua for predicting such a disaster.

Six days later a flash of clarity occurs with the Transfiguration. Mark does not explain why Yeshua takes Peter, James, and John up a mountain; the starkness of the account suggests it is specifically to reveal himself as the Anointed, which is certified by the vision of Moses and Elijah in conversation with him. Coming down from the mountain, Yeshua warns the apostles "to tell no one what they had seen until the son of man had risen from the dead." The three closest followers have witnessed the second moment of immanence after the Baptism, with God's voice again calling Yeshua his treasured son.

As the setting moves to Jerusalem, Yeshua understands that miracles and preaching are not enough. For his message to take hold in the world there must be something more, something inexorable and horrifying. He arranges to enter the holy city mounted on a colt, in a deliberate echo of Solomon riding to his installation as king of the Jews. The hosannas and the spreading of palm fronds before him proclaim him as David's heir. These exaltations, however, lead to predictable disaster, since he is studiously provoking the Temple establishment with signs of his messianic status. Whereas the first half of the story conveys a growing success, with more followers and more powerful acts, in Jerusalem Yeshua is imbued with a sense of resignation and fatality. On the Hill of Olives before his betrayal, he prays for release from his bitter destiny. Kneeling in great sorrow in Gethsemane—a flat area where oil presses stood, *gethsemane* meaning "oil press" in Aramaic—he accepts that he must face his fate alone. Of course he hopes, even expects, that God will resurrect him, but he accepts in a moment of spiritual crisis that a terrible death is necessary to seal the new covenant. In the trial before the Sanhedrin at first he refuses to answer the High Priest's questions, but when asked directly if he is the Messiah he says yes. With Pilate he answers more ambiguously, but by refusing to deny the charges against him he knows he will be condemned. In first-century Roman Judea, with its collaborating Temple authorities, declaring oneself anointed by God could lead only to one place, the place called Skull.

He learns, he accepts, he declares. In Galilee he learns how to minister to the evils people suffer in the distressed world. In Caesarea Philippi and on the road to Jerusalem he accepts the burden of his calling. In the two trials he finally uncovers the secret that he is the Messiah.

To me it seems strange that the text does not examine the significance of Yeshua's revised form of messianism. There are only two occasions that suggest his death will have redemptive value. The first is on the road to Jerusalem when he says, "For the son of man came not to be served but to serve, and to give his life as ransom for many" (10.45). The second is at the Last Supper with his words over the cup of wine, "This is my blood of the covenant which is poured out for many" (14.24). In Jewish tradition, a Messiah who allows himself to be killed is a contradiction in terms. Mark's Yeshua tries to make clear that the liberation he brings is spiritual, interior, and apolitical. It does not involve the restoration of a Davidic kingdom, despite all the references to King David. It is instead a freedom from the self-imposed bonds of a mistaken or sinful life. The apostles do not understand it, the High Priest rejects it, Pilate in an offhand way does not bother to make the distinction, and we also might be forgiven for failing to understand it fully.

Burton Mack, reminding us that Mark was concerned with the state of the Christian movement around the year 70, not the year 30, suggests the text's incomplete notion of salvation through the cross is the result of the evangelist positioning himself between the Yeshua cult and the Christos cult—i.e., between the Jerusalem apostles and Paul.[9] I will investigate later whether the material about the Last Supper came from the oral tradition or from ritual practice, but regardless of the source of the words over the cup, it would be reasonable to expect Mark's text to reflect something of the belief in the sacrificial redemption brought by the Crucifixion. Paul had proclaimed it in the communities he founded a generation earlier. It would be even more likely if Mark wrote after the destruction of Jerusalem, when some of the restraints on the expanding beliefs of the Christos cult were loosened. Yet in his gospel the wider significance of the Messiah's death is not elaborated, just as the significance of the Resurrection is left unspoken. This may be because Mark's original audience already knew how to interpret those events, but the interpretive seeds are not in the text.

If you approach the gospel of Mark as a believing Christian who accepts, more or less, the doctrines expressed in the Nicene Creed, the habits of reading backward and reading sideways might well affect how you construe the messianic secret. You might use your preexisting belief in the salvation guaranteed by the cross and back-form it onto Yeshua's tendency to withhold information about his true identity, seeing the secrecy as an acceptable part of the overall plan. Or you might instinctively lay the other evangelists' more extended treatments of the issue onto your reading. John, for example, has his Yeshua declare he is the Messiah in the first fifth of his gospel, in the episode of the Samaritan woman at the well (chapter 4), and there is never any doubt thereafter about his purpose in the world. Following that line of thought, you could see the secrecy theme in Mark as odd but not really significant, since you already know Yeshua is the Messiah and that he soon will reveal it.

---

9. Mack, *Myth of Innocence*, 276.

But if you approach Mark as a literary object, independent of the other gospels and subsequent theology, you might recognize the uncertainty at the heart of his treatment of the principal character. It is not clear that Yeshua believes he is the Anointed One from the beginning. It is not clear that his fate is preordained or that he knows his mission will be successful or will have universal redemptive consequences. Twenty centuries on, it looks as if Mark left a lot unsaid about how Christianity would eventually understand Iesous Christos. The earliest gospel omits a great of what orthodoxy would come to accept as essential.

In fact the technique of withholding, allowing blank space, not explaining the significance of every important event, seems at times to anticipate later literary methods, especially in fiction, that consciously invite the reader to participate in the manufacture of meaning. I do not mean that Mark was a modernist, much less a postmodernist; he is closer in method to Pliny or Tacitus than to Virginia Woolf or Samuel Beckett. Yet the character he stitched together has the opaque appeal of deficiency or fallibility that the later gospels wish to dispel. Whether through artistic ineptitude, scarcity of information, or some indefinable inspiration, Mark has given us an ambiguous central figure whose superhuman powers are moderated by an interior struggle to understand his place in a divine mystery story.

Divine man. The title of Anointed or Messiah is counterpoised against two other titles in the gospel, son of God and son of man. Both are terms with complicated histories, and as usual in Mark the text is not completely clear about what they mean or if they always mean the same thing. It may be, as some scholars hold, that Mark's audience understood them in specific ways and needed no gloss, but there can be no convincing evidence of this. It is dangerous to assume what any audience understands, whether in the past or the present, and by the second or third century the meaning of son of God had already been changed by emerging consensus.

Son of God. God's voice twice proclaims Yeshua as his treasured son, at his Baptism and Transfiguration. Impure spirits recognize him as God's son in chapters 3 and 5 before exorcism, as does the centurion at the Crucifixion. When the High Priest at the Sanhedrin trial asks if he is "the Anointed, the son of the Blessed One," he answers yes, and that is as close as he comes to calling himself the son of God. What does the phrase mean?

Let's start with what it does not mean. For Mark it could not mean God the Son, the Second Person of the Trinity, as promulgated in the Nicene Creed in the fourth century. The notion that Yahweh could be divided, no mater how mysteriously, has always been antithetical to Jewish belief. *Shema, Yisrael*, begins the great Hebrew prayer, "Hear, Israel, Yahweh is our God, Yahweh is one."[10] What, then, could "son of God" mean? For orthodox Christians nothing less than the divinity of Christos is at stake, but Mark is no clearer about that than Paul is. Both tend to dodge the issue, recognizing that Yeshua has great power but treating it as a gift from God.

If Mark's Yeshua is a god or a superhero he is a very human one. He gets hungry, he needs sleep, he curses, his disregards his mother and family. He grows tired of the crowds that follow him. He gets angry and frustrated. He is intolerant with his dullard apostles, the scribes, the Pharisees, the Sadducees, his "mistaken generation," and with the gentile Syro-Phoenician woman. He destroys a fig tree with a curse because it has no figs when he is hungry, even though figs are out of season. If we apply Occam's razor to the question, searching for the simplest explanation of his status in Mark, it would be a form of adoptionism. He is a man, born of a woman with no miraculous circumstances mentioned, who is chosen by Yahweh to carry a message to his people. In line with the expectations of the Messiah, Yahweh has given him exceptional powers to prove his authenticity. Then, contrary to messianic expectations, Yahweh allows him without comment to suffer the bitter pain and humiliation of crucifixion before raising him from the dead. Does that make him divine?

It depends on how we define *divine*. In the Hellenized world people believed or half-believed in many gods and godlike humans, demigods or sons and daughters of gods. Affected by that cultural environment, some Jews probably did as well. It is often noted that the Romans were generally tolerant of other religions, such as Judaism, because they barely believed in their own, which was more a social than a theological compact. The gods have been good to Rome, its leaders thought, so we must worship them to maintain favor. In Mediterranean cultures of the time there was a widespread belief that "divine men occasionally roamed the

---

10. Deuteronomy 6.4. Hebrew does not use written vowels and in traditional use "Yahweh" is rendered by the tetragram YHWH. In its current version the opening of this morning and evening prayer in Hebrew can be translated as "Hear, O Israel, the Lord our God, the Lord is one." Among the various possible translations of Deuteronomy, the NRSV chose "Hear, O Israel: The Lord is our God, the Lord alone."

earth" for the benefit of humanity.[11] In Greek mythology gods and goddesses coupled with humans, breeding hybrid offspring with semidivine powers. A human son of a god such as Heracles was occasionally raised to Olympian rank. "Did she put on his knowledge with his power," W. B. Yeats asked of Leda, after the great god Zeus raped her in the form of a swan. Leda's daughter by Zeus, Helen of Troy, whose superhuman beauty caused the greatest war in antique legend, personifies the danger of interaction between mortals and the divine.

Pagan gods could be created at need and could be forgotten through neglect. Men or women who exhibited unexpected or unusual power could be declared gods, and no one thought this strange. After his shipwreck on Malta, Paul was setting a bundle of sticks on an outdoor fire "when a viper, driven out by the heat, wound about his hand." He was not injured and shook it off into the fire. The local people waited for him to drop dead; when he did not, "they said he was a god" (Acts 28.3-6).

In the Hebrew scriptures "son of God" is applied to some kings of Israel, to pious men, and even to Israel itself, in the sense that all Jews were considered children of God. "Son of God" was a common phrase in the ancient world in general, applied to great men from Babylonia to Rome. Rulers frequently claimed the title. After his assassination in 42 BCE, Julius Caesar was declared *Divus Iulius* (Divine Julius, figure 7).

FIGURE 7. DIVUS IULIU(S)

Silver denarius struck c. 18 BCE during the reign of Caesar Augustus

His adopted son Octavian, later known as Caesar Augustus, whose image is on the obverse of the coin, was called "son of the divine Julius" or "son

---

11. Metzger and Ehrman, *Text of the New Testament*, 291.

of the divine," and a cult of his worship developed in the empire that treated him as the son of a god.

Of course a son of a god who was a man later called divine, in a spirit world in which many divinities existed, is different from a son of the only God in the Jewish universe. In fact the Romans made a practical distinction between an immortal Olympian god or goddess (*deus* or *dea*) and an emperor or a member of his family made divine (*divus* or *diva*). In the three centuries after the death of Julius Caesar seventeen emperors were declared divine, along with sixteen members of imperial families.[12] Nonetheless, the case of Augustus is a reasonable analogy for the celestial implications of Mark's Yeshua, a man adopted by Yahweh and invested with heroic capabilities. Paul often speaks of him as "raised up" by God, which seems to mean elevated above ordinary mortals as well as raised from the dead. A third rise, to sit at the right hand of God in heaven, would make him a divine man, a son of God, without violating Paul's monotheism or forcing Mark's text to anticipate the doctrine of the Trinity.

Son of man. In the Hebrew scriptures "son of man" is a general term for a human, notable in the Psalms and Ezekiel. (The NRSV does not help by translating the phrase as "mortal" or "human being"; I have restored the original phrase in the quotation below.) There is some possibility that the term was still used in that sense in colloquial Aramaic during Yeshua's lifetime. That simple meaning was transformed in the book of Daniel (7.13–14) in one of Daniel's visions:

> As I watched in the night visions, I saw one like a son of man coming with the clouds of heaven. And he came to the Ancient One and was presented before him. To him was given dominion and glory and kingship, that all peoples, nations, and languages should serve him. His dominion is an everlasting dominion that shall not pass away, and his kingship is one that shall never be destroyed.

Daniel's dream is not easy to interpret. In context, "one like a son of man" implies a mortal being who has been exalted. Does it mean a Messiah, or a king of the Jews?

---

12. Beard, *Emperor of Rome*, 381. Bryan's *Son of God* treats the multiple meanings of the phrase in historical context.

In Mark, Yeshua uses the phrase fourteen times, and there is no scholarly agreement on which meaning is intended.[13] The probable reason for the uncertainty is that he means both blended together, simultaneously invoking his ordinary humanity and his extraordinary calling. Sometimes the term suggests his power, as in chapter 2 when he relies on it to explain his authority to forgive sins and heal on the sabbath. At other times he uses it in predictions of his suffering and death (chapters 8 and 10), emphasizing his mortality. In fact it is not clear that he always refers to himself when he uses the expression; it is possible that he occasionally entertains the idea that God would send another to institute his new reign. The final use, however, includes a direct quotation from Daniel, in answer to the High Priest's question as to whether he is the Anointed. "I am," he says, and continues:

> And you will see the son of man sitting at the right hand of power, coming on the clouds of heaven. (14.62)

The High Priest, who would have recognized the quotation, tears his clothes and calls the reply blasphemy.

I have no competence to discuss the overtones the phrase might carry from Hebrew or Aramaic into Mark's usage, yet in general "son of man" is accepted without comment by the followers in all the gospels, as if the audiences—the imagined audiences of Yeshua's speech, and the original audiences of the four evangelists—did understand both its scriptural allusion and whatever subtleties were attached to the term. I hazard a guess, based simply on the context, that its significance in Mark is primarily a literary effect. It was a way of allowing his Yeshua to speak of himself in third person, also eliminating the need to call himself son of God or Messiah. Mark left it to others, including God himself, to proclaim that for him.

Disciples. It is common in Christian history to make a distinction between the apostles and the other followers of Yeshua, though both are often called disciples. In the gospels, however, the apostles are generally called the Twelve. When the Twelve are appointed in Mark, the phrase "and called them apostles" does not appear in all ancient manuscripts. It is slightly redundant, since *apostolos* already means ambassador or delegate; its root sense is "to send out." That is how they are described: "and called them apostles so that he could send them to proclaim and with the authority to expel demons" (3.14). The number twelve is significant

---

13. Marcus, *Mark 1–8*, 528.

because it implies that when the reign of God is established the apostles will be the representatives of the restored twelve tribes of Israel. That seems to be the expectation of James and John when they ask Yeshua to prefer them above the others when he returns in glory (10.37).

The charge to the Twelve is to preach and exorcize demons. In this passage Mark unintentionally provided a basis for a Christian priesthood. Though it is nothing more than an implication, the subsequent church took the charge as sacerdotal authorization, based on apostolic succession, one generation of priests and bishops ordaining the next. It is regularly said that Jesus Christ was the founder of Christianity, but it's a great stretch to think so. Paul, the organizer, theologian, and arbiter of the first-century faith, deserves that title. Mark's Yeshua shows no interest in founding a religion in any sense, whether administrative, hieratic, or doctrinal, nor do the apostles take his meaning in that way. All thirteen, the leader and his adherents, were observant Jews, hoping for a better, holier, restored version of their ancient belief in Yahweh. Why would they want a new religion? The world was going to be transformed in their lifetime.

But twelve characters in the same functional position are too many for a reader to keep straight. A writer has to treat them as a single unit or designate a few to stand for all. Mark restricts the number to three, Peter, James, and John, with infrequent mentions of Andrew and, of course, Judas. Only the three main apostles witness the Transfiguration, have private conversations with Yeshua, and are with him in the inner scenes in Gethsemane. They are the only followers who are given basic characteristics. After the arrest, none appear but Peter, and he is present in the High Priest's courtyard only for the purpose of denial.

In terms of literary portrayal, this generalized field of undistinguished followers serves as a backdrop for the brilliant depiction of Yeshua as a multifarious figure. He is many things in the gospel, but to the disciples he is most of all their teacher. That is what he is usually called (with variations such as Rabbi or Rabbouni, both honorifics for teacher) and that is chiefly how he functions. He is a teacher of the Law or the new law, an explicator of the scriptures, a guide to moral living, and a forecaster of change to come. In fact the Greek word *mathetes*, usually translated as *disciple*, actually means student, pupil, or learner. The disciples above all are Yeshua's students, and they will be tested at the end of the course.

Bread. There is a considerable concern about food in Mark. Hardly a chapter is without a meal or at least one reference to eating or drinking, and food metaphors are scattered throughout. Given the Judaic attention to diet protocols, it is to be expected that the Pharisees, sticklers for ritual purity, would object to Yeshua dining with sinners and the disciples eating without washing their hands in the prescribed manner. That second objection prompts Yeshua to claim, against the rules of the Torah, that no food is unclean (7.14–19). On one teaching occasion "the press of people was so great it was not even possible to eat" (3.20), and after healing the daughter of Jairus, Yeshua is careful to remind the family that she should be fed (5.43). His parables and analogies are usually agrarian: sowing, vineyards, mustard seeds, wineskins. When at first he refuses to heal the daughter of the gentile Syro-Phoenician woman (i.e., a Canaanite woman), he says, "First let the children be fed; it is not good to take bread from the children and throw it to the dogs" (7.27). His disciples are criticized because they do not fast like those of John the Baptizer and the Pharisees, implying the same about Yeshua (2.18). He replies that there will be time for fasting after he is gone.

Yeshua's violations of dietary purity are on a par with his violations of the sabbath, in that he uses them to propose that the Law must be reformed to allow a new spiritual understanding of it. The images and examples of food and drink keep the divine message on an earthy level, easily accessible to his listeners, some of whom would have known hunger. The two miraculous feedings, the first of five thousand followers and the second of four thousand, are the clearest indications that Yeshua knew the body must be fed if the spirit was to be satisfied. In those cases he concerns himself with the well-being of the healthy as well as the sick. "I feel sympathy for the crowd," he says, "because they have been with me for three days already and have nothing to eat. If I send them home hungry, they will faint on the road, since some have come from far away" (8.2–3). These two miracles, the most astounding of his northern ministry, are clearly mythic in nature. It is not surprising that no one can believe them or that the apostles do not understand them. For Mark the important point is that they are social in character and large in span. Unlike walking on water or calming storms, or the oddity of cursing the fig tree—showy tricks for the closest disciples—the feedings were public events for thousands of people, dividing the two staples of the Galilean diet, bread and fish, to effortless surplus.

After the second feeding the apostles forget to bring bread in the boat, and Yeshua jokes that they must "watch out for the leaven of the Pharisees and the leaven of Herod" (8.15). These events and images prefigure the Last Supper, not only in the breaking and distribution of bread but also in that the bread is distributed for the good of others. *Do this in remembrance of me*: though those words are not spoken in Mark, the ritual practice of the eucharist was well established by his time. As the bread of the feedings was broken to satisfy all, so the bread of the final meal was broken to allow each apostle a sufficient portion, including Judas. All will be fed, all will be satisfied: again the spiritual message is framed in alimentary terms.

But in Mark food can also imply disaster. Eating together is a sign of kinship and trust, though the need for knives at table in much of Western cuisine carries the risk of danger. In some segments of French society it is still considered impolite to place your hands on your lap at table, a custom deriving from a time when you might be concealing a weapon. A number of cultures prohibit or discourage exogenous dining, and in Judaism the Passover meal in particular was (and is) a family affair. Mark indicates more than once that the apostles have replaced Yeshua's family; we hear nothing about his human father and he ignores his mother. Just before he breaks bread at the Last Supper as a symbol of his soon-to-be-broken body, with the Twelve reclining at table, he announces that "one of you eating with me will betray me." Surely not I, they all insist. "It is one of the Twelve," he says, "one dipping in the bowl with me" (14.18–20). They are dipping in the bowl with bread, of course, dividing a common dish, their fingers touching the shared food, betrayer, betrayed, and witnesses alike. The bread of the new covenant is immediately preceded by the bread of sedition: the two go together, Mark suggests, intimacy and treason, hand in hand.

The mirrored moments of the scene, the bread of death set against the bread of life, is typical of Mark's irony. The trust that Judas violates can occur only because of the confidence placed in him. In choosing Judas as his intimate Yeshua brings on his own destruction: trust is as dangerous as dining together. The Last Supper, which concludes the cycle of feeding stories, makes bread the symbol of that doubleness. As one commentator[14] puts it, "After Mark no Christian can eat the holy meal without asking himself, 'Am I myself a betrayer of Jesus?' " It is also possible to view the betrayal, which is a necessary action in the plot, as a form of sacrifice itself. Since Yeshua requires a traitor in order to complete his

---

14. Vernon K. Robbins, "Last Meal," in Kelber, *The Passion in Mark*, 40. The parallel scene in John (13.18) has Yeshua quoting Psalm 41.9: "The one eating my bread has lifted his heel against me."

mission, we might take his words at the Last Supper as permission for Judas to proceed and thereby lose everything, including his reputation for all time. Eat my bread and do what you must, Yeshua says in effect; you must sacrifice yourself so that I can be sacrificed. "Is Judas not therefore the ultimate hero of the New Testament," Slavoj Žižek asks, "the one who was ready to lose his soul and accept eternal damnation so that the divine plan could be accomplished?"[15]

The theme of bread also reflects the period surrounding Mark's composition. The miraculous feedings suggest an era of peace and plenty, bread and fish out of thin air, that contrasted with the dire circumstances leading to the destruction of the Temple, the worst event possible in the Jewish imagination. As Mack points out, Josephus in *The Jewish War* portrays the decade of the 60s as a story of "famine, social unrest, institutional deterioration, bitter internal conflicts, class warfare, banditry, insurrections, intrigues, betrayals, bloodshed, and the scattering of Judeans throughout Palestine." The rebel Simon the Zealot ruled Jerusalem near the end of the war and was executed by the Romans as the king of the Jews. During the siege of Jerusalem, which lasted from 66 to 70 CE, stories abounded of popular messiahs, prophets who decried the corruption of the Temple and the collaboration of its priests with the Romans, citizens and pilgrims in riot, assassins on the loose, wars and rumors of wars.[16] The parallel with Yeshua's prediction of the time of the end in Mark 13 is striking:

- When you hear of wars and rumors of wars, do not be alarmed. That must happen, but it is not yet the end. For nation will rise up against nation and kingdom against kingdom. There will be earthquakes throughout the lands and famines.

- Brother will betray brother to death and father, child. Children will rebel against parents and put them to death.

- When you see *the abomination that makes desolation* standing where it should not be—the one reading, let him understand—then let those in Judea escape to the mountains, let no one on the roof come down or go in to take anything out of his house, and let no one in the field return to get his cloak. It will be miserable in those days for women who are pregnant or nursing. Pray that it will not be

15. Žižek, *The Puppet and the Dwarf*, 16. See also Klassen, *Judas*.
16. Mack, *Myth of Innocence*, 315.

winter, because those days will see suffering never before endured, since the beginning of God's creation until now, and never will occur again.

Mark may have been in Jerusalem or Antioch or Rome, and he may have written before or after the year 70. In any event he would have known about the starved conditions in the city before or after its desolation, and used them to increase the contemporary resonance of Yeshua's prophesy. The gospel suggests that bread is the opposite of war and its pains. I will distribute my bread, Mark's Yeshua implies, and like the five thousand on the desolate shore, or the four thousand reclining on the ground, you will be satisfied.

Evil. A world without evil has no need of salvation. No matter if we consider evil something done to us, inherent within us, or fomented by a diabolic agency, we know all too well that terrible people and terrifying events abound in history. Evil doesn't exist in general but in specific. We might say the times are evil or this or that country is evil, but those are phrases of convenience. A savior, a liberator, a demigod needs to match himself or herself to the particularity of a perceived wickedness. In the Hebrew scriptures, the anticipation of a Messiah was prompted by a desire to destroy Israel's enemies who wreaked devastation on Yahweh's people. The prophets most connected to the hope of relief—Elijah, Isaiah, Ezekiel, Jeremiah—were most connected to disaster: the division of the Israelite kingdom, the Babylonian conquest of Jerusalem, the destruction of Solomon's Temple and the subsequent Babylonian captivity. Mark assumes as self-evident that the world of his book was in the chains of evil. Titus, whose army destroyed the Second Temple and Jerusalem after a bitter war of rebellion, was the agent of the emperor Tiberius in Rome. Titus must have seemed a re-embodiment of Nebuzaradan, whose army set alight the First Temple, Solomon's Temple, and destroyed Jerusalem after an earlier bitter war of rebellion; he was the agent of the emperor Nebuchadnezzar II in Babylon.[17] The Roman destruction of 70 CE re-enacted the Babylonian destruction of 587 BCE and provoked another Jewish exile.

That repetition, the doubleness of Israelite history, served Mark's ironic purpose: he overlaid the circumstance of the contemporary rebellion against Rome with the story of Yeshua. He makes no distinction

---

17. Nebuchadnezzar's siege and destruction of Jerusalem are related in 2 Kings 25 and Lamentations 4.

between the evil caused by Rome and the evil caused by Satana the Adversary. They operate in conjunction: Rome is Satan, Satan is Rome, and the keepers of the Temple have been corrupted by both. The High Priest is an agent of Pilate, and Pilate an agent of the High Priest. (In reality, the High Priest had been a Roman appointment since Pompey's conquest of Judea in 63 BCE.) In Mark there is a gulf between Yahweh and the world, John Painter says, and human beings cannot bridge it. Only Yahweh can do that, by affecting the world through his holy spirit (or "sacred breath"), the term used in Judaism for God's actions on earth. If he chose, Yahweh could send a new David as his Anointed, an improbable boy to slay the Roman Goliath with a slingshot.

Instead he sends Yeshua, a different improbability. He faces not Rome's generals but generalized symbols of the world's horror: illness, impure spirits, hypocritical Pharisees, legalistic scribes, a corrupt High Priest, and finally the ruling Prefect of Judea. They are all unnamed except the last, who is nominated to embody the evil of the age. The repeated exorcisms and the healing of the stream of sick men, women, and children are not only cures of social disorders but signs that "the Kingdom of God has come, overpowering the forces of evil."[18] An Anointed One of this type is not going to be recognized as a Messiah; that is the underlying irony of the story. In fact, such a savior calls into question the entire history of Hebraic expectation. He has to die to effect the change, and his death does not change the nature of the world, only the nature of the expectation. Would such a man be a Messiah at all? Have the Jews been wrong in what for centuries they have wished for? Why do they, and we, expect a superman to cure us when what we most need is correction of ourselves?

The renewed fascination with comic-book superheroes in contemporary Hollywood films might be taken as an absurd facsimile of the world that Mark depicts. Batman, Superman, Wonder Woman, Catwoman, Spiderman, even those Tom Cruise exotics Ethan Hunt and Jack Reacher—all are improbable saviors whose special powers are needed to defeat the malignity of twisted men and monsters in their American and global varieties. They are signs that normal human beings are powerless against the amalgamated forces of evil in a world without a visible God. But the analogy is imperfect because comic-book evil and its opposite are so clearly demarcated and represented by melodramatic examples.

---

18. Painter, *Mark's Gospel*, 14, 17.

A film that hints at a world closer to Mark's is Quentin Tarantino's *Pulp Fiction* (1994), a morality play disguised as a gangster movie. In its nonlinear narrative, and in the midst of the nihilistic violence of its dramatic universe, it is easy to miss that the overarching plot is focused on three acts of redemption connected to the vicious criminal Marsellus Wallace (played by Ving Rhames). First, the gunman Vincent (John Travolta) saves Marsellus's wife from an accidental overdose. Next, the boxer Butch (Bruce Willis) saves Marsellus from death, even though the gangster seeks Butch's death. Last, Jules (Samuel L. Jackson), the main hired gun, who is fond of quoting Ezekiel 25.17 just before he kills someone, under pressure of being robbed in a coffee shop saves both the robber and himself. Earlier a man emptied an oversized pistol at him and missed entirely; Jules considers it a miracle and now hopes to change his brutal life. None of these rescues is entirely selfless; selfless people do not exist in *Pulp Fiction*. There is no savior, of course, and no God; there is no superman either. Evil exists, the film tells us, it is all around us, and we have to face it alone. Any redemption, if redemption is possible, must come from within.

In Mark self-reform is one of Yeshua's chief arguments. He came into an evil world to bring the Good Message of the arrival of the new reign of God, and is killed for it. An unexpected and disappointing Messiah, he stresses the need for individual repentance much more than he proclaims that his death will provide salvation for others. His death is necessary and is revoked after the fact by God, who raises him far above the level of ordinary humans. But what his death secures is not emphasized.

Roger Caillois published a novel in French in 1961, *Ponce Pilate*, which imagines a complicated Pilate who declines to condemn Yeshua and sets him free. Yeshua returns to Galilee, continues preaching, dies in old age, and is forgotten. Without the Resurrection, Paul says, there is no salvation; without the Crucifixion, Caillois says, there is no Christianity at all. About this question Mark is strangely a little closer to Caillois than to Paul. Without the Crucifixion there is no Resurrection; with the Crucifixion—with or without the Resurrection—there is a superlative story of a man cut short for teaching a new rule of life. Mark sensed the power that lies in the story on a human level and pieced together the strands of the oral tradition to make the narrative itself convey the meaning of the tale of Yeshua's time on earth. The evangelist portrays the cross as inevitable but does not elucidate the fullness of its meaning. It's true that its meaning is implied, and perhaps Mark's original audience knew very well what it meant for them. If we stay inside the gospel as we have it, however, looking at the text purely as a literary object, we are left to wonder.

Empty tomb. Women do not play a large role in Mark's gospel. By my count there are fourteen female characters mentioned, five in serving positions, four related to cures (including Peter's mother-in-law, who is healed of a fever then serves the men), two members of Yeshua's family, two in the Herod–John the Baptizer story, and the widow who gives small coins to the Temple treasury. In addition there are three references to wives in teaching episodes. Of the fourteen women identified, most are unnamed and only two are given even elementary characterization: the Syro-Phoenician woman who argues with Yeshua that gentiles deserve his help as well as Jews, and the serving girl of the High Priest who insists that Peter is Yeshua's companion and prompts his triple denial. Those named are Herodias; Yeshua's mother, Mary (called so in 6.3, which may be a secondary insertion); and the women at the tomb: Mary of Magdala, Mary the mother of the apostle James the younger and of Joses, and Salome.

We should not make too much of this gender slight, since Mark's treatment of women reflects the circumstances of his time. Aside from the apostles, not many male characters are named either, and few are given distinctive character traits, including the Twelve; half of the apostles appointed in Mark's chapter 3 are never mentioned again. Even Judas, whose motives are a wide-open opportunity for explication, is limited to the function of betrayer. Which figures are named often seems random. Preserving all twelve of the apostles' names was clearly important, partly because the number emphasized their symbolic relationship to the twelve tribes of Israel. Preserving the names of the cured was not important, since they too are function characters; yet not only is the blind beggar on the road to Jericho named, so is his father. Why are we told that Simon of Cyrene is the father of Alexander and Rufus, who are unknown and irrelevant? These isolated bits of information are the result of the imperfect or scattered nature of the oral tradition as it came to Mark, and he probably included names when he had them to increase the verisimilitude of the incidents.

The women at the tomb stand out in function as well as importance. They are named at the end of the Crucifixion scene in chapter 15, when they are noted as part of a group of "women watching from the distance." They had followed Yeshua "in Galilee and had served him, along with many others who had come up to Jerusalem." They are placed in severe contrast to the apostles, who ran away after Yeshua's arrest in Gethsemane and were remarkable by their absence at his death. When Joseph of Arimathea placed the corpse in a rock tomb, the two Marys "watched where he was laid." Since Jewish custom required burial before the start of the sabbath at sunset on Friday, there was no time to wash and anoint the body. Yeshua had already been anointed on Wednesday at Bethany, when a woman poured fragrant oil on his head, worth about a year's wages for a workingman—a workingman like most of the apostles or Yeshua himself. He dismisses the objections to the waste: "She has anointed my body in advance for burial" (14.8). For the proper postmortem anointing, however, the three women must wait until Sunday, when they set out early in the morning with spices and oils, wondering how they will open the tomb.

So Mark begins one of the strangest and most affecting short scenes in all of Western literature. Chapter 16 has the condensed language of a lyric poem, the striking images of an unexpected dramatic turn, and the resonance of deep emotion held in check by restrained language. It also has an overtone of literary primitivism, as if the topic were too significant, too overwhelming, for the competence of the author, who could trust only the simplest words to articulate the unfathomable.

The women have come to do women's work, serving the corpse. They expect to unwrap the *sindon*, the linen cloth for burial that Joseph had bought on Friday, then wash and perfume the body and shroud it again, their final view of their teacher and master. In a prefiguring incident, a *sindon* was all the young man was wearing at the time of Yeshua's arrest, the young man who was grabbed by the mob and escaped by running away naked (14.51–52). Yeshua hung on the cross naked and now will be made naked again in sight of these women who revered him.

They find the great stone rolled away and enter the tomb. Instead of the corpse of their teacher they find another Young Man (the same word, *neaniskos*, is used on both occasions), and the women are astonished. He is sitting on the right, dressed in a white *stole*, the long robe worn by elite classes in the eastern empire. Is he an angel, a messenger from on high? Mark does not say. The Young Man speaks in naturalistic language:

> Do not be alarmed. You are looking for Iesous of Nazareth, who was crucified. He is risen, he is not here. See, there is the place where they laid him. But go, tell his disciples and Peter that he is going ahead of you into Galilee. You will see him there, as he told you.

That is all. The great event of Christianity, the impossible revival of a dead human body, is treated in the earliest of the gospels in a few short sentences. "See, there is the place where they laid him." The Resurrection is portrayed as an absence. An absence cannot prove anything except itself, but an absence is what confronts the women. The rest, Mark implies, belongs to trust.

The Young Man makes a promise on Yeshua's behalf: you will see him again in Galilee, as he predicted. Your job now, the Young Man says to the women, is to tell the disciples that the Anointed One, who cannot be anointed in death because his body is missing, just as the apostles were missing at the Crucifixion, will be faithful to them despite their own infidelity. Jerusalem, where his mission failed—or was fulfilled, depending on your point of view—is not worthy of him. He does not take the obvious course and frighten the High Priest as an apparition, or point a finger at Pilate in retribution as would the ghost of Hamlet's father. That might prove he is the Messiah, Pilate's king of the Jews. What would Pilate do, anyway—crucify him again? Instead of justifying his work and his life to the authorities who condemned him, Yeshua does something more remarkable. He walks home.

The women have not expected this. Did they not know his prophesy that he would rise on the third day? Did they not trust it, or have they forgotten it in their panic? They definitely do not know how to react. They ask no questions of the messenger, but rush out and run away from the tomb, "seized by trembling and confusion." The gospel ends with an evocative and ambiguous final line, "They said nothing to anyone, because they were afraid." Those last words (Greek *ephobounto gar*) can also be rendered as "because they were awestruck," and perhaps both meanings are implied. Awe is one of the deepest emotions, knocking us backward as Paul was knocked off his horse on the way to Damascus, and contains a strong element of fear. In classical Greek literature "fear is a common reaction to divine epiphany."[19] The women are speechless, stunned. How can they believe what they have just been told? Their expectations have been upended, replaced by a new expectation.

The syntax of the final line deserves a mention. It is unusual to end a sentence in Greek with a word such as *gar*, a conjunction used to express cause and meaning "for" or "indeed." The literary critic Frank Kermode

---

19. Collins, *Mark*, 800. A useful context for the scene is Victoria Phillips, "The Failure of the Women Who Followed Jesus in the Gospel of Mark," in Levine, *Feminist Companion to Mark*, 222–34

holds that there is no other book in all of ancient Greek that ends with *gar*.[20] Superficially that fact argues for thinking that Mark did not intend to stop at verse 8. Perhaps he did not complete the book, or perhaps his ending was lost, though guesswork gets us nowhere. As I said before, it is understandable that some early Christian authority or scribe would want to amend the ending to include the Resurrection appearances, to bring Mark in line with the subsequent gospels and the beliefs of the Christos cult. What we can know is this: the best ancient manuscripts stop after verse 8. All modern biblical scholars conclude that the longer ending is inauthentic, out of keeping with Mark's style, and polemical in nature.

We are left with a founding Christian text that does not finish the Christian story. Yeshua appears at the beginning of the gospel as a blank and disappears at the end as a blank. In a sense Mark's text works against itself, leaving a hole where the Messiah should be. What it does is something more interesting: it offers a future, an open invitation, in the midst of fear and awe. The two Marys saw Yeshua laid in the tomb and now "the place where they laid him" is empty. Within the confines of the text the women are the only mortal witnesses to the Resurrection, yet they are shown only what is not there. Mark secures belief in a strange way, by offering a scene that confounds the witnesses and sends them rushing outside, gasping for air. The promises set into the structure of the gospel are again redoubled. First there is the promise that Yeshua will meet the apostles in Galilee; that is where the proof of the Resurrection will occur, and perhaps some explanation. We long for explanation, but we do not return to Galilee to witness it. A second promise is implicit in the first: that Yeshua, son of God and son of man, will return one day on the clouds of heaven to inaugurate the reign of God on earth. The emptiness of the tomb ultimately points to a space that will remain empty until the Second Coming of the Anointed, who will transform the world, or end it.

When will that be? Mark does not ask the question.

---

20. Kermode, *Genesis of Secrecy*, 66.

5

The Oral Tradition

Since many have attempted to arrange a narrative of the events that have been entirely believed among us, just as they were handed down to us by those who were eyewitnesses and servants of the word from the start, it seemed good that I, having carefully investigated everything anew, should also write an orderly account for you, most excellent Theophilus, so you might have some certainty about the words you have been taught.

SO LUKE BEGINS HIS version of the gospel, and right away we notice a number of departures from Mark. First, the "I" of the author, which does not appear in the other synoptics, emphasizes that this is an account by a single writer, rather than an accumulation of traditional material. Second, the self-conscious literary diction of the long sentence, which borrows from classical Greek a style that contrasts with Mark's vernacular mode. Third, the implication that Luke's predecessors were insufficient; he has taken pains to make his work better and more complete, and it ought to replace them. Last, the appeal to the "many" who have told the story: who were they? Mark for sure, as Luke copied or adapted Mark for over forty percent of his own text. Matthew? According to the Two-Document Hypothesis, Luke did not have Matthew, though it is possible that he did, or at least knew of it. The assumption is that Luke had Q, that hypothetical list of sayings; the theory holds that the sayings were not tied to a narrative because Matthew and Luke put their Yeshua quotations in different plot positions. Who else had "attempted to arrange a narrative" of the life of Yeshua? Was Luke referring to texts that have been lost? Is "many" one of Luke's exaggerations, or just a conventional way of saying "others"?

What is clear is that Luke drew on the oral tradition going back to "eyewitnesses," the apostles or other original companions of Yeshua; "handed down to us" was a conventional ancient phrase about that practice in both Jewish and Greek cultures. Since thirty-five percent of Luke is material not in the other synoptics, he relied heavily on the unwritten tradition, or on his own imagination. How he received the material he doesn't say, but the "many" might include his private anonymous sources. Was he really Paul's companion on some of his missions, as implied by the "we" passages in Acts, gathering material along the way? The legends about the birth and childhood of Yeshua that only Luke relates might have been gathered from Galilean or Jerusalem sources,[1] though it is also possible that they are Lukan inventions compiled by reading backward to the prophets he cites as antecedents.

The most intriguing part of Luke's prologue, however, is the claim that he has "investigated everything anew" (or "investigated for a long time" or "from the beginning": the Greek can hold any of those meanings). What did he investigate? That's where we need to pick up the story.

Despite all the uncertainties surrounding the creation of the earliest gospel, one thing is definite: Mark based his account on information that had been passed down by word of mouth since the decade of the 30s. Luke also relied on the oral tradition, but he had Mark to guide him and provide him with the core of his account, whereas Mark had only the tradition. We will never know the nature of those sources, or which communities of the Yeshua cult in Palestine, or the Christos cult to the west, had preserved which parts of them.

Historians unanimously agree that the material had been transmitted orally. Writing down the tales and sayings of Yeshua would have been a contradiction of the movement, since the end of the world was at hand. Why preserve the notes and background of belief if Yeshua was returning in person any day to establish a new realm? The future did not need stories of his life, since the future was to be God's, a new kingdom of peace and harmony, the character of the world exalted as Yeshua had been exalted, freed from Rome and evil. Further, since Yeshua had taught only through speech, and to Galileans and Judeans who were mostly illiterate, writing would have seemed a double betrayal. He did not speak

---

1. Bovon, *Luke 1*, 8.

expecting a record of his speech. He spoke face-to-face to listeners who responded to him orally, in the moment, with questions, agreement, or counter argument. The comparison to Socrates is particularly relevant here. Socrates not only taught by speech, but in Plato's *Phaedrus* holds that writing is an imperfect means of communication. A text, Socrates says, cannot be questioned about its statements as a speaker can be. Writing cannot speak, it can only insist. You can question it all day and it will stay mute. Challenge its conclusions and it stares at you and implies, as Yeshua said to Pilate, *sy legeis*: so you say.

Nevertheless, by the time of Mark, with Jerusalem destroyed or about to be destroyed and the kingdom no closer, the future began to look more complex. Preservation of the tradition could be endangered. If the Temple could be lost, with its scrolls and gold, its treasures taken to Rome and put on display, then Yeshua's words could also be lost. Mark might well think his reed pen mightier than the Roman sword.

You may know the party game known variously as Telephone or Chinese Whispers. Players sit in a circle or line, and the leader begins by whispering a phrase or sentence in the ear of the next player, who whispers it to the next, and so on until the last player says aloud what she has heard. The result is usually a hilarious perversion of the initial statement, and part of the fun lies in learning where the breakdowns occurred. On the same subject, we have the wonderful Monty Python film *The Life of Brian* (directed by Terry Jones, 1979), with its parody of the reception of the Sermon on the Mount. The people too far away from Yeshua hear "Blessed are the Greek" and "Blessed are the cheesemakers."

More than ever we live in what Marshall McLuhan called the Gutenberg Galaxy, a world dominated by type. McLuhan thought that era was ending in the 1960s, but his prediction that media technology would replace print culture with an oral/aural culture has not proved correct. The internet, though freed from the printing press, has only increased our reliance on distributable and retrievable script and images. So much writing and so many images are in the ether that they overwhelm us and stand in for direct human contact. Whatever its benefits, it turns out that contemporary communication technology erodes shared experience, an irony McLuhan did not foresee. His global village has become a heterogeneous universe of endless information instantly available on demand, abolishing the need for remembered knowledge, suggesting by their sheer volume that words ultimately do not matter much. Because we can always Google again, words, whether written or spoken by a chatbot, fade in the mind like disappearing ink. Yet, strangely, sometimes words do matter, and even in that endless stream words can be dangerous. An incautious or impulsive post can lose an election or land you in court. A telephone conversation can do that as well if it has been recorded, another form of electronic writing.

It is difficult, perhaps impossible, for us to imagine a premodern world dependent on orality, where most information was delivered in person, by voice to an audience, with the literal meaning of "those within hearing." Our assumption now is that anything important must be written if it is to be accurately preserved. But to assume that an oral culture is bound to corrupt information is a modern misconception. If the players in the party game were allowed to query what they heard, the game would be no fun, but the repetition of the original sentence might be exact, or close to it.

Scholars have taken divergent approaches to the oral nature of the Yeshua tradition before Mark. This is crucial to understanding how the evangelist went about making the earliest gospel. What was his material like, and how did he treat it? What type of advance did he seek in breaking with the oral tradition? We need to address this if we are to grasp the radical nature of his writing.

Demythologizing. Some of the most influential research on the gospels in the twentieth century was done by the German scholar Rudolf Bultmann (1884–1976). An intellectual in the Lutheran tradition, Bultmann taught for thirty years at the University of Marburg, where for five of those years his colleague was the existentialist philosopher Martin Heidegger. Their friendship and collaboration affected Bultmann's position that the gospels must be viewed through their *Sitz im Leben*, or situation in life, which he held to be that of the time of their composition, not the time of Yeshua.[2] The existentialist needs of the early Christian communities determined what the evangelists wrote, and the aim of the commentator was to "demythologize" the gospels in order to make them meaningful to a modern world skeptical of supernatural explanation.

Bultmann's *The History of the Synoptic Tradition* was first published in German in 1921 and subsequently expanded. Along with the work of like-minded scholars, his method was called "form history" or "form criticism." Its object was to identify the earliest form of the various

---

2. Unlike Heidegger, Bultmann disapproved of the Nazi movement and never joined the Nazi party. A useful summary of his method and limitations is in the entry on him by Russell Morton in Evans, *Encyclopedia of the Historical Jesus*, 80–84.

episodes and sayings in the gospels by looking at them as individual pieces of an oral tradition. These segments, called pericopes (from a Greek word meaning cutting or snippet), were marked off as bits of remembered material associated with Yeshua. Bultmann identified them across the four gospels by type: controversy dialogues, biographical apothegms, wisdom tales, apocalyptic sayings, similitudes (parables), and so on, in an attempt to uncover their earliest formulations—though *uncover*, in this case, actually meant conjecture about. Bultmann held that the collection of this material began with the first Galilean disciples and that it was altered according to the needs of subsequent Hellenistic assemblies. "Mark was the creator of this sort of Gospel," Bultmann wrote; he saw Mark as gathering the pericopes of the tradition to give his work a unity based not on biography but on the requirements of the new faith, "the myth of the kerygma." (*Kerygma*, another Greek word, means proclamation or announcement, and is used to describe the entirety of the message preached by Yeshua or his followers.) The Christ of the gospels, Bultmann said, "is not the historic Jesus, but the Christ of faith and cult.... The kerygma of Christ is cultic legend and the Gospels are expanded cult legends."[3] He claimed that the modern world should not be distressed or alienated by the supernatural elements in the texts because Yeshua's miracles, for example, are also not historical. They are part of the mythic nature of the gospels.

For Bultmann, demythologizing did not mean abandoning trust in Yeshua as redeemer. He was a believer who held that the kerygma or article of faith preceded the gospels in significance. In this sense the gospels are a way of explaining the human basis of the faith, narrative works that allow the faith to be more completely expressed, even if they are ultimately mythic in character. They are cultic legends, but the Christos cult was based on faith in the Resurrection and what it promised for believers. Bultmann apparently was not bothered by the logical contradiction: if the elements of the gospels are mythic, why should the Resurrection not be mythic as well? It's fair to stress that in this context "myth" should be understood not as falsehood but in an anthropological sense as an explanatory or origin story, as Genesis was for many Second-Temple Jews.

---

3. Bultmann, *Synoptic Tradition*, 370–71. The principal New Testament form critics who preceded Bultmann both published groundbreaking books in 1919: K. L. Schmidt in *Der Rahmen der Geschichte Jesu* (The Framework of the Story of Jesus) and Martin Dibelius in *Die Formgeschichte des Evangeliums* (The Form History of the Gospels; English version, *From Tradition to Gospel*, 1934).

Demythologizing did not mean abandoning the basic truth (or belief in the truth) behind Mark; it meant seeing the gospel in existentialist terms, as a writer's amalgamation of remembered incidents and expanded folklore relating to Yeshua that propped up trust in him. As with Paul, the specifics of the historical Yeshua become not only irrecoverable but irrelevant. Yeshua did not propose a new religion or a new social contract or a new form of Judaism; his God was close and getting closer, coming within a generation, bringing with him the end of time, the new reign, and the transformation of the earth.

Form criticism tended to turn the evangelists into editors.[4] In Mark especially, the act of authorship was diminished to an act of arrangement, as if the evangelist had papyrus index cards of the pericopes and his task was to put them in order and provide connectives. He created the narrative, but out of material that had been well established in the forty years since Yeshua's death, some of which (the Passion story, for example) already implied a plot structure.

Bultmann freed scholarship to investigate the gospels more rigorously by asserting that the sources of the evangelists could be studied through acts of imaginative conjecture. Though the sources are not available to us—remember, even Q is a hypothesis—by investigating the gospels as collections of pericopes it is possible to identify what type of original material the sources contained. That in turn permits analysis of why Mark arranged them as he did, and why Matthew and Luke elaborated the basic story using additional sources. We might say that Bultmann and the form critics broke the gospels open to see their moving parts.

Despite Bultmann's great influence, however, there are problems with his approach. I will mention only two of them connected to the oral tradition. First, Bultmann held that the move from oral expression to a written text was a natural, evolutionary development. In his view, the arrival of Mark around 70 CE was unsurprising, indeed inevitable. This led him to think the expansion of the gospel by the subsequent evangelists was also an evolutionary development, whereas the opposite is more likely: that they were hoping to replace their predecessors. The evolutionary position is really untenable; there was nothing predictable about Mark's action. The earliest Christians had no need for a written version of

---

4. *Redaktionsgeschichte* (redaction history or redaction criticism) arose in Germany from form criticism and drew attention to the ways in which the evangelists edited the material they received from the tradition. The term came into general use through Willi Marxsen's *Der Evangelist Markus* (1956).

the Good Message. The Galileans who heard Yeshua preach were unlettered, and those who succeeded them were getting along fine with oral transmission. They conducted their meetings and teachings orally, held discussions orally, learned orally from traveling conveyors of the word, and when they received a letter from the geographically distant Paul, they heard it read aloud. "Thus faith," Paul wrote to the Romans (10.17), "is from hearing." Speaking and writing are entirely different in modality and social purpose. Writing provides a fixity of message that in oral form is supple, interpretive, immediate, and subject to query and correction. The two modes can work in harmony, as in the example of reciting Paul's letters, but they are not the same.

Although Bultmann stressed that the tradition before Mark was oral, he actually treated it as if it had been written. This is the second problem. He thought of the tradition as somehow fixed, not variable, and did not attempt to account for its fluidity in transmission. We know that different communities interpreted the proclamations of faith differently, emphasized one item over another, or misunderstood important questions. That is why Paul sent correctives to his assemblies. When Mark wrote down the traditional material he had collected, he did more than edit it. He fixed it, yes, but he also created its meaning by narrativizing it. The arrangement in itself, how one episode relates to another, is not a mechanical but a creative act. We can witness this in how the other evangelists reordered the events in the life of Yeshua to provide different emphases, even a different theology. Far from shuffling index cards, Mark took the tradition and set it alight. Or, depending on your point of view, set it in stone.

Orality. Did Christianity lose something in the process? That's the question Werner Kelber asked in 1983 in *The Oral and the Written Gospel*. Making those same objections to Bultmann, Kelber wished to explain the nature of oral transmission and the radical break that Mark made from it. He stressed that even literate cultures in antiquity remained committed to oral expression. "Because the vast majority of people were habituated to the spoken word," he said, "much of what was written was meant to be recited and listened to. The practice of writing did thus not immediately make literacy the new model of linguistic behavior, nor were oral speech forms and habits summarily extinguished by literature."[5]

---

5. Kelber, *Oral and Written Gospel*, 17. The quotations in the next few paragraphs are from pp. 30 and 91.

Kelber drew upon a considerable body of work in literary and social studies about the nature of orality.[6] He held that we not only had to drop the notion of natural evolution from the oral to the written gospel but also had to drop the quest for a single original form, because by its nature oral transmission is multiple. Each act of speaking is in itself original. If Yeshua delivered a saying more than once, "the first utterance did not produce 'the original,' nor was the second one a 'variant' thereof, because each moment of speech is wondrously fresh and new." Oral transmission is inherently multiple. But Kelber claimed more than that, because he held that in oral cultures "*tradition is almost always composition in transmission*" (Kelber's italics). The episodes in the life of Yeshua were not fixed in firm memory as if they were the oral equivalent of note cards, but as separate retellings that were capable of being altered creatively, the way a Homeric bard rearranged and altered traditional material to suit a new audience. A body of oral material existed, both historical and mythic in character, and the inheritors of the tradition continued to select from and expand it.

Mark's gospel, Kelber insisted, was a radical break with the tradition as well as a regulation of it. His summary is worth quoting:

> Mark's writing project is an act of daring and rife with consequences. To the extent that the gospel draws on oral voices, it has rendered them voiceless. The voiceprints of once-spoken words have been muted. . . . If it is agreed that Jesus entrusted his message to the oral medium, the existence of a written gospel is nothing short of remarkable. For the moment, language has fallen silent; the ground of Jesus' speech and that of his earliest followers is abandoned. . . . The text, while asserting itself out of dominant oral traditions and activities, has brought about a freezing of oral life into textual still life.

As his tone suggests, Kelber thought this a loss to the living testament. His concept assumed that the episodes in the life of Yeshua were variable

---

6. Twentieth-century orality studies go back to the work of Milman Parry (1902–1935) and Albert Lord (1912–1991) with illiterate traditional bards in Bosnia, best known through Lord's *The Singer of Tales*. The most influential scholar has been Walter J. Ong, especially in *Presence of the Word* and *Orality and Literacy*. Ong deeply affected Kelber and the subsequent orality movement in New Testament studies. Among the important works in the tradition are Dewey, *Oral Ethos of the Early Church*; Horsley, Draper, and Foley, *Performing the Gospel*; Rhoads, "Performance Criticism"; Shiner, *Proclaiming the Gospel*; and B. Wright, *Communal Reading in the Time of Jesus*. A readable introduction to the topic is Rodríguez, *Oral Tradition*. An influential text for students and general readers is Rhoads, Dewey, and Michie, *Mark as Story*.

in detail and flexible in meaning as they passed from the first to the second generation of Yeshua followers. Kelber has a case for the loss entailed by writing if we think, like the earliest Christians, that the end time is around the corner. But when time did not end, even after the destruction of the Temple and all that meant for Jews, including the surviving members of the Yeshua cult in Palestine, then the virtue of a paper version of the story seemed both logical and a blessing.

Kelber later accepted that he had gone too far in building a wall between writing and orality.[7] It is clear from the elaborations in the later gospels that Mark's version did not stop oral preaching and expansion of the tradition. In fact, Mark provided the basis for wider distribution of those parts of the tradition he set down, and therefore contributed to the circulation of the Good Message by speech and personal discussion, a practice that continues in Christianity today. Obviously there is a big difference between speech and writing, but the divide does not prevent the two from interacting. When we consider that Mark was read aloud to the early assemblies, we have to accept that the oral nature of the message was not so much curtailed as adjusted. While we cannot know if Mark wrote expressly for oral presentation, surely he knew his work would reach most people through their ears. Evidence of his awareness is in his parenthetical line, "the one reading, let him understand," or "let the reader understand" (Mark 13.14, repeated word for word in Matthew 24.15). That curious insertion can best be explained if we take it as an aside or stage direction to a person who is reciting the gospel to a group.

Public reading was common in Roman and Hellenistic culture. More to the point, it was how synagogue services proceeded, by reading a passage from the Torah or the Prophets and commenting on it. Luke (4.16–20) has Yeshua begin his ministry in the Nazareth synagogue this way. On the sabbath he is handed "the scroll of the prophet Isaiah," then locates and reads the passage in which the Lord anoints Isaiah "to announce the good message [*euaggelion*] to the poor." Yeshua then comments on the verses, declaring that the prophesy has been completed in his own mission.

We know that Paul's letters circulated in his lifetime and were read aloud to communities other than their addressees. The ending of the letter to the Colossians (4.16) asks the recipients to ensure that it reach farther: "And when this letter has been read before you, make sure it is also read

---

7. Kelber's revised thinking is summarized in "It's Not Easy to Take a Fresh Approach," an interview in Thatcher, *Jesus, the Voice, and the Text*.

in the assembly of the Laodiceans, and you should also read the letter from Laodicea." (Colossae was some fifteen kilometers from Laodicea, in the province of Phrygia in Anatolia.) Paul's authorship of Colossians is disputed, but the point about multiple recipients remains valid no matter who wrote it. After the turn of the century, the anonymous author of the second letter ascribed to Peter reveals that Paul's correspondence was still being read to various assemblies, now as sacred scripture (2 Peter 3.15, probably written between 110 and 150 CE).

Listening to a reader as a group can over time create a reading community,[8] which is one way to describe the early experience of Mark: a cluster of like-minded followers heard sections of a text codifying episodes of the life Yeshua that they believed had been passed down from eyewitnesses. To put it another way, Mark's written text created a listening audience, the same as any public audience in a church or lecture hall or theater or cinema. For a live audience in real time, it isn't only the witnessing that matters, it is the communal witnessing. For the length of the event, a hearer joins a willing gathering of other hearers. And watchers too: under usual live conditions, hearing and seeing the speaker are synonymous. Gesture, facial expression, dress, stance, and movement are as much a part of the experience as vocal tone, pace, mimicry, or volume. Listening in public appeals to eye as well as to ear. Despite our miscellaneous identities and individual understandings, as members of an audience we are united for a time in a shared visual and aural experience. We do not become one, but we do participate jointly in the singular happening. Of course it is hoped that we will carry the experience forward into our lives after the event—true for a play or film as well as for the gospel—but what matters most is the momentary community that draws us out of our private selves into the realm of what is spoken and enacted.[9]

Listening to the gospel of Mark, then, far from being a deadened textual encounter, for early Christians would have meant active engagement with living speech and display. A recitation of the gospel, or any portion of it, is a performance of the gospel. In the first century it may not

---

8. "Reading communities" is the term used by Johnson in *Readers and Reading Culture*. Keith's *Gospel as Manuscript* treats the matter in detail with regard to early Christianity. Public reading is also examined in B. Wright, *Communal Reading in the Time of Jesus*.

9. My treatment of this aspect of an audience is in the introduction to Kennedy, *Spectator and the Spectacle*.

always have been a very good performance, just as today some ministers and readers at a service are not very accomplished in their recitals of text, but it would have been a performance nonetheless. The fact that it was a sacred occasion—or, at the time, perhaps a semi-sacred occasion—does not change the basic circumstance. Public reading is performance, just as ritual reenactment of the Last Supper is performance, and we should recognize the possibility that early experience of the gospel in an assembly could easily have progressed to an expressive or dramatic action, one that would not be identical in every community.

At the same time I must admit that nothing is documented about readings from the gospels in the time of the evangelists, and very little is known in the following centuries before Constantine. One surviving instance comes from Justin Martyr's description of a mid-second-century service that mixed liturgical practice, such as baptism and eucharist, with public recital. Near the end of his *First Apology* (c. 150 CE) he writes:

> And on the day called Sunday there is a meeting in one place of those who live in cities or the country, and the memoirs of the apostles [the gospels] or the writings of the prophets are read, as long as time permits. When the reader has finished the president in a speech admonishes and exhorts us to imitate these good things. Then we all rise together and pray and, as we said before, when our prayer is ended, bread and wine and water are brought, and the president similarly offers up prayers and thanksgivings to the best of his power, and the people assent with Amen. Then follows a distribution of the eucharistic gifts [*or* the things over which thanks have been given] and the partaking of them by all, and they are sent by the deacons to those who are absent. (*1 Apologia* 67).[10]

We can assume that those Sunday readings of the gospels were excerpts rather than complete versions, in line with synagogue practice and that of the later church. Justin's "for as long as time permits" implies that no matter how lengthy the service, some limit was ultimately imposed, whether by fatigue or hunger or fading light.

Nor is anything known about how the faithful responded to the readings. Much as I would like to, it is useless to speculate about this. We have a small bit of evidence from Eusebius with regard to Paul of Samosata (200–275), overseer of the Antioch Christians until deposed for heresy. He was also accused of secularism and corruption, and the

---

10. Quoted with modifications from Bettenson, *Early Christian Fathers*, 62.

charges included the chastisement that in giving a sermon "he rebukes and insults those who do not applaud, and shake their handkerchiefs as in the theatres."[11] But it is clear that his desire for overt approval was considered abnormal.

Memory. We still haven't come to terms with the nature of the oral transmission of the Yeshua cult. What exactly was the material that Mark relied on and how was it passed on? We can't know the answer, but in trying to find one we are faced with two extremes. On the one hand we have Bultmann and the form critics treating the oral tradition as if the individual episodes had been fixed as they circulated, like bits of paper handed from one generation to the next. On the other hand we have Kelber's insistence that oral transmission is by its nature variable and flexible; there could be no fixed or certain form but only a series of original statements that included "composition in transmission." Between these extremes is an aspect of mental processing not sufficiently addressed by either side, and that is memory.

Memory is a huge topic, but I am considering only its relationship to oral transmission. To do that, I propose three categories of memory: personal, communicative, and collective. The first, personal memory, is what we each hold in our heads. It can be close to the surface and remembered frequently, or lie dormant and be activated by external triggers (photographs, letters, grave markers), or pop up internally through cognitive processes. Personal memory carries the traces of our own pasts, our interactions with the world and with the minds and memories of others.

The second category, communicative memory, involves the transmission of personal memory face to face and is the basis of information diffusion in a society that is predominantly oral. At its most direct, one person with the knowledge tells another that the emperor Vespasian has died of dysentery and his son Titus is the new Caesar. More complex is the transmission of memory from long ago. "Let me repeat what I heard when I was young," or "My father told me that once upon a time," or "I remember an old woman saying to me"—that is how such transmissions begin, face-to-face communication from recall. There is a temporal limit to how long such personal remembrance can be passed along. Jan Assmann suggests that communicative memory can span no more than

---

11. Eusebius, *Church History* 7.30.9, in Schaff and Wace, *Church Fathers*, 1:314.

three or four generations, or eighty to a hundred years.[12] That's about the length of time the Romans called a *saeculum*, an age, after which an event belonged to time immemorial, "time out of mind." My uncle remembered his mother saying that she had heard from her mother: at that point we reach the approximate end of personal connective.

In order for the memory to survive beyond that span it must be transformed into the third type, collective or "cultural" memory. The collective now holds the memory as a group. Not every person will know the item from the past or remember it accurately; sometimes a specific class (priests, historians) will be entrusted with it, but society as a whole is tasked with its retention rather than a sequence of individuals. As Eric Eve puts it, collective memory is "the external means by which a group makes use of the past to construct its own identity through ritual, monuments, oral traditions, texts, accepted ways of behaving and so forth."[13] Societies commonly remember the past in terms of stories, whose narrative cohesion makes the events easier to recall. Stories with plot frameworks that go from A to B to C can be told and retold, sometimes altering details, so long as the basic outline and function are retained.

A romantic view of the oral transmission of the Yeshua chronicle, whether in episodic or narrative form, might think of it as occurring face to face, one person telling another something of what she had learned from someone else, the way the news is spread in epic religious films such as *Ben-Hur* or *The Robe*, or how Barabbas, in Pär Lagerkvist's novel of that name, relates his eyewitness account of the Crucifixion. While such connections may well have taken place, it is more likely that the circumstances were more formal. Followers, disciples, apostles were sent out to deliver a speech about the Good Message to a local gathering, which would include some details of Yeshua's life and death. They would be following the model mentioned in chapter 6 of Mark, when Yeshua sends out the Twelve to proselytize in pairs. In the first generation, Acts of the Apostles tells us, such messengers went to the great cities from Antioch to Rome to spread the word. Paul did the same for the assemblies he founded in Greece and Asia Minor. Luke (if he was the actual author of Acts) invents classically modeled speeches for the apostles in which they proclaim the new belief. Their speeches were no doubt rougher and more improvised than Luke gives us—and sometimes may have required

---

12. Assmann, *Cultural Memory and Early Civilization*, 41.
13. Eve, *Writing the Gospels*, 106.

a translator—but however they sounded, they were performances. They were not haphazard or half-remembered reminiscences around the fire after dinner, or conversations in casual meetings at crossroads. They were organized sermons or debates that had been practiced and refined through repetition.

In the second generation, as the eyewitnesses faded and died, the passing on of the tradition would have become problematic. As long as the message remained oral it required new speakers to ensure its continuance. It is reasonable to suppose that the oral tradition, the basis of everything we know about Yeshua and his significance, continued to exist primarily through performance, when one or more speakers addressed an audience. As one writer puts it, any tradition "becomes manifest at the multiple points of its performances."[14] The Yeshua tradition, then, became actualized through the oral repetition of its elements to assemblies of men and women. Performers of a tradition rise out of a community when they have absorbed the magnitude of the message and a method of successfully conveying it. They pass along two practices: the traditional material (the history) and the tradition of how to explain it (the performance).

Since there was no established Christian church, only scattered and sometimes isolated groups spread throughout the empire, any transmitter of the Good Message could distort or mistake its features. Indeed, when the church did get organized after Constantine, it found its consensus of belief by identifying such distortions, which it called heresies. But the ideas and theologies condemned as heretical were almost always about interpretation, about the meaning or implications of New Testament events, not whether the events themselves were reported accurately. Back in the first and second generations of Christianity, control of the oral tradition was accomplished by the corrective aspect of communicative memory. The various urban assembles guarded and repeated the tradition through repetition and ritual reenactment, as the quotation above from Justin Martyr suggests. Speech that varied from the accepted norm could be corrected or suppressed. In addition, the assemblies were occasionally supervised by major proclaimers, such as Paul and his successors, who could emend errors and clear up misunderstandings.

My ordering of personal, communicative, and collective memory makes transmission sound progressive or evolutionary, logically

---

14. Kirk, *Q in Matthew*, 5.

proceeding down a road from one mind to many minds to a collective or mythic state. It would be wrong to think it so simple. In oral societies many memories must be lost along the way, and others corrupted. It's easy to imagine Blessed are the Cheesemakers moments. There is no guarantee that face-to-face communication will survive even one generation. Only those recollections that enough people consider crucial or important to their present moment will pass through time as active memories, whether or not they are written. Or those so striking as to be literally unforgettable: lighthearted ones, such as the young George Washington chopping down the cherry tree, or King John losing the crown jewels in the Wash; horrifying ones, such as the Nazi extermination camps or the atom bombs at Hiroshima and Nagasaki. For early Christians, the Crucifixion of Yeshua would certainly fit the second category. Monuments are no guarantee: the next generation can ignore or destroy a statue of a hero or forget his deeds or remember only a portion of their significance. Books can be lost in libraries or wars. Machine memory is volatile. The cyber cloud needs constant electrical current. Disasters of fire, flood, earthquake, battle, and nuclear obliteration are hazards to any form of chronicling. In our own time we tell stories in films and books and plays about the possibility, even the imminence, of the end time. If human beings survived some devastating event they might do so with the loss of collective memory, or portions of it, and, in a favorite theme of science fiction, have to start over, remaking human culture like those mythic originators Adam and Eve.

But we are concerned here with the first century, not the twenty-first, and in context the most interesting characteristic of transmission memory is Assmann's assertion that in cultures that possess writing, texts often start to appear at the point of a "tradition break" after about forty years from an event, when the original witnesses begin to die out.[15] Mark's gospel appeared just at that moment, about four decades after the Crucifixion, and close behind the martyrdoms of the major followers as related in Acts or legend. The dates of the deaths of Peter and Paul are not known precisely but likely occurred between 64 and 70 CE. According to Josephus, James the brother of Yeshua was stoned on the order of the High Priest Ananus in the year 62.[16] Those martyrdoms, the actual or

---

15. Assmann discusses the relationship between cultural memory and the rise of writing in *Cultural Memory and Early Civilization*, 70–110. Eve applies this insight to gospel writing in *Writing the Gospels*, 106–9.

16. Josephus, *Antiquities of the Jews*, 20.9.1. In this account Ananus acted improperly

anticipated destruction of the Temple, the accumulation of oral tradition, and the disagreements among the various strands of the tradition, could prompt a member of the cult to preserve the communicative memory in firmer form, in a script available for performers to recite to the collective.

Eucharist. The memory of the apostles present at the Last Supper, we assume, became the prompt for the principal rite of Christianity. The eucharist (Greek *eucharistos*, thanksgiving) as still practiced in most sects is centered around giving thanks over bread and wine and distributing them to congregants. The action elevates the bread and wine to a high symbolic position and offers the joining of Christos as savior with those who hope to be saved. Among major religions that have survived into modernity, a few continue to use alcohol as part of ceremonies, such as sake in Shintoism and wine in Judaism, but as far as I know Christianity is the only one that uses an alcoholic drink as central to worship.[17]

Mark's scene in which Yeshua is asked why his disciples do not fast is altered by Luke into a sermon for the people. In it Yeshua says, "John the Baptizer came not eating bread or drinking wine, and you say, He has a demon. The son of man came eating and drinking and you say, Look at the man, a glutton and a wino, and a friend of tax collectors and sinners" (Luke 7.33–34). The implication that overeating and drunkenness were parallel to ritual impurity is intriguing, whether applied to Yeshua or not. In Mark, however, wine has no negative connotations; it is as much a part of life as bread, and two of Yeshua's parables focus on wine or vineyards. Wine had been present in Hebrew culture for over a millennium, just as condemnations of drunkenness had been. Wine was usually diluted by a double or even triple portion of water, reducing its alcohol content to two to four percent.[18] In a warm region like Palestine, it was a cooling drink rather than an inflaming one.

---

in convening the Sanhedrin without the consent of the Roman Prefect Albinus; Agrippa agreed and removed Ananus from his position.

17. Contemporary concerns about alcohol abuse have affected the use of wine in some Christian sects. Sometimes grape juice is substituted or provided as an alternative to wine for communicants. Even the Roman church allows the use of *mustum* ("must" in English), natural grape juice in which the fermentation process has been suspended, for priests who are alcoholics.

18. For example, in Roman culture of the first century, both in Italy and in *provincia romana*, the large province that is now southern France, highly flavored wine of ten to twelve percent alcohol by volume was generally reserved for the upper classes; most wine would have been allowed to ferment to only seven or eight percent. It was Roman custom to dilute all wine, regardless of its alcohol content; it was considered barbaric to drink it neat. See Phillips, *French Wine*, 21.

Though wine is not mentioned in the Mosaic injunction to celebrate the Passover meal called the Seder (Exodus 13.3–10), it had likely been included for many centuries. Little is known about the nature of the Seder in the period, and the accounts of the Last Supper in the gospels are opaque. In Mark Yeshua sends two disciples to prepare for Passover in an upper room "on the first day of Unleavened Bread, when the Passover lamb is to be sacrificed" (14.12). That evening he goes there with the Twelve. Mark may have intended the meal to be the Seder, though there is no mention of the customary bitter herbs or the liturgy concerning the Exodus. Or he may have intended an ordinary meal (with unleavened bread) on the evening before the beginning of Passover proper.[19] Jewish rituals and the operations of the Temple tend to be generalized in his gospel, which might indicate a gentile audience or, just as likely, a determination that they were not significant to the principal theme.

Here is the section on the eucharist (Mark 14.22–24):

> While they were eating, Iesous took bread, gave praise, broke it, and gave it to them, saying, "Take, this is my body." And holding a cup, he gave thanks and offered it to them, and they all drank from it. Then he said to them, "This is my blood of the covenant which is poured out for many. In all truth I say to you, I will not drink the fruit of the vine again until that day when I drink it for the first time in the reign of God."

I mentioned in the previous chapter that the meal is the culmination of the feeding theme, transforming Yeshua from a patron of the poor and hungry to a sacrificial victim who declares that the bread and wine are his body and blood. We should also remember that in Aramaic there would have been no verb in his directive, just "Take, this my body," or perhaps "Take this, my body." Christians have argued for centuries over what his words indicate, and I'm not going to enter that unresolvable debate, which at root is an argument about adverbs: did he intend it literally, metonymically, or metaphorically? In spite of my Catholic indoctrination about transubstantiation, I'm not sure it matters much; the important

---

19. The uncertainty over whether the Last Supper was a Passover Seder probably derives from the fact that the Passover and the Unleavened Bread are actually separate feasts, one following the other in the same week. Passover marks the passage of the angel of death and the escape of the Israelites from Egypt; Unleavened Bread marks the need for haste in preparation for that escape. In practice they were merged during the Babylonian exile, and by the time of Yeshua the two terms were sometimes used interchangeably, as in Luke (22.1): "Now the feast of the Unleavened, which is called the Passover, was drawing near."

issue is whether the communicant accepts the physical sign in a spiritual sense.

What I want to get at in this section is how the words of the eucharistic action got to Mark. Before I discuss the basis of the oral tradition, it's worth making two side points. The first is that Yeshua's revelation that he is about to be betrayed by one of the Twelve, which immediately precedes the event of bread and wine, is given as much textual space as the eucharist. We've noted that treachery and redemption are intimately related in the gospel. Strictly from a narrative standpoint the betrayal is more important than the eucharist. Food and drink cease to be part of the story at the end of the supper, but since the Temple priests do not want to arrest Yeshua in front of the people, some informant is required to reveal his location after dark. John, who does not relate the eucharist, instead pays a good deal of attention to the betrayal, even having Yeshua identify Judas by giving him a piece of bread after dipping it in the bowl, an act of communion tied directly to treachery (John 13.21–28). In Mark there is no sense that Yeshua has instituted a sacrament with the bread and wine, no injunction to repeat the event in his memory, and little attention given to the salvific implications that the subsequent church considered essential. The only nod to grander significance is the phrase "This is my blood of the covenant which is poured out for many." Like the meaning of the words over the bread and wine, that cries out for explanation. It may be that the betrayal and the eucharist came to Mark as separate pericopes which he put together in the same scene as necessary opposites, combining the table as feeding image with the cross as sacrificial image, thereby establishing the mythic and ritual basis of Christianity.

The second side point is contained in the next line, "In all truth I say to you, I will not drink the fruit of the vine again until that day when I drink it for the first time in the reign of God." That sentence tends to take the accent away from the eucharist as an institutional event, making the meal a form of farewell to the Twelve. This is what I leave you with, Yeshua suggests, a memory of my body and blood, because this is the end of me. The apostles are thus invited to anticipate the imminent arrival of the new kingdom, when they will see Yeshua again and drink wine in fellowship again. The pledge he makes, never to take wine until the transformation of the world, extends to his Crucifixion the next morning, when he refuses the wine laced with myrrh that is offered him as a sedative (15.23).

Given how crucial the eucharist became in Christianity, it is a shock to recognize that the sacramental words of institution—*Do this in remembrance of me*—occur in only one of the gospels (Luke 22.19–20), and that in a passage that does not appear in all ancient manuscripts. It may well be a secondary insertion. Without the instruction to repeat the action of the bread and wine, there would be little basis for making the eucharist into the purpose of the Mass or the major sacramental rite of Christian fellowship. This a clear case in which the oral tradition took precedence over the gospel in time and authority, and did not develop by simple passed-on speech but by ritual practice.

There is no documentary evidence from the first century about the nature of the rite that reenacted the Last Supper. As in the case of the kerygma or article of faith, the earliest record comes from Paul's first letter to the Corinthians, sometime around the year 55. His words constitute the only assured scriptural reference to the memorial intention behind the bread and wine. Here is a literal translation, which I have deliberately left unpolished to be closer to the Greek expression:

> For I received from the Lord what I also handed on to you, that the Lord Iesous on the night when he was handed over took bread, and having given thanks [*eucharistesas*], he broke and said, "This is my body that is for you; do this in remembrance of me." The same with the cup also, after having eaten, saying, "This cup is the new covenant in my blood; as often as you might drink, do this in remembrance of me." (1 Corinthians 11.23–25)

"Received" and "handed on" are conventional phrases for the transmission of an oral tradition. We cannot know in what way Paul received the information "from the Lord." From a historical position it is most likely that he got it from the major disciples on one of his visits to Jerusalem, and of course Peter, James, and John were present at the Last Supper.

The important point about the passage, however, is that it reflects active ritual practice. Chapter 11 of the letter is in effect a disciplinary corrective to errors and misuses in the Corinth assembly that had been separately related to Paul. He is particularly concerned about abuses to the eucharist. "Then when you gather in once place," he writes, "it is not to eat the dinner of the Lord, for someone eats his own dinner first and another is actually hungry and another one gets drunk. Do you not in fact have houses to eat and drink in?" He instructs the Corinthians to eat at home before coming to the assembly, so that hunger will not interfere with the proper spirit and form of the ceremony (11.20–22, 33–34).

Paul's insistence on physical and spiritual correctness suggests that some form of the ritual was already well established before the decade of the 50s and that it was considered a substantial part of Christian life. Its importance is underlined in 11.26: "For as often as you eat this bread and drink the cup, you celebrate [or proclaim] the Lord's death until he might come." Aside from the words Paul gives us, we do not know what the ritual was like, but it is reasonable to conclude that it was something approaching a meal. Whether it was the same as the *agape*, the "love feast" or "goodwill dinner" mentioned in passing in Jude 12, cannot be known. (The letter of Jude, which might be as late as 110 CE, is a rebuke to improper behavior in a Jewish Christian group that is parallel to Paul's chastisement of the gentile Christian group in Corinth.) Given the diversity of the Christian assemblies at the time, it is unlikely that the eucharist was celebrated the same way everywhere, even if the crucial words were comparable. We cannot even be sure that the practice was modeled on the Last Supper, since the narratives of the Supper in the synoptic gospels were composed decades later than Paul.[20]

Similarly, we have no way of knowing what those early participants believed about the eucharist. Did they think the blessing and thanksgiving changed the bread and wine into another substance? Did they consider eating and drinking together to be a spiritual as well as a collective encounter? Did they believe that by invoking Yeshua's words they brought him closer? As promised, I am not going to speculate.

What does it mean to re-perform an event that the participants believe actually happened in the past? Theology and performance theory look at the matter differently. Christian theology has tended to explain the eucharist as a *gift*, a grace from God. Yeshua as Messiah, having died, risen, and ascended to the Father, now descends again—is reincarnated—in the bread and wine, literally or spiritually, to nourish the souls of the faithful who accept him as redeemer. The feeding theme of Mark, in other words, continues into our present moment. That way of thinking emphasizes the materiality of the meal, the need for a Christian to eat and drink in order to benefit from the divine gift. The bread and wine are simultaneously sign and substance, which is true whether one believes they are actual body and blood or a symbol of body and blood. A theological approach to the liturgy of the eucharist wants to

---

20. Bradshaw, *Eucharistic Origins*, 11–15, outlines the evidence of eucharist protocol from Paul to the fourth century. Bradshaw holds that practice was highly varied until after Constantine, and not always based on the memory accounts of the Last Supper.

uncover its *indexical meaning*. By that I mean that theology is interested in what the eucharist points to, how it reveals or uncovers the Savior's gift of salvation. The event remains physical but it stands for something else, something that cannot be seen. The performance of the ritual of the Last Supper in a gathering of believers is less an act of memorializing the past occasion and more an insistence on Yeshua's continuing, if invisible, presence. The event of the Last Supper happened once and, so long as somebody re-performs it, is continually happening.

Performance theory does not turn the theological approach around entirely, since thinking performatively still sees ritual as a communal sign of an absence. The difference lies in the relation of the ritual re-performance to the original event. In Richard Schechner's much-quoted definition, performance is "restored behavior" or "twice-behaved behavior," action that imitates an original action, whether the original was actual or fictive.[21] It does not matter if the imitation is accurate to the original, or if the original itself meant something different from the current meaning of its imitation. It does not matter if actors and audience believe in the truth of the original. What matters is that the performer and the spectator-participant are conscious that they are engaged together in a replication. From this standpoint, the eucharist as observed now is not an ongoing re-creation of the Last Supper that achieves what the Last Supper achieved, it is an *enactment of the script* of the Last Supper. And though the reenactment in the Mass, for example, involves the priest quoting Yeshua's words adapted from Mark's script, the words came to Paul and then to Mark through oral and physical repetition of the rite itself.

So the absence in Mark of the formula *Do this is remembrance of me* is not significant, since the eucharistic rite was proceeding along independently of both the oral tradition about the life of Yeshua and Mark's scribal version. Mark's audience did not need to be told in the gospel that Yeshua wanted them to re-perform the Last Supper; they were already doing it.

About a hundred years after Paul's instructions to Corinth, Justin Martyr's *First Apology*, quoted earlier in this chapter, describes a version of the rite on a Sunday, most likely in Rome, that contained both gospel reading and ritual performance of the Last Supper. "Bread and wine and

---

21. Schechner developed his theory of ritual and performance over some decades, particularly in *Between Theatre and Anthropology* and *Future of Ritual*. My critique of his position on ritual and belief is in chapter 11 of Kennedy, *Spectator and the Spectacle*. A readable introduction to performance theory is Carlson's *Performance*.

water are brought," Justin wrote, "and the president in like manner offers prayers and thanksgivings, according to his ability, and the people assent, saying Amen. And there is a distribution to each. . . ." (Note that water is specified, for diluting the wine.) In his previous section Justin calls the eucharist by name, says it is reserved for believers who have been baptized, and suggests that a type of transubstantiation was already part of the belief: ". . . so likewise have we been taught that the food which is blessed by the prayer of his word, and from which our blood and flesh by transmutation are nourished, is the flesh and blood of that Iesous who was made flesh" (1 *Apologia* 66). Justin's explanation of Christian practice, in a defense written for the emperor Antoninus Pius (reigned 138–161 CE), shows that a form of the eucharist continued in an unbroken oral tradition to his time, as it continues today. Two thousand years of replicating the same action, a very long run.

Swallowing the scroll. For most of my life I have been involved with an activity that relies on memorization and performance: live theater. I gave my first memorized speech at age twelve, at that same Saint Francis de Sales School in Cincinnati. It was an encomium to the long-serving pastor, who was celebrating the sixtieth anniversary of his ordination. The speech was written by the school principal, Sister Dorothea, so I was a reciter for someone else. Obviously, that's what an actor is: someone who makes a writer's words live before an audience. I acted throughout high school and university, then acted professionally (not very well), got the conventional advanced degrees, and moved on to playwriting, directing, university teaching, and scholarship.

What I've learned about memorizing in those sixty years in and around theatres is simple: to be convincing and intelligible in any role, Shakespeare or Spielberg, actors have to abandon the book and make the words entirely their own. Actors are the focal point of the great paradox of playmaking: they learn written lines so they can speak them *as if they had not been written*. That requires a kind of memorizing that in rehearsal gradually incorporates the text into the actor's body. But if actors make the words their own, how accurate to the text will their words be?

At the start of his prophesy about 593 BCE, Ezekiel gives a frightening account of how he was chosen as Yahweh's spokesman. A vision of a crystal throne in the heavens appeared to him and a voice charged him to instruct the Israelites ("that rebellious house") to repent. A hand stretched out from the throne holding a scroll, written on both sides with "words of mourning and woe." A voice spoke:

> He said to me, son of man, eat what is offered to you; eat this scroll, and go speak to the house of Israel. So I opened my mouth, and he gave me the scroll to eat. He said to me, son of man, eat this scroll that I give you and fill your stomach with it. Then I ate it; and in my mouth it was sweet as honey. He said to me: son of man, go to the house of Israel and speak my very words to them. (Ezekiel 3.1–3)[22]

Eating the writing is an extreme enforcement of the desire for textual accuracy in a speaker. Yahweh does not trust his prophet to remember his words exactly and entirely, human memory being both imperfect and unpredictable, so Ezekiel is commanded to incorporate the words literally. Of course, alimentation is no cure for bad memory, despite Ezekiel's metaphor. Nonetheless, that is what actors must do: swallow the book, in the sense of making the words part of themselves. If that means an occasional imperfect delivery of the text, a thorough theatre professional—Shakespeare, for one—probably wouldn't care.

There is a surprising similarity between biblical textual scholarship and Shakespeare textual scholarship. In fact, the first serious studies of Shakespeare's texts borrowed the philological methods of nineteenth-century biblical studies in search of the same goal: the discovery of the original form, the earliest readings, the most authentic text that could be connected to the author. There are huge differences, naturally, between ancient biblical codices and plays printed within or soon after an author's lifetime. In both cases, however, the originals are lacking. There are no manuscripts of Mark before about 300, and there are no manuscripts of Shakespeare, whether in his hand or a copyist's. There are also large differences in the purpose of the writing and the communities meant to receive it. Yet Shakespeare textual scholars worry over the questions of primary form, corruption, variant readings, copying errors (printers' errors rather than scribes' errors), and the establishment of a genuine text just as their biblical counterparts do.

Take the case of *Hamlet*. Modern editions are based on three printed versions from the early seventeenth century. Two were published singly in quarto size (1603 and 1604), a few years after the play was first performed; the third is one of the thirty-six plays printed in the First Folio edition

---

22. The NRSV translates the Hebrew "son of man" as "mortal," and I have once again taken the liberty of restoring the original. The image of eating the scroll is also used in Jeremiah (15.16) and recalled in Revelation (10.8–10). I discuss the paradox of speaking written text in Kennedy, "The Spectator, the Text, and Ezekiel."

of 1623. Each differs significantly from the others. The First Quarto, sometimes called the Bad Quarto, was a pirated edition, unauthorized by the author's acting company, that took advantage of the play's popularity. One theory holds that the text was printed not from playhouse papers, which would have been held securely, but by "memorial reconstruction": a few actors trying to piece together the lines as they remembered them, a parody inversion of Mark's reliance on oral tradition. The Second Quarto, rushed out the next year, probably by Shakespeare's company, then called the King's Men, seemed designed to correct the considerable errors and jumbled lines in the first. The First Folio, edited by two members of the company, with a verse preface by Ben Jonson, was published as a memorial seven years after Shakespeare's death.

Which is the authentic text of *Hamlet*? Most modern editions are amalgamations, like Tatian's harmonization of the gospels, taking the best or clearest passages from the three *Hamlet* samples and pasting them together (though editors draw little from the First Quarto). Despite effort by scholars over many decades to establish a correct version, one believed to represent Shakespeare's actual intentions, the truth is that none of them is original and all of them are original, because "original" had no fixed meaning in the rough and collaborative world of London commercial theatre around 1600. When merged, the character of Hamlet has five well-known soliloquies, though all five are in none of the three main texts. A "complete" version, such as Kenneth Branagh presented in his four-hour film of 1996, would never have been seen in Shakespeare's time. Branagh thought his screenplay to be fidelity itself, but what he filmed was a script without textual authority.

A similar problem exists for the two texts of *King Lear*, a quarto of 1608 and the First Folio of 1623, which differ considerably in length and material. Was the second Shakespeare's revision of the first, or do they indicate two separate performance texts? Is an amalgamation of them justified or an editorial perversion? In the face of editorial anxiety I want to emphasize that in performance it doesn't much matter. An ordinary audience is unlikely to care if Hamlet says "Oh, that this too too sallied flesh would melt" (Second Quarto) or "sullied flesh" (editorial correction) or "solid flesh" (First Folio). I'm not sure they would even hear the difference. It doesn't much matter if the actor bungles the line entirely, so long as he doesn't dry up and leave a gap in the scene that embarrasses the audience on his behalf.

In making this comparison I do not mean to imply that Mark's words do not matter or that exactitude in uncovering them is mistaken. Clearly a true text, one that gets as close as possible to what the evangelist wrote, does matter, especially for the many Christians who consider the gospels a form of holy revelation. Nor do I wish to denigrate the significant work done by Shakespeare editors, who have in the past fifty years produced both texts and a social context for the texts far superior to those accepted earlier. Want I wish to indicate is that in speaking a text, whether in a contemporary theatre or in an early Christian assembly, the totality of the performance makes the impression on an audience, not the complete accuracy of the speaker to the written words.[23]

Did Mark understand this when he wrote a gospel that would be recited aloud? It is probable that he did. One indirect bit of evidence is his vernacular style. It is usually assumed that Mark's basic Greek and the simplicity of his diction indicate that he was not an accomplished author, that Greek was not his first language, and that he was chosen by his community or took the job on himself because no one better was available. But what if his low style was a deliberate choice? What if, knowing most people would encounter the gospel by hearing it, he purposefully kept his syntax easy to follow and his vocabulary immediate? What if—and here I swim the sea of speculation—he consciously worked as a dramatist does, in full knowledge that someone else would deliver his words to a live audience? I have mentioned before that curious aside in Mark 13.14: "The one reading, let him understand" (or "let the reader understand"). I recall it here because it can help *us* understand what the evangelist himself probably understood: that the oral presentation of his work required a style of writing that could be comprehended in the moment of hearing.

If so, it would have been right and proper for the "reader"—that is, the reciter—to swallow the scroll, internalize the words, and deliver the Good Message as if it were breaking news, happening now, in the way that reenactment ritual, while recalling the past, happens only in the present. It would have been right and proper for the reader to speak the words like a storyteller, as if they had never been written. Then Mark's written gospel, far from being a text for private contemplation that broke the living connection to Yeshua, would actually carry on the public condition of its heritage. The written gospel would not have been the end of the oral tradition but its rescue.

23. A direct comparison of New Testament performance to Shakespeare performance is made by Holland, "Playing to the Groundlings."

6

Myth and History

On Sundays the ladies sometimes went to Mass, to hear some good music or a well-known organist: neither of them was a practicing Catholic, but the faith of others helped them to ecstatic enjoyment of the music. They believed in God just long enough to enjoy a toccata.

—Jean-Paul Sartre[1]

The claim that Mark did not break the oral tradition is further supported by noting that he wrote in a culture that often treated writing as a prompt for the spoken word rather than a substitute for it. In offering versions that differed from Mark, the later gospels can be thought of as accumulations, adding new episodes and details that helped to confront new circumstances. We could think of the process as a written continuation of the elasticity of the oral message. Matthew and Luke built their versions on Mark's words and outline, elaborating the basic story by investing Yeshua with more birthright, more authority from the Hebrew scriptures, more sermons and parables, and greater divine agency. The urge to elevate Yeshua is even clearer in the case of John, whose theological orientation often determined how he revised the Markan story. The synoptics present Yeshua as a prophet and preacher of the Good Message, while John makes him into the message itself. In the resonant words of Rudolf Bultmann, in John the proclaimer became the proclaimed.

1. Sartre, *Words*, 19.

As we have seen, in the second century the fledgling Christian movement took the four gospels together as the apostolic message and subsequently preserved them equally. Each gospel was an attempt at capturing what its author considered essential; none was comprehensive or encyclopedic, which means each participated in the *incompleteness* of passed-on knowledge. That they differed in detail meant that the early Christian movement could continue to be flexible about the nature of the message, again preserving some qualities of the oral tradition. It is best to see Mark as part of the ongoing history of the tradition, which developed and changed over the next few centuries.

Legends. The oral messaging itself did not stop when Mark wrote some of it down. Because the second-century texts, with the exception a few letters, were not admitted to the canon, it is easy to ignore how they expanded the Christian story by filling in blanks left by the authorized evangelists. We can take as examples the "infancy gospels," a genre of works dealing with the birth and early life of Yeshua and his mother. The Protoevangelium of James, also called the Infancy Gospel of James and sometimes just the Gospel of James, was written in Greek around the middle of the second century and widely translated. The author maintains that he is James the brother of Yeshua—actually his stepbrother from an earlier marriage of Joseph's, a distinction made necessary by the author's assertion of Mary's perpetual virginity. The text relates the birth and childhood of Mary, her chaste marriage to Joseph, the supernatural birth of Yeshua in a cave near Bethlehem which leaves Mary's hymen unbroken, the visit of the Magi, the slaughter of the innocents, and concludes with the martyrdom of Zechariah, the father of John the Baptizer. The account is filled with extraordinary events, reflecting the convention that miracles were proof of the full divinity of Yeshua.

Paul does not mention Mary and says only that Yeshua was born of a woman (Galatians 4.4). Mark mentions her twice, the second time naming her Mary (Maria in Greek, Miriam in Hebrew, the name of the sister of Moses and one of the most common Jewish female names; there are six separate Miriams in the New Testament). The text makes clear that she has no confidence in her son and that he has little regard for her. Matthew treats Mary with respect and says she was a virgin who conceived by divine intervention (1.16). Where did Matthew get this notion? A partial explanation comes from the Hebrew scriptures, since he takes her virginal pregnancy as fulfilment of a prophesy of Isaiah (7.14). As Matthew quotes it from the Septuagint, the Greek reads "Behold, the virgin will have in her womb and bear a son and they will call his name Immanuel." Here is another case where an accidental difficulty of translation prompted major doctrinal trouble. Isaiah's word in Hebrew is *almah*, which means young girl or maiden. It contains the general implication of virginity before marriage in the same way that English "young girl" does. Isaiah meant she would be a maiden until she conceived; he surely did not intend to suggest that the young girl would conceive without sexual congress and give birth while remaining a virgin. The Septuagint put *almah* into Greek as *parthenos*, which has a stronger sense of an unmarried and virginal girl, and that is the word Matthew copied.[2]

In reading backward for prophetic authority, Matthew either started or, more likely, solidified a tradition that the child was conceived while Mary continued to be a virgin. We have no record of anyone talking about her virginity until then, in about 80 or 85 CE. That doesn't prove there was no tradition asserting it, only that Paul and Mark did not know of it or think it important. By the time of the Protoevangelium of James around the year 150, the tradition had expanded into a belief that Mary gave birth as a virgin and remained a virgin thereafter, creating the desexualized vision of the Mother of God common in devotion and religious art. The perpetual virginity of Mary is a doctrine which the Roman church still insists on, despite Matthew's implication that Joseph had sex with her after the birth of Yeshua ("and did not know her until she had produced a son, and he called his name Iesous," 1.25).

The other noncanonical gospels of the second or third centuries continued to elaborate the Yeshua legend, often by attaching further miraculous occurrences to the basic narrative. Is this characteristic of information passed on orally, to explain by expansion and invention? I don't know, though the evidence suggests that retold stories lean toward addition, not subtraction. We can't know whether authors like the pseudo-James relied on actual tradition or simply made things up. Was it common to tell tales of little Yeshua shaping birds out of clay and making them fly, or bringing a dried fish back to life? Those are two of the events in the Infancy Gospel of Thomas,[3] and I heard both from nuns in school,

---

2. While it is clear in context that Matthew in 1.23 intends *parthenos* to mean virgin, the confusion over the word extends to contemporary English translations of Isaiah 7.14. Most versions render *almah* as virgin, making the Old Testament conform to the New. A few (including NRSV) prefer "young woman."

3. The texts of the infancy gospels and other noncanonical works are contained in Ehrman and Plese, *The Apocryphal Gospels*.

told as fact. When the church got around to establishing the canon, the consensus gave precedence to the first-century texts, chiefly because of their presumed apostolic authority. But sometimes the more legendary treatments, excluded from the New Testament, influenced doctrine anyway, as with Mary's virginity.

The tradition itself: what was the reality behind what it preserved in the four decades after the Crucifixion before Mark and the six or seven decades before John? How did the evangelists and early Christians think of the truth of the story of Yeshua they inherited? Was it "cultic myth" to them, in Bultmann's words? Was it history in the sense of an accurate depiction of events or a reliable biography? It is impossible to answer those questions but we can make some assumptions, and the first thing to say is that in the ancient world the distinction between myth and history was not absolute. Very often myth *was* history, and sometimes real events became myth. The mythic mode, after all, is simply another way of expressing what is true, or what is thought to be true, in a memorable or poetic fashion. As Jan Assmann puts it, "Myth is the past condensed into foundational narrative."[4] Since the rise of science we no longer think that way. We make a firm distinction between premodern mythic knowledge and modern verifiable knowledge. History and biography may be "soft" subjects in that they are interpretive discourses dependent on argument and persuasion, but we still expect their basic facts to be verifiable. If we apply scientific ideas of accuracy to the events in the New Testament, as a modern historian would do, they will not stand up very well, and that makes it hard for a modern mind to take them literally.

Not so long ago it was common for English-speaking families to have copies of two early seventeenth-century books, the King James Bible and the complete works of Shakespeare. They might sit side by side, often bound in soft leather, about equal in size and presumed value. But of the full Christian bible the New Testament is a small portion, less than a fifth of the whole, and Shakespeare's works are more than six times its size. While earlier I remarked that we are lucky to have so many first-century Christian documents, they still amount to very little. The New Testament, most scholars will agree, is insufficient. Just as Mark often says less than orthodoxy wants him to say, as a whole the New Testament leaves us wanting more: more clarity, more explanation, more certainty.

---

4. Assmann, *Cultural Memory and Early Civilization*, 61.

That it is completely lacking in external verification also disturbs us. Believers in the Good Message or not, we are children of the Enlightenment, raised in the age of science. Most major world religions date from antiquity, arose out of alleged revelation or other supernatural occurrence, and lack doctrinal exactitude. They resist rationalization. Their founding texts—the Torah, the Bhagavad Gita, the Buddhist Canons, the New Testament, the Qur'an—usually combine the mystical and the practical, the invisible with the visible, and tend to be open rather than closed. Their wide interpretative range has permitted reassessment over centuries as circumstances change, but at the same time has prompted dissension and sectarianism.

In Christianity different religious leaders, reading the same small body of authorized texts, have regularly achieved opposing conclusions. Biblical scholars are no exception. As Burton Mack puts it, modern New Testament scholarship seems to accept that it is in search of something out of reach, because the texts available cannot reveal the point of their origins. "The origins of Christianity," he writes at the beginning of his book on Mark, "are known to lie on the other side of limits set by the nature of the texts at the scholar's disposal and the nature of the history that can be reconstructed from them." The most sophisticated methods of historical analysis and literary criticism prove inadequate. The few allusions in first-century non-Christian records are confusing, and the oral tradition leaves no material trace outside of the texts it influenced. Thus, Mack says, the critical study of the New Testament is a paradox, "a scholarship in quest of an objective known to be unreachable by scholarly tools and methods."[5]

Faced with this difficulty, there are really only two ways for a commentator on the gospels to proceed. One is to accept that the origin of Christianity lay in a unique event in the history of mankind, an intervention by the creator that altered the nature of time and, in the person of Yeshua, defied human mortality and ordinary human understanding. The second is to proceed as a historian, as I am trying to do, separating what can be proved from what cannot. None of us can know if Yeshua was raised from the dead. What we can know is that his immediate followers believed he was, or at least said they believed it. Most Christians observe that belief, but to think that belief, no matter how firmly held, is

---

5. Mack, *Myth of Innocence*, 3, 4.

the same as knowledge is to confuse mythic understanding with historical understanding.

Believing the Resurrection. From its first recorded stages in the letters of Paul, as many as two decades before Mark, the Christos cult had extended Yeshua's unique Resurrection from the dead to all believers in it, offering the righteous the promise of revival into God's kingdom when it arrived on earth. The first sectarian conflict, that between Paul and the apostles remaining in Jerusalem, was over whether the promise pertained to Jews alone, or could be extended to other peoples without the need for male circumcision and obedience to the Mosaic law. The compromise they achieved might have broken belief in Yeshua as Messiah into two separate strands, one a reformed sect of Judaism centered in Jerusalem, the other a Hellenized mystery cult centered in Antioch or Rome. But history intervened, Titus destroyed the Temple, and the Pauline way subsumed the Jerusalem way.[6]

We have seen that the kerygma or article of faith had been circulating orally before Paul wrote it down in the decade of the 50s. I quoted its first section in chapter 1. Figure 8 is the full version with Paul's additions, arranged by lettering the elements of the creed.

FIGURE 8

For I handed on to you the most important thing that I also received:
A. *That the Anointed [Christos] died for our sins according to the scriptures,*
B. *and that he was buried,*
C. *and that he was raised on the third day according to the scriptures,*
D. *and that he appeared to Cephas, then to the Twelve.*
E. *Then he appeared to over five hundred brothers at one time, most of them remaining still, though some have fallen asleep.*
F. *Then he appeared to James, then to all the apostles.*
G. *Then last of all, because born at the wrong time, he also appeared to me.*

The Pauline kerygma (1 Corinthians 15.3–8)

---

6. Among the Jewish-Christian sects that developed after 70 CE, the best attested is a group called the Ebionites ("the poor ones") that lasted for several centuries. Though very little is known about them outside of condemnations by the early church fathers, they seemed to accept Yeshua as a human (not divine) reformer of the Law, traced their origin to his brother James (James the Just), and a lived an impoverished life.

A few explanatory notes are needed. Cephas (Peter) was one of the Twelve, but immediately after the Resurrection there were only eleven apostles including him; the Twelve has to be taken as a synonym for the apostles as a group. The appearance to over five hundred is not in the gospels; Paul is perhaps referring to the day of Pentecost in Jerusalem, the Jewish pilgrimage festival of Shavuot, fifty days after Passover (*pentekoste* is Greek for fiftieth). As related in chapter 2 of Acts, on that day God's spirit descended on the apostles in tongues of flame, witnessed by Jews from around the empire, though there is no mention there of an appearance by the resurrected Christos. The James cited must be the brother of Yeshua, since the two apostles named James would have been included in the appearance to the Twelve, but there no reference in the gospels or Acts to a separate appearance to James.

Laying the text out this way reveals three matters of significance: that the core belief was simple (A to C); that reading backward for support in the Hebrew scriptures was important to the tradition (A and C); that Paul considered proof of the Resurrection to be so crucial that he outlined all the appearances he had heard of (D to G). A few verses later he refers to the preaching of the apostles and concludes that the kerygma is uncontested in the movement: "No matter whether I or they, so we all proclaim and so you believed."

So we all proclaim and so you believed. This letter cannot be dated precisely, though 55 CE is a reasonable compromise, as I have said before. In any case it seems that chapter 15 represents the conviction of the original apostles and the oral tradition they started, which Paul received from them and from others. The mentions of the postmortem appearances of Yeshua are without detail and feel exaggerated. Five hundred brothers is clearly excessive, unless Paul means the witnesses at Pentecost, who were Jews but not brothers in belief; Acts (1.15) states that the "brothers" of the faith at the time numbered about 120. Paul makes no distinction between the appearances immediately after the Resurrection and his own vision on the road to Damascus, two years or more later. These problems are typical of the trouble we encounter when we take a rational approach to expressions of belief.

Mark gives even less information about the Resurrection appearances—he omits them entirely. The Young Man in the tomb has a great message for the women arriving to prepare Yeshua's body: he has risen. No information is given about how that happened, only that he is not here. The Young Man says, "But go, tell his disciples and Peter that he is going ahead of you into Galilee. You will see him there, as he told you" (16.7). Why does Mark not detail the manifestations? As we saw in chapter 2, Adela Collins suggests that the gospel was written when the tradition about the appearances was in the process of forming, when it "did not seem to be an integral part of the story of Jesus." Yeshua's own predictions of his death and resurrection do not mention any anticipated displays of his revived body. Mark's audience would know of the manifestations already, Collins holds, so it was necessary only to have the Young Man predict Yeshua's presence in Galilee. Mark stopped after the first part of the kerygma (died, buried, raised) and took the second part (appeared) for granted. Only after the next three gospels included the appearances did "the ending of Mark seem deficient," which led to the addition of the longer ending in the second century or later.[7]

Of course the absence of the corpse in Mark can also be explained in naturalistic terms: either Yeshua was not really dead, or he was and someone stole his body. The first option is a kind of Houdini trick: that a man could look dead on the cross, lie down for a while, then recover and claim he'd been resurrected. Yeshua had been accused of diabolic magic during his Galilean ministry, particularly by the scribes from Jerusalem ("He has Beelzeboul inside him and by the power of the chief of demons he expels demons," Mark 3.22), and playing dead for two nights and a day would fit into that conjuror's frame. In the second option accusation would focus on the apostles, as it does in Matthew (28.11–15); they had reason to take the body and claim that Yeshua had returned to life as he had predicted. Mark's ending did not anticipate such charges, and the subsequent evangelists thought they better correct it.

How they corrected it is a classic example of the disagreements among the gospels. It is why the Greek philosopher Porphyry around 270 CE accused them of complete invention. "The evangelists were fiction writers," he said in his tract *Against the Christians*, "not observers or eyewitnesses of the life of Jesus. Each of the four contradicts the other in writing his account of the events of his suffering and crucifixion." He disparaged the oral tradition as mythical, based on "secondhand reports" that combined details from "several crucifixions."[8] It's unlikely they made up all of it, but Porphyry was right about the contradictions. The

---

7. Collins, *Mark*, 800. Remember that the longer ending of Mark is not in the best ancient manuscripts, or it is marked in some way to question its authenticity.

8. Porphyry, *Adversus Christianos*, 11.12–15, in *Porphyry's Against the Christians*, 32–33.

basic story of the Resurrection is the same, but each evangelist tells it differently.

Mark 16. Just after dawn on Sunday, Mary of Magdala, Mary the mother of James, and Salome arrive at the tomb to find the stone rolled away, Yeshua's body gone, and a Young Man sitting on a stone inside. He tells them that Yeshua has risen, and they should tell Peter and the others he has gone before them to Galilee, where they will see him. The women leave the tomb and stand outside, trembling and afraid.

Matthew 28. About dawn on Sunday, Mary of Magdala and "the other Mary" (likely the mother of the apostle James) arrive at the tomb and witness an earthquake as a shining angel appears and rolls away the stone. The guards, struck with fear, "became as dead." The angel tells the women that Yeshua has been raised and they must tell the disciples to meet him in Galilee. As they run away, suddenly Yeshua stands in their path and repeats that the disciples should meet him in Galilee. The guards report the event to the chief priests, who bribe them to say that the disciples have taken the body away while they slept. That story became widely known among the Jews, Matthew writes, "as far as the present day." The eleven apostles go to Galilee and see Yeshua at a mountain location, "though some doubted." Yeshua then gives them authority to spread his message to all peoples.[9]

Luke 24. Very early Sunday three women followers discover the stone already rolled away; they enter the tomb and find it empty. Suddenly two dazzling angels declare that Yeshua has risen; the women report this to the apostles, who think the story "idle talk" and do not trust them. Luke identifies the women as "Mary of Magdala, Joanna, and Mary [the mother] of James." The same day, two unnamed disciples are walking to the village of Emmaus, "sixty stadia from Jerusalem" (about eleven kilometers or seven miles), when Yeshua joins them unrecognized. They discuss his death and the rumor of the Resurrection. Yeshua chides their slowness to understand that these events were foretold by the prophets. In the village near evening they press him to eat with them, and as he

---

9. Some scholars suspect that the conclusion of Matthew (28.19–20), containing the "great commission" to evangelize the nations (*ethne*, which can also mean gentiles or foreigners), is a gloss later tacked on to the end, chiefly because it contains the only Trinitarian statement in any of the gospels ("baptizing them in the name of the father, and of the son, and of the holy spirit"). Since the concept of the Trinity developed in the second century, and was not confirmed until the Council of Nicaea in 325, the formula appears anachronistic. It is necessary to note, however, that these verses appear in all the best ancient manuscripts.

breaks bread "their eyes were fully opened" to his identity and "he vanished from their sight." They return to Jerusalem, to the Eleven and the rest of the disciples, to find that the Lord has appeared to Simon. Suddenly Yeshua stands among them. They are terrified and "thought they saw a phantom." He shows his hands and feet and tells them to touch him; "a phantom does not have flesh and bones as I have." The disciples are still unconvinced, so he asks for something to eat; they give him part of a grilled fish and "he ate it in front of them." He opens their minds to understand the scriptures regarding the Messiah and tells them to proclaim the message to all nations. They are to wait in Jerusalem, where he will send "the promise of my Father to you." He takes them to Bethany and "was removed from them." They return to Jerusalem.

John 20–21. Early Sunday morning Mary of Magdala finds the stone moved away, and hurries to Peter and John to report the body is missing. The two apostles run to the tomb, find it empty, and go home, leaving Mary behind. Two angels in white appear in the tomb and ask why she is weeping. "They have taken my Lord away," she says, "and I do not know where they have laid him." Yeshua then appears and asks whom she seeks. Thinking he is the gardener, she begs him to tell her where the body is. Yeshua calls her by name and she recognizes him. "Do not touch me," he says, "because I have not yet ascended to the Father." He sends her to the disciples with the message that he is going to God. She tells them she has seen the Lord. That evening the disciples, "in fear of the Jews," are assembled behind locked doors when Yeshua appears among them and shows them his hands and side. They are filled with joy. Yeshua breathes on them and gives them the power to forgive sins. Thomas, not present at that time, refuses to believe Yeshua has risen. Eight days later Yeshua again appears through locked doors and directs Thomas to put his finger in the wounds of Yeshua's hands and his hand into the wound in Yeshua's side, and believe. Thomas calls him Lord and God. Yeshua says, "Because you have seen me you believe; happy are those who have not seen but have believed." Later, at the Sea of Tiberius (the Roman name for the Sea of Galilee), Peter goes fishing at night in the boat with Thomas and another disciple. In the morning Yeshua is on the shore and calls out, asking about the catch. They do not recognize him and say they caught nothing. He directs them to cast to the right side and they bring in a net loaded with fish. They recognize Yeshua and rush ashore to find a coal fire with fish and bread on it. Yeshua says, "Come and eat." After they dine, he tells Peter to care for his flock, predicts Peter's martyrdom, and asks him to follow him.

Acts of the Apostles 1. Luke makes an adjustment to the end of his gospel by saying that Yeshua showed himself many times to the apostles over a period of forty days before he ascended to the Father. They ask Yeshua if this is the time of the end, when "you restore the kingdom to Israel." He says it is not for them to know times or seasons which the Father has put in place. He tells them to remain in Jerusalem until the holy spirit comes to them, then to carry the message "to Jerusalem, and in all Judea and Samaria, and to the farthest part of the earth."

In addition to the desire to correct Mark, the differences in these versions are surely due to differences in the oral tradition. Some are relatively small variances, such as the names of the women at the tomb and their number, an earthquake, the number of angels, the presence of guards. Those are the kind of details that separate strands of oral transmission might learn differently. Some are larger matters: did Yeshua speak to Mary of Magdala, did she recognize him, did any apostles go into the tomb? The core belief that Yeshua was raised from the dead and showed himself alive to his followers before finally disappearing is present in all three of the later gospels and Acts, yet the manner of his postmortem appearances varies considerably.

Matthew has no Sunday-evening visitations to the apostles in Jerusalem; following Mark's lead, the Eleven go to Galilee to meet Yeshua, whose bodily manifestation is not described. Luke adds the evocative story of Emmaus and introduces the theme that the disciples cannot recognize Yeshua until he breaks bread; then he disappears before their eyes. His second appearance, to Peter alone, is only reported. On the third occasion, in the locked room in Jerusalem, he frightens the assembled disciples, who think he is a spirit. Then he displays his physicality, and eats a piece of fish to prove that he is human. In John he tells Mary of Magdala in the morning not to touch him, then in the evening suddenly appears in the locked room and shows his wounds. About a week on he proves the physicality of his resurrection to Thomas. Later, on the beach in Galilee, he is again not recognized until the miraculous catch of fish is hauled into the boat, then he eats with the apostles. By the time of Acts, it seems the tradition had developed that the Ascension took place forty days after the Resurrection, which forced its author to write that Yeshua appeared to the disciples during all of that period.

There are ways to explain the differences that stay within the parameters of belief: the events were so overwhelming that the participants were confused; different eyewitnesses, awestruck by the vision, told the tale as they best remembered it but differed; the details accumulated piecemeal over time; at the point of writing, the need for proof did not register the same way because each evangelist was responding to the requirements of his time and community. And, of course, it is possible the Resurrection did not happen at all, that the apostles were delusional, made up the details to certify that it did, and that the subsequent traditions followed different lines because the story was never invented comprehensively.

Speaking of the four gospels in general, Francis Watson holds that the choice is simple: either select one as a "historically reliable guide," or accept that the truth of the four "is not to be found at the literal-historical level." The fourfold gospel, he says, should mark "the end of all attempts to reconstruct the life of the historical Jesus."[10] We cannot harmonize the gospel accounts of the Resurrection because the details are not harmonious. Most retellings in sermons or literature collect bits from each of the sources, reading sideways by habit. Artistic representations have worked their way deeply into Western culture and influenced how people for centuries have thought of the Resurrection, Christians and non-Christians alike. Painters and sculptors, too many to list, tended to prize the most pictorial elements regardless of source or context: the blinding light, the dazzling angel, the meeting of Yeshua with Mary of Magdala, the journey to Emmaus, the supper there, doubting Thomas.

The more theatrical moments, especially those requiring dialogue, have worked their way into dramas up to the present. The record begins in the tenth century with the Quem Quaeritis trope, an elaboration with music of the visit of the women to the empty tomb that formed part of the Easter liturgy in some monasteries. (The phrase *Quem quaeritis in sepulchro*, Latin for "Whom do you seek in the tomb," is a variant of the angel's words in the synoptics or Yeshua's words in John.) The record continues with the biblical cycle plays of the middle ages, which were still being staged in England when Shakespeare was a boy, and up to the Hollywood epic films of the 1950s and 1960s. Almost all visual representations of the resurrected Yeshua find difficulty in defining his corporal presence. A good film of 2016 called *Risen*, directed by Kevin Reynolds—which incidentally uses the name Yeshua—avoids showing the Resurrection

---

10. Watson, *Gospel Writing*, 550. Barton discusses the point in *History of the Bible*, 211.

itself and solves the dramatic problem by having Yeshua look exactly the same as he did before. It even manages to make a striking scene out of the breakfast of fish on the shore.

Proving the Resurrection. The manifestations of the risen Messiah, taken all together, question themselves. He could be seen in bodily form, but on three occasions is at first not recognized. In three other cases he arrives or disappears like a ghost. Once he says do not touch me, twice he says touch me, once he breaks bread, once warms it, twice eats fish. In the most famous and gruesome case, he tells the apostle Thomas to enter his wounds, invade his body with finger and hand as if opening the injuries anew, to prove he is the crucified one, yet breathing. The only clear conclusion I can draw from the totality of the appearances is that the risen body is both alive and not alive. Walking through locked doors, being present without recognition, frightening the disciples like a phantasm, yet speaking in his own voice, physically touchable, eating meals—all those examples make Yeshua similar to his premortem self and at the same time demonstrably changed. He is not exactly a body and not exactly a spirit. He is a carnal apparition, a ghost with a body.

In some threads of Buddhism, after the body's death and before the spirit's rebirth into another body, the soul or spirit exists for a time in a transitional condition. In Sanskrit the condition is called *antarabhava* ("intermediate state"), but the notion is particularly strong in Tibet, where the term is *bardo*. In Tibetan theory, bardo is a liminal position between two lives on earth. It offers the spirit an opportunity for liberation toward the ineffable before a higher rebirth, but can be a danger for the unprepared soul and lead to a lower rebirth.

Without implying Buddhist influence, I see in the concept of bardo a way to understand Yeshua's resurrected state as reported in the gospels, and perhaps explain why they vary so much about its details. According to Acts, Yeshua lived on earth for forty days before he ascended to heaven. That's a long time to be in between one form of existence and another, and it's not surprising that Acts avoids specifics about his bodily form. I would put that statement in the category of events in Acts that are the result of legends that grew up near the end of the first century, similar to supernatural events related in the pagan myths of the Hellenistic world. The gospels make the period seem much shorter, a matter of no more than days. Matthew says nothing about the Ascension, though his final scene takes place on a mountain as soon as the apostles get to Galilee, and contains a sense of farewell. In a conflict with Acts, Luke's gospel implies that Yeshua departed from the apostles at Bethany almost immediately after the episode of eating the grilled fish, which occurred the evening of the Resurrection.[11] John also omits the Ascension, though he implies that Yeshua departed from the apostles after the breakfast of fish on the shore in Galilee, which was eight days after Easter.

The evangelists after Mark needed to provide proof of the Resurrection. The best they could do was emphasize that his followers saw Yeshua alive, heard him, touched him, ate with him. The tradition of the appearances that they inherited did not provide an account of the moment of the Resurrection nor a coherent image of what the apparitions were like. Since Yeshua's bardo-like state was taken to be unprecedented, there were no literary models to draw on that the evangelists could trust, whether classical or biblical. They tried to explain something that was inexplicable. It made sense, therefore, to keep the descriptions brief, to accent simple emotions like fear and joy, and to end Yeshua's transitional or intermediate period as soon as they could. None of them envisioned a resurrected man walking the earth for forty days.

It made even more sense not to relate it at all. To describe the supernatural in naturalistic terms is a great challenge for a writer. In *Paradise Lost* John Milton found a humanized Satan much more interesting than the abstract spirit of God. The evocations of the Passion and Crucifixion in the gospels are more convincing than those of the Resurrection because suffering is a shared human experience and rising from the dead is not. The more Yeshua's revived body is particularized, the less I want to accept the accounts as honest; in seeking verisimilitude, they lose the ring of truth. Trying to bolster belief in the reality of the Resurrection, the evangelists made it more difficult to believe.

Mark's empty tomb has great power on a number of levels. The absence of the body adds further mystery to the event of the Resurrection, suggesting that just as the characters in the story are unable to explain it, so neither is the evangelist. From a theological standpoint, the absence points to the Second Coming; the missing body is the nothing we have until the return of God's anointed, which will mark the re-creation of the world, or its ending. And from a biographical standpoint, the lack of a corpse or a restored man leaves the actuality of the Resurrection open, an ambiguous emptiness lying between human experience and divine

---

11. Luke 24.53 is clearly a moment of farewell, but the phrase at the end of the verse, "and was taken up into heaven," does not appear in all ancient manuscripts and is probably secondary.

mediation. To believe that Yeshua has been raised we must accept the Young Man's word. And who is he? Literally, he is an angel since he is a messenger, but even in that crucial case Mark makes him more human than the other evangelists do.

In omitting the postmortem appearances, merely instructing the apostles to meet Yeshua in Galilee, Mark kept the Resurrection out of the realm of evidence and in the realm of faith. He implies that you either believe in the Resurrection or you don't: ghost stories about a dead man eating fish or passing through solid walls are not likely to change your mind.

To repeat: what we can know is that the apostles believed in the Resurrection, or said they did, and then convinced others to believe. Miracles played a part in their proselytizing, if we can accept the legends related in Acts of the Apostles. Paul was transformed by his personal vision of Yeshua and converted others by argument, chiefly by reading backward to show that Yeshua had been predicted in the Hebrew scriptures. But preaching and argument go only so far; any number of self-proclaimed prophets did that. It was the Good Message itself that made the difference. The message was more than good—it was astounding, transformational: a promise of eternal life in exchange for trust in Yeshua as Messiah. It was especially attractive to some diaspora Jews who thought the Temple corrupt. It was also attractive to the "God fearers," gentiles who had tired of the pagan gods, attended the synagogues, and already held at least a partial belief in the God of Abraham, Isaac, and Jacob. A thriving new religion grows exponentially, as adherents make other adherents and circumstances allow their dispersion. The success of Christianity by the time of Mark had many causes. Ultimately, however, I suspect that most early converts believed not because they were convinced by the proof of the Resurrection but because they desperately *wanted* to believe in the possibility of salvation.

The post-Constantine church has rarely worried over what the contradictions in the gospel accounts of the Resurrection might imply, preferring to accept the article of faith over the notations of the evangelists. We can see this clearly in the first version of the Nicene Creed (figure 4, chapter 2), which ignores the appearances entirely and says only that Iesous "suffered, and on the third day he rose again." The manifestations of the walking Yeshua to the apostles were in the initial kerygma as Paul set it down. Why were they not mentioned in the formalized creed? The answer seems to be that belief was independent of proof. It may even be that the bishops who composed the creed in the fourth century felt that proof brought a divine mystery too close to human questioning and, following Mark's lead, thought it better to leave it out.

Help my distrust. At the time of Moses the archaic Hebrews *believed* that many gods existed; Yahweh demanded that they have *faith* only in him. He had chosen them as his people, and required that they respond by trusting in his protection and worship him alone. Put aside your concerns for those gods of the Canaanites, Ba'al Hermon, El, Moloch, he commanded; they are no longer relevant to you. "I am the Lord your God, who brought you out of the land of Egypt, out of the house of slavery; you shall have no other gods before me" (Exodus 20.2–3). I will make a contract with you, a covenant, a testament, based not on belief but trust.

Belief is one thing, faith a bigger thing. In ancient Greek thought belief is simply opinion (*doxa*) while faith is trust (*pistis*). I can believe my brother is a thief—maybe he is, I can't be sure—and yet have faith that he will pay back the money I lent him. As Slavoj Žižek puts it, faith is "the symbolic pact between the two of us, a binding engagement," something more than simply believing in gods or the existence of angels.[12] Faith is hope with a handshake: faith grants you the expectation of a beneficial reward based on the contract you signed when you said *credo*: I believe.

In Christianity the two concepts got merged: belief leads to faith, and faith reinforces belief. Paul believed in the Resurrection, and that belief gave him faith in the promise of salvation from his own death. He was sure God would keep his part of the bargain, if only Paul would keep his. In Mark, and in most of the New Testament, *pistis* is used for both belief and trust. When Yeshua asks someone to believe, he is not referring to *doxa*; it is not opinion he requires, but trust. He asks for trust in him before he completes the social contract (of healing, of the promise of the kingdom), but only because he is the delegate of Yahweh.[13] Trust in me, he says, and you trust in the Father; then all things are possible. Thus the social act of trust in Yeshua as patron of the poor becomes a theological act of trust in God. For that reason, in my translation of Mark I rendered all uses of *pistis* as "trust."

The developing church turned the meaning of *doxa* around and made orthodoxy (literally, correct opinion) a matter of faith. But we can still make the distinction. Unlike Paul, I can believe in the Resurrection

---

12. Žižek, *On Belief*, 109–10.
13. Morgan, *Roman Faith and Christian Faith*, details the uses of *pistis* in Mark, 348–65.

without having faith that it will bring me to heaven. And I can disbelieve in the Resurrection and yet have faith that Christianity's promise of heaven is true. Neither belief nor faith are fully rational: each is a state of mind based on untested premises. If I say I believe it is raining, you can check and determine that it is not, that my belief is wrong, though I can stubbornly persist in believing it is true. You shake your head and call me a fool. But if I say I believe in the Resurrection, you cannot check the veracity of my belief. You might share it, you might even have faith in its historicity and its promise of eternal life, but you cannot certify it. Both the belief and the faith remain unverifiable. We are all agnostics in the literal sense of the word: unknowing.

Why would I continue to believe it is raining when you have shown it is not? Because I *feel* inside me that it is raining. Maybe I smell rain in the air, maybe the sky is dark gray, maybe my knee aches. In other words, I perceive internally the phenomenon of precipitation, though I cannot explain its source. That is not a mental state but an emotional one, and I have permitted the emotion to obscure my ability to observe the weather. I have allowed a subjective state to overwhelm an objective event.

I said in the previous section that either you believe in the Resurrection or you don't, but perhaps it is not so simple a binary. Perhaps belief in the Resurrection, or in rain, can be graphed on a Doubt Scale with absolute belief at the top and total disbelief at the bottom. That would appear to be the meaning of the passage in Mark (9.23–24) about the father who begs Yeshua to heal his epileptic son. When challenged to accept that "everything is possible for someone who trusts," the father shouts, "I do trust; help my distrust." That phrase, which Augustine of Hippo took to heart, sets *pistis* against its antonym *apistia*, trust against distrust, belief against disbelief, and suggests it is possible to believe sometimes or with varying degrees of assurance, sliding up or down the Doubt Scale. Belief might be considered a shifting emotional state that depends on subjective probabilities: what will be the benefit for me if I accept an unverifiable thing as true? What will happen if I'm wrong? There can easily be a spectrum of credences that incorporates the kind of analysis we make when betting on a horse race, a decision that is usually both intellectual and affective.[14] The "leap of faith" that is necessary to have trust in a promise is a leap from rationality to emotionality.

14. The notion that belief can exist on a scale of credence is taken from Bayesian epistemology, based on probability theory. See Peterson, *An Introduction to Decision Theory*.

Betting brings to mind Pascal's famous wager. You my not fully believe in the Christian message, he wrote, you may think the whole thing made up, but it's better to act as if you do believe. If there is no final judgment, no heaven and hell to worry over, you haven't lost much by leading a righteous life. But if it turns out to be true, and you've lived immorally and are sent to hell for eternity, then you have lost a great deal. The odds may be even, but the punishment/reward ratio is heavily in favor of belief. That still leaves the problem of acquisition. How do you gain belief if you do not have it? Pascal held that the rational mind that denies belief can be conquered by force of habit. If you doubt, he says, do what others have done: "they acted as if they believed, took holy water, had masses said, etc. This will make you believe naturally and mechanically" (*vous abêtira*, will debase you, or make you like animals; i.e., you will act on instinct).[15] Do the required rituals and belief will come to you, or at least move you up the Doubt Scale. Perform belief and you will find it.

Not many Christian churches would agree that an emotionless outward show of faith, which is a political and social action, substitutes for inner spiritual commitment, despite the long history of their demanding Sunday attendance regardless of true belief. Since we can never know for sure what is in the mind or heart of others, we have to judge them by what they say and do. But Pascal is certainly right that belief needs to be exercised, just as the larger faith needs to be nurtured. Public shouts of "I believe!," often used in parody of the Christian experience of conversion, are common in charismatic churches that seek to raise belief by generating intense emotions of love, fear, community, hatred of evil, awe of divine power, or hope of reward. But rhythmic sermonizing, chant, mantras of repetitious prayer, music, song, dance, incense, unusual costumes, processions, candles, bells, stained glass, paintings, sculptures, ancient languages, eating the bread, drinking the wine—at least some of these emotional triggers have been part of most Christian sects over the centuries. They assist belief or strengthen it, but they have to be repeated often in rituals and ceremonies, preferably weekly, or their power will fade.

It looks to me that belief is intimately involved with emotion. We can make an intellectual decision to believe, but for belief to take effect it must be felt. It must make us want to rise up and shout, even if, as in the mainline churches, the shout is ritualized into hymn or prayer. The emotional side of the equation can be deceptive, of course, even dangerous;

15. Pascal, *Pensées*, 44.

martial music in a massed parade of soldiers can stir up a population to an unjust war. Similarly, the music and the performance of worship in church can in the moment move us to feel we believe in something our minds may later dismiss as a false impression. To take hold of us fully, the mental experience must be united with the emotional experience.

There is yet another side to the question. Many people believe because they have inherited a tradition of belief; they belong to a family or social group that for generations has believed, and its members feel an obligation to maintain the allegiance. In the history of Christianity this has led to sectarianism and sometimes to ethnic or cultural tribalism, where the gathering of the community around the details of belief is more important than the belief itself, forgetting that its major premises are actually shared across the divide (Catholic vs. protestant, Anglican vs. Methodist, and so on). Individual members of the group may or may not have faith in their hearts but continue to believe, or say they believe, and follow the established protocols for the sake of the larger social identity. This is a form of deferred or citational belief, in which the responsibility to believe is transferred to the group. The citation that others believe frees individuals from having to investigate the nature or degree of their own trust in the message.[16] It is not Pascal's performance of belief in the hope that belief will come, though there is a performative element in the deferral, neither is it full belief with an emotional component.

We might compare this type of belief with that of eight- or nine-year-old children who have begun to doubt the existence of Father Christmas or Santa Claus, but continue to believe in a determined manner because they want the myth to be true, or because they think their parents want them to believe. And of course there is a practical benefit to the belief, if Santa fills their stockings for Christmas morning. That seems to be one lesson from Pascal: will yourself to believe and you will believe. Perhaps this works sometimes, perhaps not; but it does recognize that a proclamation of belief, or following the prescribed protocol associated with a belief system, can hold your place in the community of belief regardless of personal doubt. And for many people it is enough to publicly demonstrate that they are fulfilling an obligation.

If, as happened to me long ago, you eat the bread of thanksgiving in the midst of fellowship and heightened public emotion and still feel an

---

16. The concept of citational belief comes from Michel de Certeau, though he treats it in a different context. See Certeau, *The Practice of Everyday Life*, 186–89, and "What We Do When We Believe."

outsider, separate from rather than joined to the community of saints, you have slid to the bottom of the Doubt Scale and there is no longer a reason to keep the faith. Instead, I suppose, you make up for the loss by writing a book such as this one, thinking about the Good Message instead of trusting in it.

Saved. I'm confident that the writer of the gospel of Mark believed in the Resurrection of Yeshua despite his omitting any representation of it. What is absolutely certain is that Paul believed in it and had trust—*pistis* again—that it guaranteed his salvation. His own vision of Yeshua on the way to Damascus was all the proof he needed. As a Pharisee before his conversion, Paul would have already believed in the resurrection of the bodies of the righteous when God's reign was established. He argued that Yahweh gave his first example of this in raising Yeshua from the dead, and concluded that this opened the possibility to all who trusted in the Good Message. As he writes in Romans (10.9-10), ". . . for if you accept by saying with your mouth, Lord Iesous, and trust in your heart that God raised him out of the dead, you will be saved [or rescued]. Indeed in the heart trust leads to right living, but in the mouth acceptance leads to safety [or rescue]."

Saved from what? Historically, Christianity as an organized religion was based on the premise of salvation from death and, despite major changes in the details and practice, continues to work the same way. Its great proselytizing accomplishment lay in its explanation of why life is hard: it is a test and, to put it bluntly, if you pass you will get a prize. To summarize Simone Weil, Christianity succeeded because it offered not only an explanation of suffering but a reward for it.

But if we go back to the only documents we have from the first generation after the Crucifixion, it is remarkably difficult to construe from Paul's letters what his expectation was, other than a form of union with God and his Anointed One. The developing church later concluded that Paul meant salvation from an eternity without God, which is the simplest definition of what would ultimately be called hades or hell. Paul could just as well have meant salvation from oblivion, the fate of unbelievers. But—and here I speak as a reader, not a theologian—I do not find in the seven authentic letters of Paul[17] any clear indication of what an afterlife

---

17. Most scholars accept that Paul wrote Galatians, Romans, 1 and 2 Corinthians, Philemon, Philippians, and 1 Thessalonians, while the authorship of 2 Thessalonians, Ephesians, and Colossians is disputed. The letter to Titus and the two to Timothy are pseudepigraphic (deliberately ascribed to Paul's name for the sake of his authority, a

might be like, whether as an eternity of happiness or of suffering, or even if the rescue from death would be eternal. If our visual imaginings of hell as fire and torment were created by Dante, supplemented by Hieronymus Bosch, could heaven have been an invention of Paul's? The word he uses, *ouranos*, is a catchall that can mean the heavenly powers or simply the sky. In Jewish tradition, the celestial realm was the location of God and his angels, not a place for mortals. Perhaps a few humans might be elevated there, like Moses and Elijah, but the usual expectation was that Yahweh's reign, when it came, would be a kingdom on earth led by an earthly king of the Jews.

Mark also uses the word *ouranos* in both senses at different times. Concerned with the life of the man Yeshua, Mark does not treat the connotations of commitment to the Good Message, but he implies throughout that trust in it will bring his audience to an enlightened understanding and a hope of their rescue through the agency of the Anointed. His book is a promissory note, though the nature of the promise is left almost unspoken. I assume that Mark and his community knew at least some of Paul's letters, and they would certainly have known the articles of belief; Mark was writing for a group that had accepted the Pauline premise and had been instructed in its consequence. From this standpoint the evangelist did not need to detail what the result of declaring trust in Yeshua would bring; he needed only to provide a reasonable ground for holding on to the trust.

My object here is not to enter into the debate about the meaning or nature of the afterlife, or to analyze Paul's or Mark's understanding of salvation, areas that have been only too well covered in the history of Christianity. I'm not competent to treat those subjects, and to be honest they frighten me a little after all those hellfire sermons from priests and chastisements from nuns I endured in my youth. I'm content to leave them to others.[18] Instead I would like to think about the meaning of commitment, what Paul in the passage above calls *homologeo*: acceptance, declaration, proclamation, what the churches would call the confession

---

common practice in antiquity). The letter to the Hebrews, once ascribed to Paul, is also anonymous. It was probably written in the decade of the 60s, before Mark and before the destruction of Jerusalem. It contains one of the earliest expressions of the idea that Yeshua can grant "eternal salvation" to believers in him (5.9). The phrase may derive from Isaiah 45.17, where it refers not to personal salvation but to the salvation (or rescue) of the people of Israel.

18. On the history of concepts of the afterlife, see Ehrman, *Heaven and Hell*; and Finney, *Resurrection, Hell and the Afterlife*.

of faith. To do that I turn to another contemporary philosopher, Alain Badiou, whose *Saint Paul: The Foundation of Universalism* is one of the great recent books on Christianity, albeit written by an atheist.

Badiou sees Paul as the ultimate example of faithful commitment. Having declared belief in the Resurrection, he chose thereafter to define himself entirely by it. For the world to change from the command of evil, exemplified by the imperial Roman death machine, Paul thought it necessary to pronounce that as Yeshua defeated death, so death can be defeated by everyone who accepts the legitimacy of the Resurrection. The Roman power as crucifier will change to God's power as resurrector. The crucial verse is from Galatians (3.28): "There is neither Jew nor Greek, there is neither slave nor free, there is neither male and female, for all of you are one in Iesous the Anointed." If everyone is equal in sin regardless of birth or circumcision, then everyone is equally eligible for salvation through belief.

But Badiou the philosopher does not believe in the Resurrection as fact, or that Yeshua continues to exist in a godlike form. What meaning can Paul's commitment have for nonbelievers? They can make their declaration and follow it, a commitment based not on belief in an unverifiable event but on the "event" of commitment itself. If we cannot accept the myth of Christianity, Badiou writes, we must abandon "the content of the fable" and examine what is left. What is left is this: Paul as subject erased his selfhood and redefined himself by allegiance "to an event whose only 'proof' lies precisely in its having been declared by a subject." It's not whether the Resurrection is true that matters; what matters is Paul's *declaration* that it is true.

Badiou admires Paul exactly because he remained faithful to a premise that could not be proved. Truth is subjective, yes, but the important thing is commitment to the subjective truth. "Fidelity to the declaration is crucial," Badiou says, "for truth is a process, and not an illumination."[19] This is not postmodern relativism, because Badiou insists that even though what he calls "truth" is subjective, it is still necessary to be faithful to our declaration of what we accept as true. Truth is a process, just as belief is a process, and both require ongoing renewal and practice. "There can be truth only in the situation where truth insists," Badiou writes in another context, "because nothing transcendent to the situation is given to us."[20]

19. Badiou, *Saint Paul*, 5–6, 14–15.
20. Badiou, *Theoretical Writings*, 122.

For a practicing Christian, Badiou's equation of subjective truth with belief in the Resurrection is not likely to be acceptable, and I am not naïvely pretending that declaration to a subjective order is the same as declaration to an objective order. But we must all be honest here: the Resurrection of Yeshua is not objective fact. It is a matter of *pistis*, trust. No one can know positively, without question, without equivocation on the Doubt Scale, that Yeshua rose from the dead or that his rising offers us all a rescue from death. What we do know is that Paul believed it, and so thoroughly that he gave his life to that acceptance.

Mark accepted it too, and wrote out a biographical rationale for that belief, offering his work to the growing number of first-century followers. Yet—and for me this is the most distinctive aspect of the earliest gospel—Mark shows again and again just how hard it is to trust fully in the Good Message. The dullard apostles, stubborn in their misunderstanding; the demanding Galilee followers, accepting help without giving much back; the shouts of Hosanna in Jerusalem turning to shouts of Crucify Him; the priests and Sanhedrin preferring their collusion with Rome over a chance of reform; the last apostle betraying his teacher while eating with him; the first apostle denying he knows the accused; Pilate killing off the threat before it could grow: almost everything in Mark is stacked against belief. Yeshua met failure of trust at turn after turn. And then, the empty tomb, where the absence of a body stands for the Resurrection and shows in a final few lines just how hard belief in the impossible can be. To the women at the tomb the claim of a risen dead man is above all a shock, and they are afraid.

Calculating faith. I have done a good deal of the work for this book on the top floor of a fairly new library at Trinity College Dublin, in an attractive room with a large skylight and a wall of windows. The floor houses the open-shelf books on Christianity, and some of the most important works on the New Testament sit at my back, begging for use. The building is called the Ussher Library and is named after James Ussher (1581–1656), one of the earliest graduates of Trinity College, which was founded by Queen Elizabeth in 1592 as the first English colonial protestant university. (It is no longer English, colonial, or protestant, though some citizens of the Republic of Ireland have doubts.) Ussher, a fervent reformer, became Anglican Archbishop of Armagh and Primate of all Ireland. He was also a serious scholar of early Christianity.

But he is remembered for one infamous accomplishment: he calculated the day God created the world. "Which beginning of time," he wrote, "according to our Chronologie, fell upon the entrance of the night preceding the twenty third day of *Octob.* in the year of the Julian Calendar, 710." Converted to our standard Gregorian calendar, that is the year 4004 BCE. He acknowledged that a certain amount of intelligent guesswork played a role in choosing the precise day, but he was confident about the year 4004. Since Ussher's chronology was often printed in editions of the King James Bible, it achieved for some time a quasi-doctrinal status in the protestant tradition. What is more interesting than the date itself, however, is how he computed it. For the first books of the Old Testament he relied chiefly on the genealogies, adding all the begats and lifespans together. But later books are inconsistent about genealogy, and the Hebrew writings stop after Ezra and Nehemiah, about 400 years before Yeshua. So Ussher compared the biblical numbers he could deduce with historical research. For example, he accepted the extraordinary longevity of the patriarchs given in the Torah, but blended dates from the book of Kings with historical documents to establish the year of Nebuchadnezzar's death. He knew that the date of Anno Domini 1 was wrong, recognizing that Yeshua was born during the reign of Herod the Great (from Matthew) and that Herod died in 4 BCE (from Josephus).

Although Ussher was a churchman of his time in thinking the Old Testament literally true, the inspired word of God, he was also a thinker of his time in applying systematic methods to that word. Whatever his flaws, he was one of the first scholars to employ a critical approach to the separate texts of the Old Testament, recognizing when the genealogies or regnal dates had to be adjusted. To put it another way, he accepted the bible as inerrantly factual, but that did not stop him from investigating the nature of its fact.

There is another twist to the tale. A longstanding eschatological tradition equated the six days of creation with six thousand years for the earth's potential existence, based on an overly literal reading of the verse "one day with the Lord is like a thousand years" (2 Peter 3.8). If Yeshua was born in the year of Herod's death, then the Messiah came exactly four thousand years after creation, leaving two thousand years after his birth as the date of doomsday (which would have been 1996 CE, not Y2K as many people feared). Was Ussher pushed to arrive at a predetermined conclusion, his detailed calculations a mask for an inherent bias? It's possible, though I doubt it, chiefly because Herod reigned from 37 BCE—Yeshua's birth could have happened any time from then to Herod's death and still be within Matthew's time frame.

Ussher's chronology was published in London in Latin (1650), and in English as *The Annals of the World* (1658). It was not the first attempt to fix the age of the earth through the bible, and others of the era achieved remarkable proximity to Ussher's dates,[21] but Ussher had wide influence because of his account of method. For its time, the chronology was a remarkable achievement. Though he could not have intended it, his application of critical logic to the holy book anticipated the rationalist methods of the nineteenth century as applied to the relationship between archeology and biblical study. At the opposite pole, his chronology is still used today by anti-Darwinists and biblical literalists to deny the evidence of evolution.

Creationists aside, to most people now the chronology looks ridiculous. Yet it is dangerous to fall into the trap of presentism, assuming that because we now know so much more about the age of the earth, not to mention the age of the universe, Ussher was as foolish as an alchemist, sailing an impossible voyage. Even by scientific standards, his only major error was to equate mythic knowledge with historical knowledge. This is a problem inherent in the study of the sacred scriptures of any living religion, where the frame of the ancient writing, its fabulist or theoretical mode, has guided the faith into a present era that sees the world through different conceptual eyes. Sacred texts that have been successful over time tend to be elastic about their meaning, permitting or even encouraging reinterpretation without altering the words, or without altering them very much, just as secular poetic texts, such as those of Sophocles or Shakespeare, can be renewed to fit changing circumstances and new systems of thinking. When placed under the interpretative control of the guardians of a particular sect or cult, however, the openness of sacred texts tends to get closed, their meaning restricted to an authorized doctrine. Nonetheless, over time the texts remain available for further renewal and revaluation.

In both rabbinical and Christian traditions, John Barton notes, the bible was considered "a special book that required special principles of interpretation."[22] As a holy object it was set aside from other texts, literary or historical, reserved like a sacred vessel from contamination by the

---

21. Similar seventeenth-century chronologies were made by John Lightfoot, Joseph Scaliger, Johannes Kepler, and Isaac Newton. Ussher's attempt had been preceded by Jose ben Halafta and Bede. Gould reviews the Ussher chronology and its background in "Fall in the House of Ussher."

22. Barton, *History of the Bible*, 339.

hands of the vulgar. The chief method of interpretation was doctrinal exegesis, a practice of textual analysis designed to interpret difficult passages or troubling narratives according to an orthodox point of view. As we have seen, the habit of reading backward by Christian exegetes, starting with Paul and flourishing in the Middle Ages, construed Old Testament texts in a metaphoric or allegorical fashion to make them prefigure an aspect of the New Testament. The interpretation was almost always in the control of the theologically committed.

Biblical scholarship in the late nineteenth and early twentieth centuries began a radical break from earlier exegetical customs. Rationalizing or demythologizing the scriptures was at heart a process of applying to biblical writings analytical methods that are applicable to any ancient writing, treating the bible not as a special book but as another set of texts subject to code breaking. The process has continued to the present; now, most scholarly commentators on the gospels who are believers use the same methods as those who are doubters, despite reaching different conclusions. Though many priests and ministers also learn about these methods in seminaries and divinity schools, there has been resistance from the pulpit in promulgating them to the faithful, perhaps out of an understandable anxiety that historizing one aspect of the bible might lead to questioning its entirety.

Christianity has traditionally tiptoed around the problem by claiming that the bible is not only different from other books, but that certain matters contained in it are revelations, mysteries of God's otherness incapable of human understanding. In the New Testament, the virgin birth of Yeshua, his calling by God, the miracles, the Resurrection, the appearances, the Ascension: we cannot expect to comprehend such events because they are not human in origin but divine. The events may be mythic in expression, but since they came from God they are true.

Faith lends itself to mythmaking, just as skepticism lends itself to history writing. But whose purpose is served by pretending that mythic understanding is equivalent to historical understanding? The churches would be truer to their mission and the faithful truer to their faith if they acknowledged that aspects of Mark's gospel are mythological in both senses of the word, as legend and as belief propaganda. The same can be said of all the gospels, and that admission would actually help in understanding the works as religious documents. It would not mean that all aspects of the Good Message, as Mark first set it down, are corrupted or inevitably false. It would simply mean conceding that Mark wrote in a world context that did not make the same distinctions between fable and reality that we now make.

From this standpoint, Christianity, built on belief in the Resurrection as fact, has a shaky premise at its core. The Resurrection is not historical fact, and in the context of Christian history can be proved as fact only by a Second Coming. If that happens, if Yeshua descends on the clouds of heaven to establish a new kingdom, then those alive on earth will know that God anointed him for his short mission in ancient Palestine and really did raise him from the dead. In the meantime, what Christians have—as Badiou said of Paul—is the *declaration* that the Resurrection is fact. Its "truth," in other words, lies in its having been declared to be true.

We will never get beyond Mark to the historical Yeshua, or know what Yeshua considered to be his ultimate mission, or understand in what sense he thought he was the Messiah or the son of God. What we have is the sum of what Mark made of those topics, as a writer of his own time dealing with the sources at his disposal in a movement that was only forty years old. We should be able to recognize that the earliest record of the prophet from Nazareth is not a tale compete and reliable in itself, caught as it is between two modes of knowledge, the factual and the fictive.

7

Tragedy and Epic

VLADIMIR: We'll hang ourselves tomorrow. [*Pause.*] Unless Godot comes.
ESTRAGON: And if he comes?
VLADIMIR: We'll be saved.

—SAMUEL BECKETT, *Waiting for Godot*

YET THERE ARE SPACES in human life where myth and history regularly combine: in dream and imagination and memory. That's where art enters, since art both replicates the world and reinvents it. Art and its twin, entertainment, make possible the interruption of normal time and place for the sake of diversion, understanding, and the transforming emotions of wonderment, laughter, and awe. Great films, novels, plays, and poems, overwhelming music and dance, or paintings and sculptures, can manage, sometimes despite their creators and their era, to give us, when we are receptive, the experience of stepping outside ourselves and the mundane concerns that fasten like leeches onto our lives. It's not permanent, this suspension of the physical; we have to put down the book, leave the theater, look away from the image, turn off the music, and reenter the ordinary. But for a time, if we allow it, we can be sent elsewhere.

Human beings come equipped with the ability to analyze what is and to imagine what is not. I don't know why the second facility is useful from an evolutionary standpoint, but it has allowed us to wander in our minds and discourse to other worlds, concocting gods and monsters, imagining orders of being that we desire or fear. The American novelist

Samuel R. Delany has said that his task is "the incantatory naming of nonexistent objects" as he creates planets and realms that do not exist but might. It isn't only in science fiction that artists rename the objects of the earth and name their imagined duplicates. Art in general seeks that, helping us to calculate or understand how and why we exist and what we should do with the short time we have. The moral function of art—how to behave in the world—is usually attached to its aesthetic function, if only indirectly.

This may have been true from the earliest examples of human creation. In the Western tradition the two most compelling forms of literature from the ancient world, the tragic play and the epic poem, set out to investigate how men and women should act when under duress, and what the consequences of their choices might be. Classical Greek tragedy, which flourished during the height of Athenian power, was written chiefly between the final repulsion of the Persian empire by Athens (the battle of Salamis, 480 BCE) and the defeat of Athens by Sparta (the end of Peloponnesian War, 404 BCE).[1] Framed by these major political events, the tragic poets investigated the responsibilities of power, the duties of citizens, and the relationship of people to the spiritual or unseen powers that were thought to order their lives. If the surviving plays of Aeschylus, Sophocles, and Euripides are representative, Greek tragedy was concerned again and again with the moral state of great figures whose actions lead to personal disaster with social consequences. Athenian tragedy was a communal form, performed publicly during festival periods in the city and supported financially by wealthy citizens in a system of semi-voluntary taxation. It was based on a shared mythology and offered instances of proper communal behavior through positive and negative examples. Though the three surviving dramatists differ significantly in approach, their common theme is the need for reform, whether personal, familial, or collaborative.

The epics of *The Iliad* and *The Odyssey*, which predate the tragedies by some four centuries, contain a similar emphasis on appropriate behavior in an era of embattled existence. Though their immediate subject is virile endeavor in war and its aftermath, the epics judge their characters and events by social standards based on the consequences of individual

---

1. Standard dates for the extant tragedies run from Aeschylus' *The Persians* (472 BCE) to Euripides' *The Bacchae* (405 BCE). The surviving texts, however, constitute only a small portion of the total output of tragedies performed in Athens during that period.

action. Gods and goddesses choose sides and have favorites and influence outcomes, so that a supernatural element or divine overseer recurrently affects human affairs, but in the end it is personal choice—honorable behavior in line with acceptable social morality—that delivers success or failure. Ascribed since antiquity to a poet named Homer, the epics were composed orally by singers over time for public or aristocratic performance and later written down. They are usually dated toward the end of the eighth century BCE. Their mythic material, however, is much older, with its roots in Mycenaean culture of the Bronze Age, perhaps as distant as 1200 BCE, the traditional date of the start of the Trojan War.

Both the Greek epics and Greek tragedies were composed to be performed before audiences in an oral culture, as was the case with almost all ancient poetic texts. That they share this circumstance with the earliest gospel is not surprising, but they share much more, as a number of New Testament scholars have advocated. Unlike some of those commentators, I do not contend that Mark's book belongs to the genre of epic or tragedy; such an overarching claim is not helpful in understanding the gospel as art or as proclamation. It should be clear by now that I think Mark is essentially a biographical work that draws on other conventional forms from Hebrew and Greek. Based on a resilient oral tradition of belief, it is a new literary genre that its ancient manuscripts call the Good Message. But there is no doubt that Mark's gospel is attuned to epic and tragedy. Whether the evangelist was conscious of the similarity, whether the backdrop of prior Greek literature rose to the level of influence, are hypothetical questions that resolve nothing. Instead of an argument over genre, in this chapter I propose simply to highlight the ways that epic and tragedy can help us understand Mark better.

The tragic mode. Thinking of tragedy as a mode rather than a genre it makes it possible to include work that does not have the form of dramatic tragedy, whether enacted or read. By the tragic mode I mean a method of representing the world that accents the death of a single good or noble person in a plaintive manner. The meaning of life is that it ends, Kafka said, and that is the philosophy of classical tragedy. How the end comes about, and how the protagonist meets that end, are its ostensible subjects. Just as comedy foregrounds life in all its bodily flaws and frustrating absurdities while celebrating the continued generation of those absurd bodies, so tragedy sees death as the ultimate injury and its inevitability a cause for anguish. Classical comedy accents the survival of the species and likes to end with dance, song, and coupling in the marriage bed. Tragedy accents the termination of the individual and tends to end with elegy, mourning, and the earth bed. Farts and fart jokes are out of place in tragedy; in comedy they are, as it were, fundamental.

As we have seen, Mark gives plenty of attention to the body and its functions or malfunctions: food, wine, blood, epilepsy, blindness, deafness, skin disease, disablement, demons inside people, even a reference to defecation in the latrine (7.19). The book is hardly a comedy, though the first half suggests a heroic figure whose growing fame might in other circumstances lead to a happy conclusion. When the story turns to its downward action the protagonist's own body becomes the center of attention, leading to the extremity of bodily humiliation and pain the Romans could devise, then to the battered and entombed corpse, and ultimately to its absence with an expectation of the damaged body's return. Mark's concern with corporeality shapes his hero's rise and fall, and comprises the tragic action. The structure of Mark as I diagrammed it in a triangle (chapter 4, figure 6) is the rhythm of tragedy. In fact, my triangular model is borrowed from nineteenth-century dramatic criticism and could be used to outline the action of many plays and prose fictions from antiquity to the present.[2]

Mark starts his book with the hero's maturity as he begins his journey. A Greek tragedy, on the other hand, begins near the end the story, usually on the day of the protagonist's death. Sophocles' *Oedipus the King* (c. 429 BCE) was Aristotle's model of the structure, chiefly because he admired the plot. Oedipus, the king of Thebes, is already at his high point in the first scene, but his power is threatened by a plague that is decimating the city. According to the blind prophet Tiresias, the plague persists because the killer of Laius, the former king, lives within the community, polluting it ritually and actually; if civic life is to be whole again, he must be discovered and cast out. Look inside yourself, Tiresias tells the king, but Oedipus is too proud, too blind, to consider the possibility that he is the criminal.

The dramatic climax is directly connected to self-knowledge. The action moves Oedipus from ignorance to insight, its turning point (Aristotle's *peripeteia*) occurring when at last the protagonist understands the truth about his birth and the horror of what he has done. Aristotle's term

---

2. The diagram I use is a variation of the "Freytag Pyramid," devised by Gustaf Freytag in 1863 to analyze the five-act dramatic structure as introduction, rise, climax, fall, and catastrophe. It can be applied to conventional three-act structures as well, and remains the basic model for contemporary Hollywood screenplays.

for the plot revelation that accompanies the turning point is *anagnorisis* (literally, to make known), usually translated as recognition.³ Knowing the full story at last, Oedipus blinds and exiles himself as punishment for having failed to see beyond his pride into the truth of his life. He knows the need for punishment is absolute; that he acted in ignorance does not matter. He killed his father, he had sex and children with his mother, Jocasta: together these constitute a grave mistake (*hamartia*). He has violated two of the most absolute codes of tribal identity, patricide and maternal incest. No god or exterior power is needed to exact punishment; Oedipus, ruler of the city, is the cause of the civic infection and must take revenge on himself. Death would be relief but insufficient. He must instead endure his remaining days as a wandering blind beggar, an exile from the society he has led, and all other society as well.

While the action and purpose are obviously different, the parallels to Mark are notable. First there is the emphasis on secrecy and ignorance. Oedipus' true identity, concealed from him from birth, connects with the Messianic secret and the larger theme of withholding Yeshua's full identity. Yeshua's growing awareness of his mission on earth—or his acceptance of it, if you prefer—reaches a point of clarification or *anagnorisis* at the Transfiguration and at Caesarea on the road to Jerusalem. Thereafter, like Oedipus, Yeshua recognizes his end as inevitable and goes about triggering it in Jerusalem. He has committed no heinous mistake or sin (*hamartia* is the word in Mark, as in Aristotle), but on a purely human level his provocations in the face of the Jewish establishment lead directly to his condemnation and death. From Aristotle's standpoint, that is a mistake and it brings catastrophe. Yeshua has not only provoked retaliation, he has voluntarily submitted to it, as Oedipus submits to his punishment. In terms of human life the Crucifixion is a tragic fall, in Christian theology it is a glorious self-sacrifice. Whichever way we consider Yeshua's death, in Mark it is a counterpart to the end of classical tragedy, with Mark's final chapter leaving the women at the tomb, who stand like the chorus of elders of Thebes after the catastrophe, struck in fear and awe at incomprehensible events.

Pointing out that the structure and some of the themes of Mark are similar to those of a tragedy is not the same as saying the gospel is a tragedy. Despite his unsettling final chapter, Mark's overarching narrative

---

3. Aristotle's discussion of tragedy in the work now called *Poetics* is a sketchy and incomplete treatment that may have been put together from a set of lecture notes. I rely on the translation and commentary by Else, *Aristotle's Poetics*.

directs us toward hope of rehabilitation and rescue, qualities uncommon in classical tragedy or in most later models of the form. But the parallels go beyond issues of structure and theme to the heart of tragic action, which normally represents a conflict between irreconcilable forces. The latest book to claim tragic status for Mark makes conflict its central argument. Adam Wright, drawing on Hegel's notion that collision is the essence of tragedy, argues that Yeshua is exemplified by his deliberate clashes with the established order. In the first part of the gospel he provokes the scribes and Pharisees by healing on the Sabbath, dining with tax collectors and sinners, and arguing about the meaning of the Torah, the necessity of food laws, and ritual purification. These actions appear to be deliberate and, Wright thinks, are not historical events but literary effects designed to build a basis for the eventual confrontation with the Judean authorities. He puts the miracles in the same category: striking deeds that call attention to Yeshua's singularity and his disregard for contemporary Jewish conventions. No need to believe the miracles were actual, since the evangelist used them as further incitements against the corrupt Temple state.

The second part of the gospel more clearly fits the pattern of tragedy. We have seen already how Yeshua's provocations in the Temple and his testimony in the two trials, when taken together with his predictions to the apostles of his imminent suffering and death, combine to make his execution inevitable and expected. Wright notes that Mark presents Yeshua's actions in the Temple as premeditated.[4] On his first visit (it seems he had never been there before) he merely looks around, observing the practices. When he returns the next day, after working up his anger at the barren fig tree, he immediately overturns the tables of the money changers and dove sellers, prompting the chief priests to plot his death (11.15–18).

The provocations that follow in chapter 12 are not aggressive but fortify the desire of the authorities to kill him. They consist of teaching that indirectly condemns the priests in the parable of the leased vineyard, besting the Pharisees and Herodians over Caesar's image on a denarius, shaming the Sadducees about the resurrection of the body, a discussion about the true meaning of the commandments, and a condemnation of the hypocrisy of the scribes. Pharisees, Herodians, Sadducees, scribes: Mark is usually imprecise about the Temple institution but here is careful

---

4. A. Wright, *Of Conflict and Concealment*, 85.

to nominate the separate divisions of the Judean establishment, showing that Yeshua has enraged all of them. The chapter ends with the incident of the widow's mite at the Temple treasury, when Yeshua implies that true sacrifice comes not from showy gifts but from the small hidden gestures of the poor. As he leaves the Temple that day at the start of chapter 13, he predicts that the great complex will fall: "Not one stone upon stone will be left here, all will be demolished."

The prediction of the destruction of the Temple, which would be its second annihilation in history, would echo loudly in Hebrew memory and is the clearest indication that Yeshua considers the current state of affairs to be unacceptable. Though the comment is made privately it is apparently overheard, since one of the false charges leveled against him is that he claimed he would tear it down and in three days build another "not made by hands." The conflict is thus established: Yeshua against the corrupt Temple, two forces incapable of moderation or compromise. The authorities, who fear the reaction of the people and pilgrims in Jerusalem for Passover if they arrest him publicly, look for an opportunity. To complete the tragic action, the narrative needs an external stimulus and the simplest one is a defector. He arrives in the form of the last apostle, without characterization, without justification, without plot function other than betrayal. Judas approaches the chief priests with a proposal, they are delighted and promise him money though he does not ask for it; a reward seems incidental. The other gospels expand on the matter a little. Satan enters Judas in Luke and John, the amount of money is specified in Matthew (thirty *argyria* or silver pieces, perhaps meaning shekels), but the general effect of the four treatments of Judas is that he is a utility, not a motivated character.[5]

Judas facilitates the catastrophe in the way a messenger does in Greek tragedy, as the old shepherd does in *Oedipus the King* when he relates the real parentage of Oedipus and his abandonment as a baby many decades before. That story must be forced out of the shepherd, whose strongest instinct is to remain silent about the dreadful truth he carries. In Mark, however, Judas is a volunteer, a rebel without a cause, his only action in the betrayal scene a kiss, his only word "rabbi": teacher. He is a student betraying his master; perhaps, as I said in chapter 4, with his master's consent. Then Judas, like the old shepherd, disappears from the

---

5. John is a slight exception in that his Judas is partly motivated by money. As the keeper of the apostolic purse, Judas objects to the anointing of Yeshua with expensive oil because, John says, he regularly stole from the pot (12.4–6).

text. There is no suicide as in Matthew (27.5), or death by burst bowels as in Acts (1.18). For Mark, Judas is a function in the tragic action; once the function is completed, there is no need for him.

Like Mark, *Oedipus* is framed by promises. The play begins with a promise that the disease infecting Thebes will be cured when the murderer of Laius has been driven into exile, and ends with the promise of restoration brought by the exile of Oedipus. Such a frame is not unusual in tragedy, or in the wider literature of any age; it is common in the late tragedies of Shakespeare, for example. Mark's use of it, along with his other parallels to Greek tragedy, draw the evangelist into a literary tradition. Regardless of whether he was aware of the tradition, his gospel carries the tragic mode into the center of his treatment of Yeshua and his fate.

Oedipus is often thought of as a tragedy of character, the fall of the hero brought about by a deficiency in his human nature. In this view his obstinate pride leads to an inability to see the truth of his motives or recognize the disguised reality behind the prophesies about his fate. The idea of a tragic "flaw," a much-repeated mistranslation of Aristotle's *hamartia*, has been given new value by the modern notion that bad conduct is rooted in childhood trauma or personality disorder. But for Aristotle it is action that defines character in tragedy, not the other way around. We can know the essence or core of Oedipus only by virtue of what he does, and we can say the same of Mark's Yeshua. Though John makes Yeshua's divine spirituality the source of his conduct, in Mark we understand the central figure not through personality revelation but through deeds. His cures and exorcisms, the feedings, the promises of a new world, are generally social in nature—we understand that he cares for his people because he actually helps them become better. He *wants* them to become better. His conflict with the Temple is also revealed through action; the priestly authorities are threatened by him because he does things and says things that challenge their influence and status and their rigorous interpretation of the Law. They (and we) understand his essence not because he radiates holiness but because he performs works that mark him as separate and distinct. That's what makes him the Other, the one who can be proscribed. In the terms of tragedy he does not have a flaw in character that elicits the disaster since the disaster is what he seeks.

Yet Mark's Yeshua does make a mistake. His *hamartia* is not the tragic conflict with the Temple that leads to the cross, which the gospel sees as a fulfillment rather than error. Yeshua's mistake is proclaiming that the kingdom was near when it was not. For the Jews of his nation, what followed in 70 CE was not a revived and glorious Israel under God but devastation, diaspora, and death at the hands of the same Roman order that killed the young preacher from Galilee. Where was their protector? It seemed that Yahweh had abandoned his people once again. As Jacob Wright notes in a new book, the Hebrew bible is a history of the Jews losing and trying to make sense of loss.[6] That story continued with great force in the empire of the next century. The growing distance of God's reign, together with the increasing Hellenization of the Christos cult, forced the third generation of followers to transform the nature of the promise contained in Paul and Mark. The writer of the gospel of John around the end of the first century already implies that the promised kingdom is within: within Yeshua as savior, within the eternal truth of his message, within the hearts of his believers. Early Christianity, arising out of the ashes of the Temple and maintaining an oral tradition about the life of the Messiah, eventually conceded that the kingdom was not immediate after all, that it was a kind of metaphor for godly living and a promise of an afterlife to be shared with God in heaven in a hybrid existence: of human bodies that are not quite our own with a spiritual joy that is ineffable because humanly unknowable.

To hold that the kingdom is distant, mysterious, a possibility after death, is to contradict what the Yeshua in the earliest gospel, and the earliest supporting theology in Paul, actually expected: an imminent arrival, a world transformation, the son of man on the clouds of heaven sitting at the right hand of God. That's what Mark's hero promises, not an ever-receding horizon of hope. Was Yeshua authorized by God, or just a charismatic but deluded man imagining a reckoning that he wished for himself? I don't know, and of course I don't know if Yeshua will make a return visit—*parousia* is the Greek word, meaning royal appearance—but in Mark he is the prophet of an event that did not occur in the next two generations as he predicted. Yeshua was right about many things, but about the arrival of the kingdom he was mistaken. Though it may seem harsh to say it, Yeshua's mistake is the one that Christians have lived with for twenty centuries.

Another question is also legitimate: if he is coming, what is he waiting for? For us to end the world in fire ourselves, along with a civilization built partly out of his message? To me the error of calculation at the heart of the gospel makes Mark's Yeshua less mysterious, all the more

---

6. J. Wright, *Why the Bible Began*.

sympathetic, all the more human and thus all the more heroic. He goes to the cross convinced his death will bring about a new world within a few decades. It did not. If the Resurrection, even in its tentative form in Mark, cancels Yeshua's death and glorifies him above all people, his mistake about when God is coming makes his human fate all the more tragic.

Then they crucified him. In both Greek tragedy and epic, the manner of a character's death is part of its significance. Is it valiant like Antigone's or Hector's, characters who are killed in a noble cause? Or is it shameful like Agamemnon's, the great king tied up in a bath and stabbed by his vengeful wife? "Count no man happy," chants the concluding chorus of *Oedipus the King*, "until he is dead." You have to know the end, the end of a life and the end of the tale, to know what the life means for the teller. Whether through their own mistakes or not, tragic heroes do not fade away, they finish in flames and the flames illuminate their condition of virtue.

In Roman use the appalling punishment of crucifixion was generally reserved for serious crimes committed by the lowest classes: slaves who struck or injured their masters, foreigners or outcasts guilty of theft, pirates, and rebels against the state. It was a public spectacle of mortal torture, prolonged and literally excruciating, designed to be a warning to others. It was execution with maximum humiliation, the naked body exposed to the stares of all, to flies and crows and dogs, defenseless, dropping sweat and blood and piss and shit, hanging sometimes for days in agony, and often left to rot on display.

Considering how central the manner of Yeshua's death has been to Christian theology and devotion, surprisingly little is known about the pragmatic details of Roman crucifixion. Classical writers avoided the topic almost entirely, perhaps out of shame over the practice, as Joel Marcus suggests in claiming that "the passion narratives of the Gospels are our most elaborate accounts."[7] Yet the gospel accounts detail the flogging and mock tribute more than the cross. They skip over the gruesome horror of hammer and nails, the lifting of the body on the crossbeam, and the architecture of the cross. We know the torture was variably exercised; since death usually came by asphyxiation due to the stretching of the chest from the body's weight, the centurion supervising the detachment of executioners had a certain amount of liberty in prolonging or hastening the end. The upright pole could be variably made, the crossbeam

---

7. Marcus, *Mark 8–16*, 1131.

located differently or even eliminated, the arms of the condemned fixed with iron spikes through the wrists or by rope. Sometimes a small seat and a footrest would be provided on the upright to elongate the torture by preventing rapid asphyxiation, forcing the condemned to raise his body by reflex and thus endure more pain. Breaking the legs of the crucified, obviously intensely painful, was nonetheless an act of mercy. No longer able to support his weight on the footrest, his death by asphyxiation came soon.

Mark is characteristically swift: "They offered him wine laced with myrrh, but he did not take it. Then they crucified him and divided his clothes, throwing lots to decide who should have what. It was the third hour when they crucified him" (15.23–25). Then they crucified him: the Greek literally means "then they staked him" or "impaled him," and no elaboration of the method is given. It's a very quick handling of what in reality could be a lengthy and horrendous procedure. Most of the rest of the short scene concerns the behavior of the onlookers and the few words spoken by Yeshua from the cross. There may be two reasons for the evangelist's restraint. The first is that crucifixion was practiced throughout the empire for some centuries, and was such a common event—in a restless, occupied colony perhaps a daily event—that Mark's audience needed no instruction about its ferocious methods. The second reason may be the result of literary decorum, or the propriety of the belief system behind the oral tradition, which wished to promote the passivity of sacrifice over the particulars of its implementation.

For later audiences of Mark's gospel, the result is a curious doubleness about the death scene. The narrative purpose of the episode is to relate the miscarriage of justice and gratuitous cruelty perpetrated by the Temple and the Romans, yet the language pulls away from detailing that cruelty in order to highlight Yeshua's comportment on the cross as important to his redeeming martyrdom. The treatment makes his death much more like Antigone's than Agamemnon's. Antigone goes willingly to her death to protest the rule of an inflexible tyrant; Agamemnon, expecting the welcome of a returning conqueror, is surprised by a sneaky bloodbath. The centurion's line at the cross, "Truly, this man was God's son,"[8] often interpreted as a declaration of Yeshua's divinity, in context

---

8. In the Greek text there is no article before "son," thus the phrase can also be translated as "a son of God" or "the son of God." The meaning of the phrase became a matter of theological importance, but how it portrays Yeshua's relationship to God is incidental to the scene and the character of the centurion as executioner.

seems directed to the dignified manner of his end. Mark places his hero's death in the tragic mode by an ambiguous reticence that allows us to fill in what has been left out.

There has been no such reticence in subsequent eras, which have filled in the scene in grisly detail. Beginning as early as the fourth century, with the legend of the discovery of the true cross by Helena, the mother of Emperor Constantine, by the year 1000 the Eastern and Western churches had become reliquaries of the implements of the Passion. Known as Arma Christi, or the Arms of Christ ("Arms" in the heraldic sense), the display of relics or imitations of relics relating to the torture and execution of Yeshua has greatly influenced devotion and the general understanding of the Passion. The rapid treatment of the cross in Mark and the other gospels was elaborated in later writings, paintings, and sculpture into a cult of agony.

Nuns and priests subjected me to distressing analysis of the Crucifixion, and the depictions must have seeped into my psyche and nightmares. But in my waking life the gruesome lectures, usually with the theme of "honor what Jesus did by redeeming you through his terrible suffering," worked contrary to their purpose. Who asked him to? my cynical twelve-year-old self wondered. Why did the omnipotent God choose to save his children by having one of them tortured to death? It was beyond me, and logically led to my questioning why the church would want to promote the contradiction of a God who can do anything against a God who does nothing to prevent evil, one of the great imponderables of the three Abrahamic religions.

Among the pious totems in our family was a statuary figure of the Arma Christi on a circular wooden stand, protected by a glass bell jar that could be lifted off. I don't know where it came from or why it was hidden in a closet, but I found it at around age eight or nine and was fascinated. Under the glass was a wooden crucifix about a foot high with a bronze corpus and the implements of the Passion represented in miniature: crown of thorns, lash, scourging pillar, hammer, spikes, tongs, garments, ladder, spear, the inscription INRI. Some pieces were removable; I would take them out, then try to set them back in their proper places, as in a game of building blocks. I was especially attracted to throwing the tiny pair of dice, though it was impossible to decipher the markings on them. Forbidding as the total effect of the object was, for a child it was gruesome fun. Playing with it anesthetized me against the terror and pain it represented.

The more realistic the representation of the Passion is made, the harder it is to see beyond the blood and scars of the distressed body to its meaning. Though there is a long and continuing custom of using the Arma Christi and other images of suffering for devotional purposes in both the Catholic and protestant traditions, the objective reminders of Yeshua's human fate can have the effect of distancing the viewer entirely from their intended purpose. The maximum expression of physical horror, as depicted in Mel Gibson's film *The Passion of the Christ*, for example, places the viewer in such a vulnerable position that its exemplification tends to drive out the tragic import of the event or its redemptive agency. Mark was on to something when he left out the gore and permitted us to enter into the tragic circumstance with our imaginations.

The tragicomic mode. Despite the Crucifixion, Mark's gospel has a happy ending. Though the Resurrection is only reported, and though the scene is suffused by fear rather than joy, it makes little sense to call a work a tragedy if its hero is glorified. Though Mark's finale works against itself emotionally, there is no doubt that readers and hearers of his gospel were encouraged to celebrate the happy news it conveys. That brings it closer to a different type of play, one that combines the terror and pity of tragedy with the joyful release of comedy. Tragicomedy, as it was named by John Fletcher in 1609,[9] blended elements of both into the plot, which often involved a supposed death followed by restoration. Under classical influence, it arose in Italy in the sixteenth century, and then in London late in Shakespeare's career. His last plays fit easily into the category; *Cymbeline*, *Pericles*, *The Winter's Tale*, and *The Tempest* each contain the restoration of one or more characters thought to be deceased. They are wish-fulfillment plays that fulfill the dream of the bereaved, granting the dead second life.

As a genre, tragicomedy was anticipated in ancient Athens, and a number of plays performed in the tragic festivals actually have happy endings, or at least endings that do not contain death or a sense of irretrievable loss. Some of them, starting with Aeschylus' *The Eumenides* (458 BCE), involve the sudden appearance of a god or goddess who solves an irreconcilable human dilemma, a tactic known by its Latin

---

9. John Fletcher, in the preface to his first play, *The Faithful Shepherdess*: "A tragicomedy is not so called in respect of mirth and killing, but in respect it wants deaths, which is enough to make it no tragedy, yet brings some near it, which is enough to make it no comedy." Fletcher's play is a loose adaptation of Giovanni Battista Guarini's *Il Pastor Fido* (1590) combined with material from other pastoral sources. Fletcher became Shakespeare's collaborator for *Henry VIII* and *The Two Noble Kinsmen*.

name, deus ex machina. "A god from the machine" refers to the practice of lowering an actor playing a god by a crane situated on the upper level of the stagehouse in the theater in Athens. The expression is now used to describe any conclusion that relies on an unexpected force arriving from outside the previous terms of the narrative in order to conclude the story.

That is a reasonable description of the ending of Mark. A god—that is, Yahweh—sends his messenger in the form of a Young Man to deliver the news to the women at the tomb. They thought Yeshua was dead, they knew he was dead, and expected to find his corpse beginning to rot on a stone slab. What they find is that the tragic end they witnessed has been superseded. It has not been averted, the way that Orestes is saved in *The Eumenides* by the appearance of the goddess Athena; it has been subverted, entirely undone. The women do not expect this turnabout, which ends Mark's tale through an irrational or superhuman force not seen before.

It is an unusual ending in the history of literature, for plays of restoration do not normally involve the supernatural—their repaired characters are only thought to have been dead, not dead in actuality. But Mark's ending is not unique. In drama its closest predecessor is Euripides' *Alcestis*, which was presented in 438 BCE as the afterpiece to a trilogy of tragedies, a spot normally reserved for a satyr play, which was a raucous sexual piece intended to lighten the mood of the audience after a daylong bout of tragedies. The story of *Alcestis* is from Greek myth: King Admetus has been granted escape from death, but only if he finds someone to take his place on the appointed day, which he fails to do. Even his elderly father turns him down. However, the king's wife, Alcestis, agrees to substitute for him out of loving duty, and the character Death leads her away. At this point the demigod Heracles, an old friend of Admetus, arrives for a visit. Unwilling to break the rules of hospitality by displaying his grief, Admetus does not inform Heracles of his loss and instructs the servants to stay silent. Heracles gets drunk and misbehaves and a servant rebukes him, blurting out the news of the death of Alcestis. Ashamed, Heracles leaves, wrestles with Death, returns with a veiled woman, and asks Admetus to take her hand. She is revealed as Alcestis, brought back from the dead. She is in a bardo state, unable to speak for three days, after which she will be fully alive again.

The parallel scene in Shakespeare's *The Winter's Tale* of twenty centuries later presents the heroine Queen Hermione, presumed dead, as a statue that moves and is revealed to be the body of the living woman. Her husband, King Leontes, had falsely accused her of adultery when she was pregnant sixteen years before, and she is reported to have died of grief. But she was not dead, only hidden away for that time, to give him adequate space for repentance. Compared to *Alcestis*, Shakespeare's play is Christian in attitude, suggesting that atonement is possible and that what is wished for, even the impossible, can be granted through suffering and sacrifice. "It is required / You do awake your faith," the character Paulina says, asking for *pistis* before commanding the statue to come alive. Despite their differences, both *Winter's Tale* and *Alcestis* are tragicomedies that toy with death, denying its finality, allowing exceptions to the rule of mortality.

Mark's gospel is clarified by comparison to both tragedy and tragicomedy without belonging to either genre. In the final analysis, the genre of the gospel tells us little about its intention or reception. What we can say for sure is that in the literary sense Mark presents a story of a great hero, misunderstood and rejected, whose fall is disastrous but whose death is repealed. Despite the opacity of the ending, the reported restoration of Yeshua turns despair to hope, loss to gain. A deus ex machina ending becomes a deus ex sepulchro ending, a manlike god descending from the machine to announce a godlike man rising from the tomb.

Being and perception. To get to the books on the New Testament in the Ussher Library, I must go through another Trinity College Dublin building, the Berkeley Library. It is named for George Berkeley (1685–1753), who, like James Ussher, was a graduate and eventually a bishop in the Church of Ireland. I should say *was* named for him, because in 2023 the Berkeley Library was "denamed" under pressure from students. For a short period Berkeley owned a plantation in colonial Rhode Island and held a number of enslaved people; worse, he wrote a pamphlet in defense of slavery. In his own time, however, he was one of the most notable philosophers in Europe. His influence was wide—so wide that, when the University of California was founded in 1868, Berkeley was chosen as the name for its location.[10]

Berkeley's philosophy was a form of Platonic idealism that he called immaterialism. He held that objects in the world, including organisms and human bodies, exist only as ideas in the mind, or the mind of God,

---

10. To be precise, the city was so named because one of its founders recalled a line from the last stanza of Berkeley's poem "Verses on the Prospect of Planting Arts and Learning in America" (1728): "westward the course of empire takes its way." As far as I know, there are no plans to change the name of Berkeley, California.

and have no actual substance. Their heft and texture are experienced as the result of a mental operation; nothing material exists in any way unless it is encountered by a mind. Our senses are not deceptive, but they are merely perceptions triggered by cerebral endeavor. His most famous dictum, *esse est percipere* (to be is to be perceived), was reconsidered in the twentieth century and sat well with Einstein's theories of cosmic relativity and the experiments in subatomic physics that are inaccessible to our normal senses. It also affected a number of thinkers concerned with the nature of the self, personal identity, and psychological perception. If we are not seen or sensed by someone else, do we even exist?

The question runs contrary to common sense, as Berkeley's contemporary Samuel Johnson insisted. Johnson kicked a stone on a London road and said of Berkeley's thought, "I refute it *thus*." The point remains, however: I cannot enter into your experience, and you cannot assume that your experience is exterior to yourself. Perhaps there is something in the mists of Ireland that encourages this kind of spinning circularity. The major scholar of Berkeley of the twentieth century, who revived his reputation and partially reinvigorated immaterialism, was the Trinity philosopher A. A. Luce (1882–1977). More strikingly, Luce was the tutor (or academic counselor) of an undergraduate named Samuel Beckett, who took his degree in 1927. Beckett's relationship with Trinity and Ireland was profound but deeply ambiguous, yet he eventually found through Berkeley a way to express the discontents and disaffections of postwar and Cold War life: life without God, without religion, without spiritual purpose, characterized by speed and loss and an inarticulate anxiety that preoccupy us as we wait for the end. Beckett's themes of incompetence and emptiness are enlivened by his tone, which alternates between or mixes hilarity and despair. In other words, a modernist tragicomic mode.

Waiting for. Beckett's first play, *Waiting for Godot*, was written in French soon after the war, produced in Paris in 1953, and subsequently translated into English by the author. Its well-known plot (or antiplot) is also its theme: two lost and homeless characters wait by a road for someone called Mr. Godot, who never arrives. A boy messenger comes each evening with the promise that Godot will be there the next day without fail. The two acts, which effectively replicate each other, suggest a perpetual inertia; waiting, like exile, is a no-time, preventing significance while encouraging inconsequence. The waiters—Vladimir and Estragon, nicknamed Didi and Gogo—are torn between expectation and despair. They are charged with passing the time (entertaining themselves to forget their misery) and with passing the time for an audience (entertaining us with their misery). And what will happen when Godot comes? As Didi says, quoted in the epigraph to this chapter, "We'll be saved." Saved from what? In the context of the play the only rational answer is, saved from waiting.

The actual or realistic background for the work was Beckett's experience in the French Resistance in the south of France during the Second World War, when food was short, meetings with others risky, and sleeping in a trench by the side of the road not unusual. Waiting was the common condition of resisters: waiting for a signal, for a parachute drop, for a colleague who might not arrive, for the sudden appearance of the Gestapo. Though Beckett dismissed his contributions as "Boy Scout stuff," he was on the run more than once, narrowly escaped arrest by the Gestapo when his Resistance circuit was compromised, and was later honored for his work by the French government.[11]

More directly connected to Mark, though, are a considerable number of religious allusions in *Waiting for Godot*: not only saved and savior but also goats and sheep, barefoot Christ, Christ have mercy, crucifying quick, the four evangelists, and the two thieves at the Crucifixion ("One of the thieves was saved. It's a reasonable percentage"). This fact led some early spectators and commentators to interpret the piece as a perverted allegory of Christian hope, seeing God in Godot, and waiting on earth as the condition for entrance to an afterlife. Beckett was at pains to discourage such readings, claiming that the play and the figure of Godot represented nothing other than what the text says overtly. And we should remember that in French the name Godot does not contain the name of God. Beckett was a little disingenuous, or perhaps a little naïve, in insisting that an audience should not make the religious connection. Even if the salvation Didi and Gogo hope for is an earthly one—relief from suffering, from endless anticipating, from the vicious cycle of repetition—they are still asking for a *parousia*, a first or second coming, a deus ex machina, to alleviate their impotence and incompetence. Waiting, as I've said before, is a fair description of the history of Christianity.

I could go on about this, drawing a relationship between the boy messenger in *Godot* and the Young Man messenger in the tomb in Mark who reports that Yeshua is not coming today, or between the promise of the absent Godot's return and the promise of the absent Messiah's return.

---

11. For a treatment of Beckett's work in the French Resistance, see Knowlson, *Damned to Fame*, 278–90.

Or I could note that the dead tree in the first act of the play, which mysteriously sprouts a few leaves in the second act, is a reverse image of the fig tree that Yeshua curses in Mark, which the next day has withered leaves. Or that the character named Pozzo, who is sighted in the first act and blind in the second, reverses Yeshua's process of healing. There is little point, however, in belaboring the parallels; they are not all that helpful, and I do not think Beckett was consciously drawing on the gospels for his plot.

Yet there is a deeper connection between Beckett and Mark, one that brings us back to Berkeley. In Berkeleyan terms the great problem of theology is that God is unseen. *Esse est percipere*: if we cannot perceive God, does he (or she or they or it) exist? The good Bishop Berkeley would answer that we exist because we are in the mind of God, but we might as well turn that around and say that God exists because we can imagine him (or her or them or it). The divine appears only through the human, whether in revelation or judgment, and remains immaterial, unperceived. Even Mark is careful to keep God's voice disembodied. It is the job of a religion to make its god's presence felt; in Christianity, through sacramental bread and wine, through evocations of his invisible omnipresence, stories of visions and voices, supernatural occurrences, martyr myths, and pronouncing the Good Message. But God adamantly refuses to appear. In fact, it is his absence, together with the promise of his appearance, that holds the Christian faith together.

Like expectant early Christians, Didi and Gogo's rescue is continuously deferred. They have no idea who Godot is or what he will do for them or why he will come or not come. They don't know positively that he exists. They don't know if *they* exist outside of the perception of the other characters, who may not remember them tomorrow. Their most pressing anxiety is that *they are not seen*. They quiz the messenger in each act about whether he has seen them, whether he has seen them before, whether he sees Mr. Godot, what Mr. Godot looks like (he has a white beard, the boy says). Near the end, when the boy asks them what he is tell Mr. Godot, Didi replies, "Tell him . . . [*He hesitates*] . . . tell him you saw me and that . . . [*He hesitates*] . . . that you saw me."

Beckett developed the theme of existence through perception further in his later work, particularly in the play called *Play* (1963) and the film called *Film* (1965), but it is already richly exhibited in *Waiting for Godot*. Godot never enters, yet he is the most important character; his absence takes center stage. Beckett's grand achievement is the uncanny enactment of absence as presence, making what is not here more felt than what is. For a believer, could there be a better description of God? It is God's absence from earth that makes it possible to believe in him, makes it *necessary* to believe in him. With the appropriate changes, this is the essence of the ending of Mark's existentialist gospel. The absence of Yeshua's body in the tomb renders him so powerfully present that the women visitors are speechless with terror. The shock of his dying is overwhelmed by the greater shock of his rising, which is rendered in the most dramatic fashion by his nonattendance.

Beckett's material is human anxiety, suffering, and loss, the human body tortured and in pain. This is Mark's material also; the difference is that Beckett dispensed with the rescuer. His work is art after Auschwitz, art made from chaos and despair, from remorselessly looking death in the face without the narcotic of hope or salvation. Yet his characters still pray. And why not? Even if we know there is no hope of rescue, we still hope: for a last-minute pardon, for relief from pain, for another day, for admission to the land of eternal happiness. I do not believe that God or the universe cares an iota about individual life, but I still say "Saint Christopher protect us" on takeoff and landing. Even the Catholic church admits that Christopher ("Christ bearer"), once the official patron of travelers, never existed, but that doesn't stop me from invoking him or running through a quick Hail Mary when in trouble. Robert Frost noted that prayer is just saying to God, "Me! Pay attention to me!" Even so, why not pray? Why not give ourselves the illusion that we are important enough to be rescued?

Longer ending. If you think my analogy to Beckett is appropriate, then you understand why some second-century follower stuck the longer ending onto Mark's abrupt finale. A great biography that ends with the jolt of absence was not a sufficient rendering of what Christians had come to believe and what the later gospels had narrated in varying detail. What was needed in Mark's chapter 16, the author of the inserted epilogue thought, was a quick summary of the week after the Crucifixion that established the certainty of the Resurrection.

> [9]Now having risen early on the first day of the week, he appeared first to Mary of Magdala, from whom he had cast out seven demons. [10]She made her way and spoke to those who had been with him, who had been mourning and weeping. [11]But they, hearing that he was alive and seen by her, distrusted it. [12]After that he appeared in another form to two of them, as they were

walking in the country. ¹³Going back, they spoke to the rest, but they did not trust them either. ¹⁴Last he appeared to the eleven as they were reclining at table and rebuked their distrust and hardness of heart because they had not trusted those who had seen him risen from the dead. ¹⁵And he said to them, "Make your way into all the world and proclaim the good message to all creation. ¹⁶The one who trusts and is baptized will be rescued; but the one who does not trust will be condemned. ¹⁷Now these signs will follow those who have trusted: they will cast out demons in my name, they will speak in new languages, ¹⁸they will take up serpents in their hands, and if they drink any deadly thing it will not harm them. They will lay hands upon the sick and they will be made well." ¹⁹After speaking to them, then the Lord Iesous was raised up into the heavens and sat at the right hand of God. ²⁰And they went out and preached everywhere, the Lord working together with them and confirming the word with attending signs.

It is a curious addition on many levels, the strangest being that the anonymous writer does not appear to be aware of the contents of the gospel he is correcting. He makes no effort to compose in Mark's style or expand his existing details. There is no mention in Mark of casting out demons from Mary of Magdala, no sense that baptism was a necessary condition of salvation, and definitely no indication that the apostles and their designated followers would be granted supernatural abilities of speech, extraordinary powers of healing, or security from poison. Those are clearly legendary elements, prompted by passages in Luke (10.19), the day of Pentecost and Paul's encounter with a snake in Malta in Acts (2.1–13 and 28.3–6), and probably by the ongoing oral message. (The snake-handling and poison-drinking injunctions encouraged imitation in some independent churches in the American Pentecostal tradition; one conservative edition of the bible, fearful of dangerous adventures in the name of scripture, notes that the passage "does not command" deadly experimentation, "it merely promises protection if such a thing were to occur.")¹²

As we discussed before, ending at verse 8 makes the gospel feel incomplete only in light of the endings of the later gospels, which were likely based on a tradition subsequent to Mark that had made the Resurrection appearances a crucial part of the Yeshua myth. In Mark, Yeshua

12. *ESV Student Study Bible*, 1329.

promises that after his death the apostles will see him in the north: "But when I am raised I will walk ahead of you to Galilee" (14.28). There is no promise of a postmortem appearance in or near Jerusalem, much less the four appearances narrated in each of the last two gospels (in Emmaus, Jerusalem, and Bethany in Luke, Jerusalem and Galilee in John). I imagine what most disturbed the corrector of Mark was concluding the tale on a motif of absence. The correction sought to turn that absence into a presence, a perceived demigod rather than an implied one, an unveiled Alcestis, guaranteeing that the gospel would be taken as a tragicomedy, not a tragedy. Though the additional ending does not appear in all ancient manuscripts, and though now it is common to tag the passage as secondary or at least questionable, for a long time it was printed in bibles as the authentic ending of Mark, as it is in the Textus Receptus and the translations dependent on it, including the King James Version. After more than two centuries of critical textual scholarship on the gospels, accepting the longer ending as a part of Mark is a bit like revising the finale of Beckett's play to show the sudden arrival of a smiling Mr. Godot on a Triumph motorcycle. Sorry to have kept you waiting, he might say.

The epic mode. Even if he was not a practiced writer of Greek, the author of Mark lived in a widespread Greco-Roman culture. In organizing those parts of the oral tradition about Yeshua that had come to him, or appealed to his purpose, Mark also had Greek examples, in writing or in memory, of well-plotted stories, developed themes, and actions rendered into literary patterns. Writers, after all, draw on what surrounds them as much as on what is in front of them. He may not have known *Oedipus the King* or *Alcestis*, but he may have known of similar plays and stories, and it is yet more reasonable to assume he knew something of the Homeric epics. It would have been difficult for a literate person in the Hellenized world not to be aware of some of the episodes and incidents in the epics that formed the mythic backdrop of life in the Roman empire and were objects of imitation in Hellenistic education. We could compare that milieu with the position of Shakespeare in Western culture today; many people, even if they have not read or seen any of his plays, might well have heard something about Hamlet's hesitation or Macbeth's witches. That Mark does not mention the polytheistic universe represented in Homer or Virgil shows that he was addressing an audience, Jew or Greek, who dismissed the pagan gods as obsolete idols. It does not prove that he was ignorant of the stories that pervaded his world.

Mark did not mimic Homer any more than he consciously emulated Sophocles. Odysseus was not a model for Mark's Yeshua, and the gospel is not an epic poem in disguise. The differences in form, purpose, and conclusion are too significant to ignore. I stress this point because the scholar most insistent on Homeric impact repeatedly mistakes parallels for influence. Dennis R. MacDonald holds that "Mark wrote a prose epic modeled largely after the *Odyssey* and the ending of *Iliad*."[13] His study places a series of episodes from the epics against the gospel, noting similarities of language, character, action, and setting in an attempt to demonstrate that the evangelist used the epics as models for a number of pericopes and treatments of theme. But analogies and similarities abound in any literary tradition; that is what a literary tradition means. Tellers of tales repeat certain story and character types, or develop them in new ways, because they correspond to our experience of the world and give us the pleasure of the familiar. MacDonald not only travels too far in gathering evidence of influence, what he brings back is not particularly useful.

What would Mark's gospel look like if it were a Homeric epic? First it would be in verse (dactylic hexameters), be lengthy (about 12,000 to 16,000 lines), filled with many well-drawn characters of differing nature, be dotted with repeated epithets (catchphrases like "wine-dark sea"), and contain episodes of mortal combat with details of ships, horses, arms, and defensive gear. Most of these are connected to the fact that the epics were composed and performed orally, the details acting as mnemonics for a singing bard, and none of them apply to Mark. Yet the grand arc of the epics could still provide reference points for the evangelist's story, and can be seen to place another conventional context around his work. Like the *Odyssey*, Mark is based on a single charismatic and resolute character whose life connects heaven and earth, and whose exploits involve magical or supernatural events, a challenging journey, and obstacles and enemies out to deflect, delay, or destroy him. His hero is determined but misunderstood, is frustrated in achieving his purpose, encounters deaths and near-deaths, and finally is tenuously apotheosized. The endings are congruent in event and tone. In the *Iliad*, when the great Trojan warrior Hector is killed, his funeral pyre concludes the poem, lending a sense of irretrievable loss and foreshadowing the defeat of his city. In the *Odyssey*,

---

13. MacDonald, *Homeric Epics and the Gospel of Mark*, 3. MacDonald's approach has not received wide acceptance, but is a therapeutic corrective to an earlier tendency in scholarship to emphasize the influence of the Hebrew scriptures on the gospels while ignoring the effect of secular Greek literature.

the hero gets home, kills Penelope's many suitors, and is restored to her, his son, and his father, but the finale is equivocal. The families of the suitors murdered by Odysseus rise up against him, a battle begins, and a continuing cycle of revenge slayings is prevented only because Athena, in a dea ex machina conclusion, arrives to stop it. In dramatic terms the *Iliad* falls into the tragic mode, the *Odyssey* into the tragicomic mode, and the gospel of Mark lies in between.

Do the resemblances actually help us understand the work? Perhaps they do, less in particular and more in general. If Mark was writing a new kind of biography that combined Hebrew prophetic conventions with wise sayings and end-time promises, he was also in a long tradition of ancient narratives that relied on quest tales, fantastic occurrences, and a strong sense of morality or acceptable social behavior. Like an epic superman, his protagonist faces trials and obstacles that attack his self-assurance and reveal his human fallibilities. His goal is spiritual renovation, and his message is strikingly opposite to the warrior ethics of the Homeric champions, yet his short life is emboldened by his distinctive, heroic otherness.

The strangest similarity, however, is not literary but historical, and in the first century would have been most unexpected: Yeshua became celebrated in song and memory through the ages, more than Achilles, more than Odysseus. That fact does not make the gospel into an epic, but it does suggest that Mark's arrangement of the story has an epic sweep that subsequent writers could build on. As a result of certain accidents in the history of the Roman empire, this first Yeshuan chronicle laid a basis for the elevation of a minor preacher from the hinterland into the most important spiritual figure of the past two thousand years. We have seen that the article of faith, with its trust in the actuality of the Resurrection, existed before and independently of the earliest gospel. What Mark did was to create a persona who gave the belief a living exemplar, an origin figure to place at its center, to make the faith accessible to its adherents. Paul lay the philosophic groundwork for the religion we know as Christianity, but it's worth repeating that it was Mark, drawing on the memories, speeches, and whispers in the oral tradition, who invented in written form the character we know as Jesus Christ.

Epilogue

WE LIVE IN A skeptical age that is often called post-Christian. The term can refer to many features of our time, from the decline of traditional morality to the death of God. The "post" might be a little premature, given that various forms of conservative, fundamentalist, or radically self-centered Christianity are flourishing, especially in the Americas, but it is true that many people have grown tired of some of the Christian principles and platitudes that characterized Western culture for more than a millennium. Others have fallen away from inherited commitment through secularization, narcissism, or historical and scientific rationalism, sliding down the Doubt Scale like me. In addition, a number of people, including committed believers, have been offended by ecclesiastic political positions, while sexual or human-rights abuses, especially of children, have weakened the moral authority of certain religious institutions and some of their ministers. And the Catholic church is running out of priests and nuns.

In Europe, the historical seat of the Roman, Eastern Orthodox, and reformed branches, church attendance has notably diminished in the last fifty years, even in Ireland. Starting in the age of exploration, Europe was the dispersal point for Christian proselytizing to the Americas, Africa, and South Asia, but in contemporary Europe the conviction that Christianity was a legitimate aspect of the conquest of indigenous peoples is now recognized as a colonizing hypocrisy. If we can trust the surveys, belief in God has also diminished, along with confidence in the efficacy of faith. Many Europeans, and many others as well, have abandoned the rites and rigors of traditional Christianity. When a culture begins to shift like a tectonic plate, the alteration may be noticeable only here and there, in small earthquakes and mudslides. When the break becomes undeniable, when a gap opens in the ground, the change is undeniable.

I understand why fixed believers are disturbed by the change, and why some view contemporary Western secular culture as decadent. In many ways, Western secular culture *is* decadent and narcissistic, at least by traditional standards. Though a number of remaining adherents are Christians in name only—CHINOS, we could call them—they belong to what is still the world's largest religion, with about 2.4 billion devotees. Despite that number, close to a third of the world's population, I doubt that organized Christianity will ever again have the spiritual and political hold on its faithful that Catholicism had when I was a boy at Saint Francis de Sales school.

Instead of expressing shock at the change, it is more reasonable to wonder why it has taken so long to occur. Two millennia of expectation of rescue by a returning Messiah, in a belief system that anticipates an unconditional judgment after death leading to eternal reward or punishment, is a very long time for any order of thought that claims to hold absolute truth. Is this era of belief about to end? I don't know, but I have argued that Mark's gospel anticipates the difficulty of faith, showing how many of his characters fail to trust, or trust sufficiently, in the Good Message. Mark recognized that to doubt is human; doubt is a self-protective mechanism that guards against liars, frauds, and fake messiahs, those creative challengers that Yeshua warns about in his prediction of the end time. Since prophesy is about the future, who can tell the false prophet from the true?

And so it is with gods. If we look at religion as history rather than as belief system, we see gods born and gods die; gods accepted as real and later deliberately abandoned, or just forgotten. In his meditation on the movement from Judaism to Christianity, Harold Bloom asks an incisive question: what happened to Yahweh?[1] Bloom relies on literary analysis bordering on theology, two methods that are actually close since both attempt to interpret textual intention and meaning, matters that cannot be known definitively. He wonders if Yahweh committed suicide to make way for Jesus and the Trinity. More a metaphoric than a substantive question, it's nonetheless an intriguing idea. In the Christian era, as I see it, God the Father, supposedly coincident with Yahweh, is not the jealous and demanding God of the Hebrew scriptures. Though distant, God the Father is a kingly old man with a white beard (like Godot) who has mostly retired from active duty in favor of his Son, who over the centuries became the knowable aspect of the unknowable God of Jewish

---

1. Bloom, *Jesus and Yahweh*.

tradition. This Son is the approachable face of the three-personed God. He is probably what most Christians think of when they pray or offer divine worship. For many believers he is a caring, loving, and merciful figure who is congenial to sentimental renderings (the sweet suffering Jesus of the sacred heart), but he is also the expected stand-in for the Father's judgment when doomsday finally arrives.

There is an inescapable clash between these two visions of God, one the dulcet pardoner of human mistakes and the other the ultimate assessor of the worth of a human life. The conflict is between the compassion of the martyred Son and the otherness of the distant Father. *Sanctus, Sanctus, Sanctus* is the shout that introduces the consecration segment of the Mass: Holy, Holy, Holy. We usually think of holiness as piety, sanctity, saintliness, but at root the word marks extreme difference. The Sanctus exclamation comes from Isaiah's vision of God enthroned, surrounded by seraphim who sing praises to him in ancient Hebrew. A simple phonetic transliteration:

> *Kadosh kadosh kadosh* YHWH *tsevaot*
> *melo khol-haarets kevodo*

Literally this reads:

> Other, other, other, Yahweh of the armies,
> all the earth is filled with his glory. (Isaiah 6.3)

"Other" is the root meaning of *kadosh*, which the Septuagint rendered as *hagios*, the Vulgate as *sanctus*, and the King James Version and all subsequent English bibles as *holy*. Abraham is chosen by a God who calls himself the absolutely powerful (Genesis 17.1), who later tells Moses he is existence itself: "I AM who I AM . . . you shall say to the Israelites, I AM has sent me to you" (Exodus 3.14). "I am what is" might better convey the sense. Yahweh is all that is not human, a being set apart, original, unapproachable, unknowable, without blemish.

What an astonishing idea it was for early Christians to blend Yeshua the sacrificed mortal into an immortal aspect of Yahweh, thereby forcing the Jewish Other to become the Christian Father of the Forgiver. And then to make the Hebrew term for God's action on earth, holy spirit (or sacred breath or breath of the Other), into the third member of a triune God. Among the mighty paradoxes and enigmas brought by the concept of the Trinity, God's otherness seems almost lost, as if Yahweh did commit suicide after all.

The contradiction of a humanized god was manifest on the day of my first communion in Cincinnati, age seven. My class had been instructed for a year in the meaning and sacredness of the action, which acknowledged our advancement into what the church considered the age of reasoning, defined as the ability to understand the difference between good and evil; in other words, to be capable of sin through consciousness. A first confession, a search for some fault to reveal to the patient priest, occurred on Saturday. On Sunday, everything marked the event as a time set apart: fresh haircut, new white suit with two-toned shoes (white on top, brown sides), presentation prayerbook (hardshell covers marbled in black in a leatherette slipcase, rosary in a facing pocket), godparents present, church filled with May flowers. We gathered in the school in a buzzing hush of anticipation. In those days Catholics were forbidden to take anything by mouth the morning before communion, so the water fountains were tied with cloth to prevent a child from becoming ineligible at the last minute.

I understood little of the meaning of the sacrament but I did understand that Jesus entered me in the form of the consecrated host, a round wafer, a strange tasteless thing distant from food. I suppose I thought of it as a kind of medicine, a very large pill to be swallowed. It came with a rigid protocol that prohibited chewing it, spitting it out, or touching it with the fingers, and an instruction to use the tongue to dislodge it should it stick to the roof of the dry mouth. Based on belief in transubstantiation, other etiquettes were scrupulously applied: gold sacramental vessels to hold wine and wafer, gold-plated paten on a handle for the altar boy to set under the chin of each communicant to catch the wafer should it fall, the celebrant rinsing his fingers after communion over the cup and then drinking the residue in case it contained flakes of wafer. After Mass he would rinse the purificator, a linen towel used to wipe the chalice, and only in the piscina (Latin for fish tank or basin), a special sink in the sacristy with a drain directly into the earth, to ensure that no trace of consecrated wafer or drop of wine was sullied in the sewer lines. These extreme sacerdotal controls certainly mystified the event, and at the same time made the priest look bizarrely domestic, like someone washing up the dinner dishes. We heard of a boy in the previous year who, probably nauseated from unaccustomed fasting, vomited in the pew right after swallowing his first-communion wafer. The priest had to clean the mess himself.

But eating Jesus, that was the most outlandish thing of all. I felt both elated at the privilege and invaded by an alien force. I can say those words now, now that that Sister Dorothea can no longer condemn me to hell, as she once did when her spies caught me using a bad word at recess. I had been told again and again that taking the eucharist was the holiest I could be in life, as God had lowered himself to become part of my body. It was only a scrap of something pretending to be bread, but I had been taught to believe it was much more. I suppose I expected an instant change, a rush of blood to the brain, some transforming emotion, a spiritual knowing. Instead I felt nothing other than the great worry that I might accidentally bite Jesus. I didn't feel revulsed, I didn't want to vomit, but I did wonder what advantage was attached to swallowing God. As Jacques Lacan might say, I could not recognize myself in what I was supposed to be. The accent in my training had been so focused on the personal, redemptive attribute of communion that I had not even begun to grasp its collective attribute, the thanksgiving union with the congregation and the larger community of saints, living and dead. But perhaps it was simply unrealistic for a child of seven to experience anything other than the stiff texture of the foreign body in the mouth.

After mass there was a family party at our house. Uncle Cliff took me, still in my white suit, on a beer run in his laundry van. He said, "Den, this will be the happiest day of your life." Even at age seven I thought that a melancholy forecast. But maybe Cliff was right. Maybe an innocent acknowledgment of God's presence is a necessary condition for experiencing the happiness, or the moments of joy, that can be felt through complete trust in in the Other, the *I AM* who is everything that is not me. Mark's Yeshua implies as much when he says that "whoever does not accept the reign of God as a child, shall never enter it" (10.15). That line exposes the paternalistic nature of first-century Judaism that remained solidly part of Christianity, with the Father expecting filial devotion and offering safeguard in return. But that is what most gods offer, a trade between worship and rescue.

In Mark, Yeshua frequently offers such an exchange. Trust in me, he says, and you trust in the Father, and then all things are possible: the sick will be cured, the blind see, the deaf hear, the disfigured made whole, the hungry fed, the demon exorcized, and through the example of his own person, the dead will rise. It's a pretty good trade: believe in the Anointed and receive the promise of the kingdom. That's what Christianity made of it, anyway, straddling its way across the centuries between the implacable

God of Abraham and the comforting God of Jesus. If Yahweh could be transmuted into a communion cracker, if the absolute Other could descend into my seven-year-old body, then even I, wretch that I am, stained by the blood of Adam, could climb the height of Sinai, be washed in the blood of the Lamb, and lifted up in the promise of a second life.

Of course for a young boy the promise of a second life, when he had barely begun a first one, was almost meaningless. My larger point is not how the Catholic church of my young self treated the eucharist but rather that young Christianity had already obscured *kadosh* in *sanctus*, transforming the complete otherness of God into a holy but benevolent accessibility. It thus became necessary for the church to conclude that the Yeshua of the gospels had two natures, divine and human; he was not a man exalted or a demigod, but a being both from before time and in time, immortal and mortal, a desperately mysterious union of incompatibilities. Once theology had traveled that far, it hadn't much further to go to conclude that human spirits, once created, were also indestructible, semidivine, and would live forever in one place or another.

By the time Augustine of Hippo had made this clear, less than a century after Nicaea, and theorized the concept of original sin as an explanation for man's fallen state and the corresponding need for Christ's redemption, the flourishing church was well along the path of justifying belief by philosophic argument rather than scriptural authority, or using philosophic argument to interpret scripture in a predetermined way. We have seen this earlier in the book; it is what orthodoxy means, correct opinion. What happened in the Yeshua and Christos cults after Mark is absorbing: the later gospels expanded the genealogy, power, and authority of Yeshua and added the details of his Resurrection; second- and third-century believers augmented his life story; early fathers of the church began to impose theological order on the contradictions in the New Testament; and ultimately Constantine's patronage enabled the fourth-century creeds that cemented belief in the divinity of the Messiah and claimed eternal life for all people. Those developments are essential to the history of Christianity, but none of them are in Mark.

Nor are they very clear in Paul, despite the fact that his letters (and those letters once ascribed to him) have been regularly used to support subsequent theology. We have no idea what Paul might have said had he sat down to write a considered treatise on the new philosophy of salvation he promoted, for a sect that he claimed was both under the Jewish Law and liberated from it. But we can say with some assurance that Christianity would look very different were it restricted to its earliest writings. Dating two to four decades after the Crucifixion, while the oral tradition was forming and expanding, Paul and Mark are both indecisive about Yeshua's nature. To Paul he was a man whom God "raised up." Paul is clear that salvation awaits believers, based on what he received from the apostles in Jerusalem and the kerygma or article of faith he gathered from the tradition. His own Damascene vision of the risen Yeshua, which occurred a few years after the Crucifixion, had convinced him that the apostles had also encountered the crucified man in what I have called a bardo state. Paul took this as a sign that eternal life, or at least a second life, awaits those who follow the teaching he outlines. Much of Paul's teaching, however, is not directly ascribed to Yeshua; it consists of Paul's interpretation of the meaning of the Resurrection, using what amounts to a Hellenistic philosophy of reparation. Most significantly, in the ranks of the saved Paul included gentiles who were "grafted in" the tree of Israel to replace "some of the branches broken off"—that is, Jews who refused to accept Yeshua as Messiah (Romans 11.17). But whether God's kingdom will be on earth or in heaven, how humans will be judged and selected, whether nonbelievers will punished or simply obliterated; Paul states none of that objectively or absolutely.

Mark too hedges his bet about the nature of Yeshua, presenting him as a man anointed by God to deliver the Good Message and to command Jewish repentance before the end time, a man sacrificed so that he can be redeemed into a second life. The gospel is even less clear about the kingdom, except for the prediction that it will come very soon and be accompanied by great suffering, before peace will reign for a long time. In my reading, Mark's Yeshua supposes it will exist on earth, and include the resurrected bodies of righteous Jews, in some version of the ancient promise of the restoration of the nation of Israel. There is an occasional sideways hint that others might be included, in that Yeshua heals two gentiles, but he never directly offers the kingdom to those outside the Mosaic covenant.

Would that be enough to build a new religion on? Possibly, but a strictly Pauline and Markan Christianity would lack more than half of the articles of faith stated in the final version of the Nicene Creed, including crucial beliefs about Yeshua's miraculous virginal conception, his divinity, his consubstantiality with the Father, the existence of the Trinity, and the universality and apostolic foundation of the church. The first two of these are expressed or implied in the later gospels or the later letters in the New Testament; others arose and grew in importance in the second and third centuries. They were not plucked out of the air in Nicaea or Constantinople but, like most theology, they *were* plucked; that is, they were inferred, deduced, or invented. As it developed after Constantine, official Christianity seemed to agree with the ending of a tale I once heard from a traditional Irish storyteller: "And everything in my story is true. Even the parts I made up are true."

What if the gospels are not true? What if they are true selectively, or haphazardly, or true in the way myths are true? They support a cult made up of "cult legends," as Bultmann said; can the cult survive without the legends? Christianity, now almost exactly 2,000 years after its Christ died, exists inside a world that is violent, secular, acquisitive, self-destructive, and disdainful of the natural world: an era now called the anthropocene. We have seen that faith in the Resurrection preceded Paul and the gospels, and that the New Testament texts are insufficient support for some of the most important elements of belief. Biblical scholarship often questions both the making and the meaning of the texts, and sometimes the basis of the faith as well. What if Yeshua did not rise on the third day and the apostles, in the fear and anxiety of their grief, just thought they saw visions of him? What if the stories of him rising are just stories, repeated by word of mouth and then written down, to secure a feeling, a need to believe in a forgiving God and the possibility of surviving death? If so, then what is left?

What is left is this: literary works of great force, stories so powerful they have been told and retold and have convinced and bolstered Christians for two millennia. And among them, chief of them in priority and in latent force, is a tale written by an unknown author we call Mark.

Bibliography

Adams, Edward. *The Earliest Christian Meeting Places: Almost Exclusively Houses?* Revised edition. London: Bloomsbury, 2016.
Agamben, Giorgio. *The Time that Remains: A Commentary on the Letter to the Romans.* Trans. Patricia Daly. Stanford University Press, 2005.
Alexander, Loveday. *Acts: The People's Bible Commentary.* Abingdon: Bible Reading Fellowship, 2006.
Armstrong, Karen. *The Bible: The Biography.* London: Atlantic Books, 2007.
Assmann, Jan. *Cultural Memory and Early Civilization: Writing, Remembrance, and Political Imagination.* Translated by David Henry Wilson. Cambridge University Press, 2011.
Ayres, Lewis. *Nicaea and Its Legacy: An Approach to Fourth-Century Trinitarian Theology.* Oxford University Press, 2004.
Badiou, Alain. *Saint Paul: The Foundation of Universalism.* Translated by Ray Brassier. Stanford University Press, 2003.
———. *Theoretical Writings.* Edited and translated by Ray Brassier and Alberto Toscano. London: Continuum, 2004.
Barton, John. *A History of the Bible: The Book and Its Faiths.* London: Allen Lane, 2019.
Beard, Mary. *Emperor of Rome: Ruling the Ancient Roman World.* New York: Liveright/Norton, 2023.
Becker, Eve-Marie. *The Birth of Christian History: Memory and Time from Mark to Luke-Acts.* Yale University Press, 2017.
Bettenson, Henry, ed. and trans. *The Early Christian Fathers.* Oxford University Press, 1956.
Bloom, Harold. *Jesus and Yahweh: The Names Divine.* New York: Riverhead, 2005.
Botha, Pieter J. J. "The Gospel of Mark, Orality Studies and Performance Criticism." *Religion and Theology* 25 (2018) 350–93.
Bovon, François. *Luke 1: A Commentary on the Gospel of Luke 1–9.* Translated by Christine M. Thomas, edited by Helmut Koester. Minneapolis: Fortress, 2002.
Bradshaw, Paul. *Eucharistic Origins.* London: SPCK, 2004.
Brown, Colin. *Miracles and the Critical Mind.* Grand Rapids: Eerdmans, 1984.
Bruce, F. F. *New Testament History.* London: Thomas Nelson, 1969.
Bryan, Christopher. *A Preface to Mark.* Oxford University Press, 1993.
———. *The Resurrection of the Messiah.* Oxford University Press, 2011.
———. *Son of God: Reflections on a Tradition.* Oxford University Press, 2023.

Bultmann, Rudolf. *The History of the Synoptic Tradition*. Translated by John Marsh. Second edition. Oxford: Blackwell, 1968.
Caillois, Roger. *Pontius Pilate*. Translated by Charles Lam Markmann. London: Macmillan, 1963.
Campbell, Ken M. "What Was Jesus' Occupation?" *Journal of the Evangelical Theological Society* 48.3 (September 2005) 501–19.
Carlson, Marvin. *Performance: A Critical Introduction*. Third edition. London: Routledge, 2018.
Carrère, Emmanuel. *The Kingdom*. Translated by John Lambert. London: Penguin, 2018.
Casey, Maurice. *Aramaic Sources of Mark's Gospel*. Cambridge University Press, 1998.
Certeau, Michel de. *The Practice of Everyday Life*. Translated by Steven Rendall. Berkeley: University of California Press, 1984.
———. "What We Do When We Believe." In *On Signs*, edited by Marshall Blonsky. Oxford: Blackwell, 1985.
Coleman, Kathleen. "The Fragility of Evidence: Torture in Ancient Rome." In *Confronting Torture*, edited by Scott A. Anderson and Martha C. Nussbaum, 105–119. Chicago University Press, 2018.
Collins, Adela Yarbo. *Mark: A Commentary*. Edited by Helmut Koester. Minneapolis: Fortress, 2007.
Coogan, Michael D., ed. *The Oxford Encyclopedia of the Books of the Bible*. Oxford University Press, 2011.
Dewey, Joanna. *Oral Ethos of the Early Church*. Eugene, OR: Cascade, 2013.
Dinkler, Michal Beth. *Literary Theory and the New Testament*. Yale University Press, 2019.
Donahue, John, and Daniel Harrington. *The Gospel of Mark*. Collegeville, MN: Liturgical Press, 2002.
Ehrman, Bart D. *Heaven and Hell: A History of the Afterlife*. London: Oneworld, 2020.
———. *How Jesus Became God: The Exaltation of a Jewish Preacher from Galilee*. New York: HarperOne, 2014.
———. *Lost Christianities: The Battles for Scripture and the Faiths We Never Knew*. Oxford University Press, 2005.
———. *Misquoting Jesus: The Story Behind Who Changed the Bible and Why*. New York: HarperOne, 2005.
Ehrman, Bart D., and Zlatko Plese. *The Apocryphal Gospels: Texts and Translations*. Oxford University Press, 2011.
Else, Gerald F. *Aristotle's Poetics: The Argument*. Harvard University Press, 1963.
Eusebius, *History of the Church*. Translated by Arthur Cushman McGiffert. Moscow, ID: Roman Roads Media, 2015.
Evans, Craig A. *Jesus and His Contemporaries: Comparative Studies*. Leiden: Brill, 2001.
———, ed. *The Routledge Encyclopedia of the Historical Jesus*. London: Routledge, 2010.
EVS Student Study Bible. London: Collins, 2011.
Eve, Eric. *Writing the Gospels: Composition and Memory*. London: SPCK, 2016.
Finney, Mark T. *Resurrection, Hell and the Afterlife: Body and Soul in Antiquity, Judaism and Early Christianity*. London: Routledge, 2016.
France, R. T. *The Gospel of Mark*. London: Bible Reading Fellowship, 1996.
Freyne, Seán. *Galilee from Alexander the Great to Hadrian, 323 BCE to 135 CE: A Study of Second Temple Judaism*. Edinburgh: T&T Clark, 1998.

Goodacre, Mark. *The Synoptic Problem: A Way through the Maze*. Sheffield: Sheffield Academic, 2001.
Gould, Stephen J. "Fall in the House of Ussher." *Natural History* 100.11 (November 1991) 12–19.
Hanson, K. C., and Douglas E. Oakman. *Palestine in the Time of Jesus: Social Structures and Social Conflicts*. Minneapolis: Fortress, 1998.
Hoehner, Harold W. *Chronological Aspects of the Life of Christ*. Grand Rapids: Zondervan, 2010.
Holland, Glenn S. "Playing to the Groundlings: Shakespeare Performance Criticism and Performance Criticism of Biblical Texts." *Neotestamenica* 41.2 (2007) 317–40.
Horsley, R. A., J. A. Draper, and J. M. Foley, eds. *Performing the Gospel: Orality, Memory, and Mark*. Minneapolis: Fortress, 2006.
Johnson, William. *Readers and Reading Culture in the High Roman Empire: A Study of Elite Communities*. Oxford University Press, 2010.
Josephus, Flavius. *Antiquities of the Jews*. Translated by William Whiston, revised by A. R. Shilleto. London: G. Bell, 1889–1909.
Keith, Chris. *The Gospel as Manuscript: An Early History of the Jesus Tradition as Material Artifact*. Oxford University Press, 2020.
Kelber, Werner H. *The Oral and the Written Gospel: The Hermeneutics of Speaking and Writing in the Synoptic Tradition, Mark, Paul, and Q*. Minneapolis: Fortress, 1983.
———, ed. *The Passion in Mark: Studies in Mark 14–16*. Minneapolis: Fortress, 1976.
Kennedy, Dennis. *The Spectator and the Spectacle: Audiences in Modernity and Postmodernity*. Cambridge University Press, 2009.
———. "The Spectator, the Text, and Ezekiel." *The Shakespearean International Yearbook* 10 (2010) 39–45.
Kermode, Frank. *The Genesis of Secrecy: On the Interpretation of Narrative*. Harvard University Press, 1979.
Kirk, Alan. *Q in Matthew: Ancient Media, Memory, and Early Scribal Transmission of the Jesus Tradition*. London: Bloomsbury/T&T Clark, 2016.
Klassen, William. *Judas: Betrayer or Friend of Jesus?* Minneapolis: Fortress, 1996.
Knowlson, James. *Damned to Fame: The Life of Samuel Beckett*. London: Bloomsbury, 1996.
Lane, William L. *The Gospel According to Mark*. London: Marshall, Morgan & Scott, 1974.
Levine, Amy-Jill, ed. *A Feminist Companion to Mark*. Sheffield: Sheffield Academic, 2001.
Lord, Albert. *The Singer of Tales*. Harvard University Press, 1960.
MacDonald, Dennis R. *The Homeric Epics and the Gospel of Mark*. Yale University Press, 2000.
Mack, Burton L. *A Myth of Innocence: Mark and Christian Origins*. Minneapolis: Fortress, 1988.
Marcus, Joel. *Mark 1–8*. New York: Doubleday, 2000.
———. *Mark 8–16*. Yale University Press, 2009.
McLuhan, Marshall. *The Gutenberg Galaxy: The Making of Typographic Man*. Toronto University Press, 1962.
Meggitt, Justin J. "The Madness of King Jesus." *Journal for the Study of the New Testament* 29 (2007) 379–413.

Metzger, Bruce M., and Bart D. Ehrman. *The Text of the New Testament: Its Transmission, Corruption, and Restoration*. Fourth edition. Oxford University Press, 2005.

Morgan, Teresa. *Roman Faith and Christian Faith: Pistis and Fides in the Early Roman Empire and Early Churches*. Oxford University Press, 2017.

Muddiman, John, and John Barton, eds. *The Gospels*. Oxford University Press, 2001.

Myers, Ched. *Binding the Strong Man: A Political Reading of Mark's Story of Jesus*. Maryknoll: Orbis, 2008.

Nestle, Eberhard and Erwin, eds. *Novum Testamentum Graece*. Twenty-seventh edition, revised by Barbara and Kurt Aland, et al. Ninth corrected printing. Peabody, MA: Hendrickson, 2007.

Ong, Walter J. *Orality and Literacy: The Technologizing of the Word*. London: Methuen, 1982.

———. *The Presence of the Word: Some Prolegomena for Cultural and Religious History*. Yale University Press, 1967.

Painter, John. *Mark's Gospel: Worlds in Conflict*. London: Routledge, 1999.

Pascal, Blaise. *Pensées*. Edited and translated by Roger Ariew. Indianapolis: Hackett, 2005.

Perry, Peter S. "Biblical Performance Criticism: Survey and Prospects." *Religions* 10.2 (2019) 117. https://doi.org/10.3390/rel10020117.

Peterson, Martin. *An Introduction to Decision Theory*. Cambridge University Press, 2017.

Phillips, Rod. *French Wine: A History*. Berkeley: University of California Press, 2016.

Porphyry. *Porphyry's Against the Christians: The Literary Remains*. Edited and translated by R. Joseph Hoffmann. Amherst: Prometheus, 1994.

Rhoads, David. "Performance Criticism: An Emerging Methodology in Second Testament Studies." *Biblical Theological Bulletin*, Part I, 36.3 (2006) 118–33; Part II, 36.4 (2006) 164–84.

Rhoads, David, Joanna Dewey, and Donald Michie. *Mark as Story: An Introduction to the Narrative of a Gospel*. Third edition. Minneapolis: Augsburg Fortress, 2012.

Rodríguez, Rafael. *Oral Tradition and the New Testament: A Guide for the Perplexed*. London: Bloomsbury, 2014.

Rousseau, John J., and Rami Arav. *Jesus and His World: An Archaeological and Cultural Dictionary*. Minneapolis: Fortress, 1995.

Sartre, Jean-Paul. *Words*. Translated by Irene Clephane. Harmondsworth: Penguin, 1967.

Schaff, P., and H. Wace, eds. *Nicene and Post-Nicene Church Fathers*. Edinburgh: T&T Clark, 1991.

Schechner Richard. *Between Theatre and Anthropology*. Philadelphia: Pennsylvania University Press, 1985.

———. *The Future of Ritual: Writings on Culture and Performance*. London: Routledge, 1995.

Shiner, Whitney. *Proclaiming the Gospel: First-Century Performance of Mark*. Harrisburg, PA: Trinity, 2003.

Stevenson, J., ed. *A New Eusebius: Documents Illustrating the History of the Church to AD 337*. Revised by W. H. C. Frend. London: SPCK, 1987.

Tacitus, Cornelius. *The Annals*. Edited by John C. Yardley and Anthony Barrett. Oxford University Press, 2016.

Telford, William R., ed. *The Interpretation of Mark*. Second edition. Edinburgh: T&T Clark, 1995.
———. *The New Testament: A Beginner's Guide*. New York: Oneworld, 2014.
———. *The Theology of Mark*. Cambridge University Press, 1999.
Thatcher, Tom, ed. *Jesus, the Voice, and the Text: Beyond the Oral and Written Gospel*. Waco: Baylor University Press, 2008.
Watson, Francis, *Gospel Writing: A Canonical Perspective*. Grand Rapids: Eerdmans, 2013.
Wright, Adam Z. *Of Conflict and Concealment: The Gospel of Mark as Tragedy*. Eugene, OR: Pickwick, 2020.
Wright, Brian J. *Communal Reading in the Time of Jesus*. Minneapolis: Fortress, 2017.
Wright, Jacob L. *Why the Bible Began: An Alternative History of Scripture and its Origins*. Cambridge University Press, 2023.
Žižek, Slavoj. *On Belief*. London: Routledge, 2001.
———. *The Puppet and the Dwarf: The Perverse Core of Christianity*. Cambridge, MA: MIT Press, 2003.

Index

The translation of the Good Message According to Mark (chapter 3) is not indexed

Abraham, 29, 30, 88, 191, 194
absence as presence, 113, 182–84, 186
Achilles, 188
Acts of the Apostles, 11, 19, 20, 23, 29–30, 100, 126, 145, 149, 151, 153, 173, 185
Adam, 30, 88, 194
Adams, Edward, 12
adoptionism, 26, 34, 99
Aeschylus, 167, 178
Agamemnon, 175–76
agape, 133
Agrippa (Herod Agrippa II), 129
Albinus, 129
Alcestis, 179–80, 186
Alexander the Great, 5
Alexander, Loveday, 20
Ananus, 128–29
Andrew the apostle, 103
anointed as term, 7, 46; *see also* Messiah
Antigone, 175–76
Antonius Pius, 135
apostles as group, 19, 102–3, 131
Aramaic language, 5–6, 9, 13, 101–2, 130
Arav, Rami, 42
Aristotle, 169–170, 173
Arius and Arianism, 33–37
Arma Christi, 177–78
Ascension, *see* Yeshua of Nazareth

Assmann, Jan, 125–26, 128, 141
Athanasius, 33
Athena, 179, 188
audience, public, 123
Augustine of Hippo, 15, 36, 155, 194
Augustus Caesar (Octavian), 100–101
Ayres, Lewis, 35, 36

Babylonian captivity, 107
Badiou, Alain, 160–61, 165
bardo, 151–52, 179, 195
Barton, John, 9, 21, 23, 30, 38, 39, 150, 162
Beard, Mary, 101
Beatty, Chester, 44–45
Beckett, Samuel, 98, 166, 181–84, 186
belief, 144–58, 165; *see also* trust
Ben-Hur, 126
Berkeley, George, 180–81, 184
betrayal, 105–6, 131, 172
Bettenson, Henry, 124
Bhagavad Gita, 31, 143
biblical chapter and verse numbers, 48–49
biblical criticism, 143, 163–64
biblical cycle plays, 150
biographies, classical, 24
Blake, William, 5
Bloom, Harold, 190
Bosch, Hieronymus, 159

Bovon, François, 115
Bradshaw, Paul, 133
Branagh, Kenneth, 137
bread as theme, 103–7, 131
Brecht, Bertolt, 47
Brown, Colin, 93
Bryan, Christopher, 24, 101
Buddha (Siddhartha Gautama), 43
Buddhism, 151
Buddhist canons, 143
Bultmann, Rudolf, 117–20, 125, 139–40, 198

Caillois, Roger, 109
Calvin, Jean, 3
Campbell, Ken M., 6
Carlson, Marvin, 34
Carrère, Emmanuel, 92
Catholicism, Roman, 1–4, 14, 139, 184, 189, 192–94
Cephas, *see* Peter the Apostle
Certeau, Michel de, 157
Christ and Christos as terms, 7, 46
Christianity as religion, 103
Christology, 26, 34–35, 99
codex, 38
Codex Sinaiticus, 38
Codex Vaticanus, 38
Coleman, Kathleen, 42
Collins, Adela Yarbo, 24–25, 48, 112, 146
Colossians, letter to, 122–23, 158
comedy, 168–69, 178
Constantine the Great, 13, 15, 20, 32–33, 36, 45, 133, 177, 194, 196
Constantinople, Council of, 33, 36–37
Coogan, Michael D., 12
Corinthians, Paul's first letter to, 9, 12, 25–26, 33, 132–33, 144–46, 158
Crucifixion of Yeshua, *see* Yeshua of Nazareth
crucifixion, Roman, 42, 175–77
Cruise, Tom, 108

Daniel, book of, 101–2

Dante Alighieri, 159
David, King of Israel, 88, 90, 97, 108
Delany, Samuel R., 167
demythologizing, 117–20, 164
deus ex machina, 179, 180, 182, 188
Deuteronomy, 99
Dewey, Joanna, 121
Diatessaron, 40
Dibelius, Martin, 118
Dies Irae, 1–2
Diocletian persecutions, 45
disciple as term, 102–3
divine man, 98–101
doubt, 155–58, 190
doxa, 154
Draper, A., 121

Eastern (Greek) Orthodox Church, 13, 34, 36, 189
Ebionites, 144
Ehrman, Bart D., 13, 26, 37, 38, 39, 40, 100, 141, 159
Einstein, Albert, 181
ekklesia, 11, 45
Elijah, 90, 95, 107, 159
Elizabeth I, 161
Else, Gerald F., 170
empty tomb, 48, 89, 110–13, 152–53, 161, 184
end time, *see* eschatology
epic poem, 167–68, 175, 186–88
episkopos, 45
Erasmus, Desiderius, 47
eschatology, 7–8, 22, 24, 30, 92, 106–7, 122, 128, 162, 188, 190, 195
euaggelion, 10–11, 46, 122
eucharist, 9, 13, 124, 129–35
  institution, 131–32
  ritual practice, 26, 105, 131–35, 192–94
  see also bread as theme
Eumenides, 178–79
Euripides, 167, 179
Eusebius of Caesarea, 20, 33, 35, 124–25
Evans, Craig, A., 21, 93, 117
Eve, Eric, 44, 93, 126, 128

evil, 30, 93, 107–10
Exodus, 7, 130, 154, 191
exorcisms, *see* miracles
Ezekiel, 101, 107, 109, 135–36

faith, 154–55, 159–60, 189; *see also* belief; trust
faith, article or proclamation of, *see* kerygma
Farmer, William, 18
Farrer, Austin, 18
feedings, *see* miracles
Finney, Mark T., 159
Fletcher, John, 178
Foley, J. M., 121
form criticism, 117–20, 125
Freytag, Gustav, 169
Frost, Robert, 184

Galatians, Paul's letter to, 44, 158, 160
Galilee region, 5–6
Genesis, 37, 88, 90, 118, 191
gentile as term, 7, 147
Gibson, Mel, 6, 178
God fearers, 20, 153
Good Message as term, 10–11
Goodacre, Mark, 18
gospels as group, 3, 15–16, 19, 28–29, 37, 140
  authorship, 19–21
  contradictions, 146–51
  dates, 15, 21–23
  genre, 23–25
  harmonization, 39–41, 137
  reading and recitation, 123–25, 138
  term, 10–11
  translation, 12–13, 46–47
  see also synoptics
Gould, Stephen J., 163
Greek language, 4, 5, 9, 13, 14, 23, 45, 46–47, 114, 138
Griesbach, Jakob, 18
Guarini, Giovanni Battista, 178
Gutenberg bible, 13

hamartia, 46, 170, 173–74

Hamlet, 136–37
Hanson, K. C., 42
healings, *see* miracles
heaven, 155–56, 159, 174, 195
Hebrew language, 6, 13
Hebrew scriptures as term, ix–x
Hebrews, letter to, 159
Hector, 175, 187
Hegel, Georg Wilhelm, 171
Heidegger, Martin, 117
Helena, Flavia Julia, 177
hell, 156, 158–59
Hellenization, 5, 8, 99, 174
Hemingway, Ernest, 47
Heracles, 100, 179
heresy, 33, 127
Herod Antipas, 104, 110
Herod the Great, 21, 39, 162
Herodians, 171
Herodias, 110
High Priest of Temple, 96–97, 98, 102, 108, 112, 128–29
history and myth, 142, 164
Hoehner, Harold W., 21
Holland, Glenn S., 138
holy spirit as term, 33, 35, 46, 108, 191
Homer, 168, 186–87
Horsley, R. A., 121

Iesous as name, 7, 46
Iliad, 167–68, 187–88
immaterialism, 180–81
infancy gospels, 140–42; *see also* Protoevangelium of James
Infancy Gospel of Thomas, 141–42
Isaiah, 3, 30, 87, 95, 107, 122, 140–41, 159, 191
Islam, 34

Jackson, Samuel L., 109
James brother of Yeshua (James the Just), 9, 128, 144
James the apostle (James the Greater), 95, 103, 132
Jeremiah, 107, 136
Jerome, 13
Jesuits (Society of Jesus), 2, 4, 92

Jesus as name, 7
Jesus of Nazareth, *see* Yeshua of Nazareth
John Mark, 20
John the apostle, 9, 95, 103, 132
John the Baptizer, 30–31, 88, 95, 104, 110, 129
John, gospel of, 11, 19–20, 22–23, 26, 29, 33, 37, 39, 91, 97, 131, 139, 148–50, 152, 172–74, 186
Johnson, Samuel, 181
Johnson, William, 123
Jones, Terry, 116
Jonson, Ben, 4, 137
Joseph of Arimathea, 111
Joseph of Nazareth, 140
Josephus, Flavius, 19, 106, 128, 162
Joshua, 7
Judas the apostle, 103, 105–6, 110, 131, 161, 172–73
Jude, letter of, 133
Julius Caesar, 100–101
Justin Martyr, 19, 124, 127, 134–35

Kafka, Franz, 168
Keith, Chris, 144
Kelber, Werner, 31, 120–22, 125
Kermode, Frank, 38, 94, 112–13
kerygma, 25–26, 118, 144–46, 153, 159, 188, 195
Kierkegaard, Søren, 18
King James Version, 47, 142, 162, 186, 191
King Lear, 137
Kings, first book of, 7, 90, 162
Kings, second book of, 107, 162
Kirk, Alan, 127
Klassen, William, 106
Knowlson, James, 182
Koine Greek, *see* Greek language

Lacan, Jacques, 193
Lagerkvist, Pär, 126
Lamentations, book of, 107
Last Supper, 9, 12, 96–97, 105–6, 132–34; *see also* eucharist
Latin language, 6, 13–14

Law, Mosaic, *see* Torah
lectionaries, 3, 29, 49
Levine, Amy-Jill, 112
Licinius, Valerius, 36
Life of Brian, 116
literacy, 6, 38, 42, 115
Lord, Albert, 122
Luce, A. A., 181
Luke, gospel of, 10–11, 16–18, 20–23, 37, 39, 46–47, 88, 91, 114–15, 119, 129–30, 132, 139, 147–49, 151–52, 185, 186
Luther, Martin, 3

MacDonald, Dennis R., 187
Mack, Burton L., 26, 41, 97, 106, 143
Malachi, book of, 31
Marcus, Joel, 102, 175
Mark, gospel of
    authorship, 19–21
    biography, 23–24, 91, 161, 168, 184, 188
    characterization of Yeshua, 90–93, 103, 113, 174–75, 188
    date, 22–24, 107
    elements missing, 39–40, 194
    epic, 25, 186–88
    genre, 23–25, 168, 180, 187
    myth and history, 139–65
    literary document, 87–113
    longer ending, 47–48, 113, 184–86
    priority, 16–18, 25–27
    purpose, 44
    recital, 122–25, 138
    structure, 88–90, 169
    tragedy, 25, 167–75
    tragicomedy, 178–80
    translated text of, 50–86
    translation problems, 4, 46–47
    writing and orality, 25–27, 44, 87, 120, 122–23, 138, 188
    see also empty tomb; gospels as group; synoptics; Two-Document Hypothesis
Marxsen, Willi, 119

Mary mother of James, 29, 110–13, 147
Mary mother of Yeshua, 39, 94, 99, 110, 140–42
Mary of Magdala, 110–13, 147–50, 185
Mass, Catholic, 1–3, 37, 132, 134, 192
Matthew, gospel of, 10–11, 16–18, 19–20, 21, 22–23, 29, 34, 37, 39, 88, 90, 91, 114, 119, 139, 140–41, 146, 147, 149, 151, 162, 173
McLuhan, Marshall, 116
Meggitt, Justin J., 41
memory, 125–29, 135–38
Messiah, 7, 42, 94–98, 101, 107–9, 153, 165, 190
messianic secret, 94–98, 170
Metzger, Bruce M., 13, 38, 40, 100
Michie, Donald, 121
Milton, John, 152
miracles, 92–93, 96, 104, 171
Mohammed, 43
Monty Python, 116
Morgan, Teresa, 93, 154
Morton, Russell, 117
Mosaic Law, *see* Torah
Moses, 7, 90, 95, 159, 191
Myers, Ched, 93
myth, 118–19, 139–44, 164, 166, 196; *see also* Mark

Nebuchadnezzar II, 107, 162
Nebuzaradan, 107
Nero, Claudius, 22
New Testament as term, ix, 43
New Testament scholarship, 143
Nicaea, Council of, 15, 32–33, 147, 194
Nicene Creed, 33, 34–35, 37, 97, 99, 153–54, 195–96

Oakman, Douglas E., 42
Odysseus, 188
Odyssey, 167–68, 187–88
Oedipus the King, 169–70, 172–73, 175, 186

Old Testament as term, ix, 34
Ong, Walter J., 121
oral tradition, 26, 41, 44, 91, 109, 114–38, 139, 143, 149, 174, 176, 186, 188, 195
orality, 42–44, 117, 120–25, 135, 168
original sin, 194
orthodoxy, 98, 154, 194
otherness of Yahweh, 190–91, 193–94
Ovid, 87

Painter, John, 108
Papias of Hierapolis, 20, 23
papyrus, 37, 45
Paradise Lost, 152
parchment, 38
parousia, *see* Second Coming
Parry, Milman, 121
Pascal, Blaise, 156–57
Passion of the Christ, The, 6, 178
Passover, 41, 88, 90, 105, 130, 172
Paul of Samosata, 124
Paul, apostle of the Messiah, 8, 9, 10, 11, 20, 22, 25–26, 29–30, 41, 43–44, 87, 97, 99–101, 103, 109, 119, 120, 122–23, 126, 128, 132, 140, 144–45, 153–54, 158–60, 165, 174, 185, 188, 194–96; *see also* Colossians; Corinthians; Galatians; Romans
Paul's authentic letters, 158–59
Pentateuch, *see* Torah
Pentecost, 145, 185
perception and existence, 180–83
performance, 4, 122–24, 127, 133–38
pericope, 118, 131, 187
Peter the apostle (Simon), 9, 20, 25, 95, 103, 110, 128, 132, 144–45, 147, 161
Peter, second letter of, 23, 123, 162
Peterson, Martin, 155
Phaedrus, 116
Pharisees, 29, 95, 99, 104, 108, 158, 171
Phillips, Rod, 129

INDEX

Phillips, Victoria, 112
Pilate (Pontius Pilatus), 6, 41–42, 89, 96–97, 108, 161
pistus, see trust
Pius XII, 14–15
Plato, 43–44, 116
Plese, Zlatko, 37, 141
Pliny the Elder, 18, 98
Plutarch, 18, 24, 87
Pompey the Great, 108
Pontifex Maximus, 14, 33
pope and papacy, 3, 14–15
Porphyry, 146
prayer, 184
presbyteros, 45
priesthood, Christian, 103
priests of the Temple, 41, 106, 131, 147, 161, 171–72
Protoevangelium of James, 140–41
Psalms, 3, 87, 90, 101
Ptolemy II Philadelphus, 12
Pulp Fiction, 109

Q document, 16–18, 26, 114, 119
Quem Quaeritis trope, 150
Quirinius, Publius Sulpicius, 21
Qur'an, 43, 143

recital, public, 122–25, 127
redaction criticism, 119
Reformation, 2–3, 14
Renan, Ernest, 92
rescue, *see* salvation
resurrection of the body, 158
Resurrection of Yeshua, *see* Yeshua of Nazareth
Revelation to John, book of, 11, 23, 136
Reynolds, Kevin, 150
Rhames, Ving, 109
Rhoads, David, 121
Risen, 150
Robbins, Vernon K., 105
Robe, The, 126
Rodríguez, Rafael, 42, 121
Romans, Paul's letter to, 30, 120, 158, 195
Rousseau, John J., 42

Sadducees, 41, 99, 171
salvation, 3, 4, 96–97, 107, 131, 134, 158–61, 182–84
Sanhedrin, 89, 96, 98, 161
Santa Claus, 157
Sartre, Jean-Paul, 139
Satan, 108
Schechner, Richard, 134
Schmidt, K. L., 118
Schweitzer, Albert, 18
scribes, 95, 99, 108, 171
scriptio continua, 48–49
Second Coming, 113, 152, 165, 174, 182
Seder, 130
semitic languages, 5
Septuagint, 10, 12, 29, 140–41, 191
Shakespeare, William, 4, 24, 28, 135, 136–38, 142, 150, 163, 173, 178–79, 186
Shavuot, 145
Shepherd of Hermas, 38
Shiner, Whitney, 121
Simon of Cyrene, 110
Simon Peter, *see* Peter the apostle
Simon the Zealot, 106
Socrates, 43, 116
sola scriptura, 3
Solomon, 7, 90, 96
son of God, 8, 11, 34, 35, 92, 94, 98–101, 113, 165, 176
son of man, 8, 101–2, 113, 174
Sophocles, 163, 167, 169, 187
Spielberg, Steven, 135
Stevenson, J., 33
Suetonius, Gaius, 18
superheroes, 108
supersessionism, 30
synagogue, 11, 20, 95, 122, 153
synoptics and synoptic problem, 16–18, 26, 39, 114
Syro-Phoenician woman, 94, 99, 104, 110

Tacitus, Cornelius, 18, 19, 87, 98
Tanakh as term, x, 31
Tarantino, Quentin, 109
Tatian (Tatianus), 40, 137

tekton, 6
Telford, William R., 23
Temple in Jerusalem, 6, 9, 11, 22, 23, 32, 41, 95, 106, 107–8, 144, 153, 171–73, 176
testimonia, 34
Textus Receptus, 47–48, 186
thanksgiving, *see* eucharist
Thatcher, Tom, 122
Theodosius, Emperor, 36
Theophilus, 20
Thomas the apostle, 148–51
Tiberius Caesar, 107
Tiresias, 169
Tischendorf, Constantin von, 38
Titus, Caesar Vespasianus, 22, 107, 125, 144
Torah, 25, 31, 93, 104, 122, 143, 162, 171
Tov, Emmanuel, 12
tragedy, 167–75, 176–78, 186, 188
tragicomedy, 178–80, 181, 186, 188
Transfiguration, *see* Yeshua of Nazareth
translation and Christianity, 5, 12–14
transubstantiation, 130, 135, 192
Travolta, John, 109
Trinity College Dublin, 44, 161, 180–81
Trinity, doctrine of, 34, 35–36, 46, 99, 101, 147, 191
trust (*pistis*), 93, 95, 105, 154–58, 161, 180, 190, 193
Twelve as term, 25, 102–3; *see also* apostles as group
Two-Document Hypothesis, 17–18, 25, 114
Tyndale, William, 47
typology, 34

Unleavened Bread festival, 130
Ussher, James, 161–63, 180

Vespasian, Titus Flavius, 125
Virgil, 87, 186
virginity of Mary, 140–42
Vulgate, 13, 191

Waiting for Godot, 166, 181–84, 186
Watson, Francis, 150
Weil, Simone, 158
Willis, Bruce, 109
wine, 129, 131
Winter's Tale, The, 178, 179–80
women at the tomb, 110–13
Woolf, Virginia, 98
Wrede, William, 94
Wright, Adam Z., 94, 171
Wright, Brian J., 121, 123
Wright, Jacob, 174
writing, 26, 42–46, 115–20, 135, 138; *see also* literacy; Mark; orality

Yeats, W. B., 87, 100
Yeshua of Nazareth
    Ascension, 149, 151–52
    birth, ix, 21, 115
    Crucifixion, 15, 41, 109, 128, 175–77
    economic class, 8, 42–43
    historical man, 10, 18–19, 91, 118, 150, 165
    legends, 140–42
    name, 7
    natures, 194–95
    preaching, 24, 42, 92, 96
    Resurrection, 88, 109, 111–12, 144–51, 154–55, 158, 160–61, 165, 175
    Resurrection appearances, 43, 48, 145–54, 185–86
    Transfiguration, 89–90, 95, 103
    trials, 89, 96

Zechariah, book of, 90
Zeus, 100
Žižek, Slavoj, 106, 154

www.ingramcontent.com/pod-product-compliance
Lightning Source LLC
Chambersburg PA
CBHW050146170426
43197CB00011B/1980